Selected Letters of W. D. Howells

Volume 6

1912 – 1920

W. D. Howells with his grandsons,
Billy and Johnny

W. D. HOWELLS

Selected Letters

Volume 6: 1912-1920

Edited and Annotated by
William M. Gibson
and
Christoph K. Lohmann

Textual Editor
Christoph K. Lohmann

TWAYNE PUBLISHERS

Boston

1983

This volume of Selected Letters is also published as
Volume 28 of A Selected Edition of W. D. Howells

Editorial expenses for this volume have been supported by grants from
the National Endowment for the Humanities.

Published in 1983 by Twayne Publishers, A Division of G. K. Hall & Co.,
70 Lincoln Street, Boston, Massachusetts 02111

Printed on permanent/durable acid-free paper and bound in
the United States of America

First Printing

Library of Congress Cataloging in Publication Information

Howells, William Dean, 1837–1920.
Selected letters.

(His A Selected edition of W. D. Howells: v. 4, 9, 19, 24, 28)
Includes index.
CONTENTS: v. 6. 1912–1920.
1. Howells, William Dean, 1837–1920—Correspondence.
2. Novelists, American—19th century—Correspondence.
I. Arms, George Warren, 1912–
II. Title.
ISBN 0–8057–8532–9

Acknowledgmets

We are grateful for permission to print the letters in this volume, as given by William White Howells and the heirs of W. D. Howells. The following individuals and institutions have also permitted the use of letters in their collections: Alfred University, Alfred, New York; American Academy and Institute of Arts and Letters, New York City; American Antiquarian Society, Worcester, Massachusetts; George Arms, Albuquerque, New Mexico; Avon County Reference Library, Bristol (England); Brown University Library; Miller Library, Colby College, Waterville, Maine; Dorset County Museum, Dorchester (England); Harvard College Library; Haverford College Library, Haverford, Pennsylvania; Rutherford B. Hayes Library, Fremont, Ohio; Huntington Library, San Marino, California; Indiana University (Bloomington) Library; Miami University Libraries, Oxford, Ohio; Minnesota Historical Society, St. Paul; Newberry Library, Chicago; Manuscript and Archives Division and the Henry W. and Albert A. Berg Collection, New York Public Library, Astor, Lenox and Tilden Foundations; University of Pennsylvania Library; Pennsylvania State University Library, University Park; Princeton University Library; Hamlin Garland Collection, University of Southern California; Southern Illinois University Library, Carbondale; Syracuse University Library, Syracuse, New York; University of Virginia Library; Harrman Library, Wagner College, Staten Island, New York; Polly Howells Werthman, Brooklyn, New York; The Beinecke Rare Book and Manuscript Library, Yale University.

We also thank Pamela F. Lohmann for preparing the index.

Contents

A Note on Editorial Practice

Two basic principles inform the treatment of the texts of the Howells correspondence which have been selected for publication in these volumes: one, the contents of the original documents are reproduced as fully and correctly as possible; and, two, all physical details of the manuscripts necessary for accurate reconstruction of the text are reported, though without encumbering the reading text itself. Consistent with these principles, the printed versions of the letters which form the body of these volumes retain the eccentricities of Howells' spelling, punctuation, and occasionally elliptical epistolary style, and are presented without such editorial appurtenances as brackets, arrows, virgules, and *sic*'s. The printed text is, insofar as possible, that of the finished letter, after Howells revised it either locally or generally by writing over, crossing out, and interlining. Howells' errors, except for inadvertent repetitions of words or syllables, are printed as they appear in the holographs, so long as the sense of the text can be discerned.

In accordance with the principle of reporting significant manuscript information, each letter is represented by a full itemization of cancellations, interlineations, the unusual placement of postscripts and marginal comments, and the presence of nonauthorial notes and comments believed to be contemporary with the composition or receipt of the letter, as well as of those editorial revisions necessary to insure comprehension. The reader should be aware, therefore, that some few words, letters, and marks of punctuation printed in this text are not in the original letters (or in transcriptions which have been employed when the originals are no longer extant or accessible). The full record of emendations, editorial comments, textual details, and Howells' revisions is provided in the Textual Apparatus, the introduction to which explains the symbols and abbreviations used to allow for the printing of the maximum of evidence in a minimum of space. Several exceptions, however, should be noted. Howells frequently failed to lift his pen when moving from one word to the next; thus, he often joined words that were not meant to be joined. Occasionally, though not always, he would repair such errors by separating these inadvertently joined words with a vertical line. Conversely, he sometimes lifted his pen while writing a single word, or he disconnected compounds that appear elsewhere as one word. In such cases, no notation of these irregularities has been included in the apparatus, while an attempt has been made, through comparisons among the letters, to render Howells' texts as nearly as possible in the form that he seems likely to have intended.

Given the wealth of references to personal and public events in the letters and the relevance of the letters to the shape and movement of Howells' career, annotation is potentially endless. The policy of these volumes is to present only the basic information which will make the context of the letters understandable and the letters themselves useful to both scholar and general reader. Annotation is thus restricted to explanation and clarification of references to people, places, events, literary works, and other such primary data. Interpretive comment is excluded.

Since the letters in this series represent only a portion of the extant Howells correspondence, it is also important that their relationship to each other and to letters not printed in these volumes be indicated. Cross references to other letters printed in the series simply identify correspondent and date: e.g., "Howells to Comly, 7 July 1868"; references to annotation accompanying letters add to this citation the specific footnote number: e.g., "Howells to Comly, 7 July 1868, n. 4." Manuscript letters not printed in this edition but cited or quoted are identified by correspondent and date, followed by the library location or collector's name in parentheses: e.g., "(MH)" for Harvard University or "(Ray)" for the collection of Gordon N. Ray.[1] Special collections within libraries are not indicated. When manuscripts of texts cited are also available in major printed collections (e.g., *Mark Twain–Howells Letters*), publication information follows the library symbol. Publication information appearing without notation of manuscript location should be assumed to designate texts extant only in published form. Quotations from letters in annotations follow the final, revised forms, and do not include a record of internal revisions. In addition, to avoid the proliferation of annotation, information necessary to the understanding of such quoted letters is provided within brackets at appropriate points within the quotations.

To further reduce the bulk and duplication of annotation, several other conventions have been adopted. People, events, and literary works are identified in footnotes at the points where their first significant mention appears in the whole series of letters. Further annotation of these same details is provided only where the context of a specific

---

1. Libraries are indicated by the abbreviations detailed in *Symbols of American Libraries*, 10th ed. (Washington: Library of Congress, 1969).

letter demands elaboration. The basic information can be located by using the indexes to the individual volumes or the cumulative index in the final volume of letters, where major references are distinguished by the printing of the appropriate page numbers in italic type. References to books give the year of first publication; however, books reviewed in dated articles should be assumed to have been published in the same year as the review, unless information to the contrary is provided. Whenever possible, references to books by Howells identify volumes published in "A Selected Edition of W. D. Howells," signaled by the abbreviation "HE" immediately following the title; references to works not available in this form generally cite the American first edition, which is identified by date of publication.

The editors have followed a consistent policy in the use of ellipses in quotations. If the first period is close up to the word preceding it, it stands for an end-of-sentence period in the original, with the omission following it. Thus, "invention. . . . develop" indicates that there is a period in the original after "invention," with the omitted portion of the text following it. However, "hereafter . . . . Good lord!" indicates that there is more text in the same sentence after "hereafter."

Titles of most secondary sources are given in full, but a number of them are cited so often in this series that the following list of short titles has been adopted.

Cady, *Howells*, I.   Edwin H. Cady, *The Road to Realism: The Early Years, 1837–1885, of William Dean Howells* (Syracuse, N.Y.: Syracuse University Press, 1956)

Cady, *Howells*, II   Edwin H. Cady, *The Realist at War: The Mature Years, 1885–1920, of William Dean Howells* (Syracuse, N.Y.: Syracuse University Press, 1958)

Gibson-Arms, *Bibliography*   William M. Gibson and George Arms, *A Bibliography of William Dean Howells* (New York: New York Public Library, 1948; reprinted, New York Public Library and Arno Press, 1971)

James Letters	*Henry James Letters*, ed. Leon Edel, 3 vols. (Cambridge, Mass.: Harvard University Press, Belknap Press, 1974–)
Life in Letters	*Life in Letters of William Dean Howells*, ed. Mildred Howells, 2 vols. (Garden City, N.Y.: Doubleday, Doran & Co., 1928)
Lynn, *Howells*	Kenneth S. Lynn, *William Dean Howells: An American Life* (New York: Harcourt Brace Jovanovich, 1971)
Norton, *Lowell Letters*	*Letters of James Russell Lowell*, ed. C. E. Norton, 2 vols. (New York: Harper & Brothers, 1894)
Transatlantic Dialogue	*Transatlantic Dialogue: Selected American Correspondence of Edmund Gosse*, ed. Paul T. Mattheisen and Michael Millgate (Austin: University of Texas Press, 1965)
Twain-Howells	*Mark Twain-Howells Letters*, ed. Henry Nash Smith and William M. Gibson, 2 vols. (Cambridge, Mass.: Harvard University Press, Belknap Press, 1960)
Woodress, *Howells & Italy*	James L. Woodress, Jr., *Howells & Italy* (Durham, N.C.: Duke University Press, 1952)

C. K. L.

D. J. N.

Longing for Peace

1 9 1 2 — 1 9 2 0

Introduction

Like the volumes that precede it, this selection of letters from the last nine years of Howells' life focuses on his literary production as a memoirist, a novelist, a travel writer, a Harper editor, and the occupant of the "Editor's Easy Chair" in *Harper's Monthly*. They form almost inevitably a story of aging and decline, but of decline often and strikingly broken by resurgences of imagination and power and by the easy wit that may be Howells' most persistent trait from youth into old age—wit that never deserted him.

The entire extant correspondence includes an astonishing number of letters from Howells to his family: to his father (and mother while she lived), to his brother Joe, to his sisters Aurelia and Annie, to his daughter Mildred, and his son John and John's wife, Abby, and to his two grandsons. The letters to Elinor Mead Howells, his wife, are relatively few because Howells was rarely separated from her. She was nevertheless the center of his life, and his life broke in two when she died in May 1910, shortly after the death of his close friend Mark Twain. In his boyhood he and his brother Joe had been quarrelsome rivals, but long since they had become friends, as his loving concern for Joe in the letter of 19 January 1912 shows. On the other hand, Howells cared little for his rather stolid ne'er-do-well brother Sam, but he tried to understand him because he could see in Sam what he might himself have become. His relation to his son, John, and to Abby and his grandsons Billy and John was warm and rewarding, so that Howells depended on and often stayed with "JohnAbby" in the decade following Elinor's death. But it was his daughter Mildred whom he depended on most heavily; whom he traveled with and read aloud to; who remained unmarried and suffered a serious, persistent nervous breakdown in 1912 and 1913—a kind of neurasthenia that her mother had been afflicted with earlier. The elderly Howells knew that he was in some degree responsible for Mildred's breakdown, but he felt helpless to alleviate it. Although evidently the source of spiritual and financial support for an extended family, Howells was, nonetheless, a lonely old man, who missed Elinor more and more as time passed, who dreamed about her often, and who wrote of his meeting her as "the vastly most important thing in my whole life."[1]

A consequence of his loneliness was that Howells and his daughter moved and traveled throughout the decade, through England and most of Spain, much as they had revisited Italy and Germany earlier. They tried Bermuda. They boarded in Cambridge and alternated between New York and Boston. Summers they spent on the coast of Maine, at Kittery Point and York Harbor; and in the winter they often went south, to St. Augustine, Florida, Savannah, Georgia, and Tryon, North Carolina, Howells meanwhile dreaming of the long-deferred trip to New Orleans by steamboat. Travel was an anodyne for the sense of isolation, and often provided materials for Howells' special kind of "modern travel" book. Henry James was a little astonished to observe how wonderful Howells was "for bustling about," and how he and Mildred seemed to "*like* questionable inns & queer lodgings...."[2] The fact is that Howells enjoyed the "purgatory" of European travel[3] and liked to travel through New England in his early model Ford car. In this sense he singularly anticipates the rootless, restless post-World-War I generation, who Dos Passos said traveled around the world's meridians "like squirrels in a squirrel cage,"[4] looking for something else or something more.

Howells suffered through World War I, contributing a sketch to Louis Raemaker's volume of anti-German cartoons and beginning to approve of Woodrow Wilson's policies only after the president stiffened in his support of the Allies. He talked of German "schrecklichkeit" and wrote a public appeal to the Italian people for Italo-American friendship, but he refused to condemn German culture out of hand and never faltered in his belief in "the kindly German people."[5] His protesting the Irish executions by the British in 1916 is a vivid reminder that as a Swedenborgian of Welsh extraction Howells did not swim in the mainstream of American life; and it strangely recalls his courageous public stance in middle life at the time of the Chicago anarchists' trial and his youthful passion for John Brown and the abolition of slavery.

The history of Howells' last years in his letters is a history of his friendships, which were many and strong. Indeed, from the whole cor-

---

1. Howells to Laura Mitchell, 9 February 1914.

2. Henry James to Thomas S. Perry, 13 August 1913, in Virginia Harlow, *Thomas Sergeant Perry: A Biography* (Durham, N. C.: Duke University Press, 1950), p. 340.

3. See "Eighty Years and After," p. 164.

4. John Dos Passos translated Blaise Cendrar's *Panama*, including Cendrar's figure of the "squirrelcage of the meridians." He cites the metaphor again in *Orient Express* (New York: Harper & Brothers, 1927), pp. 157–58.

5. Howells to Anne H. Fréchette, 13 September 1914.

respondence one gets the impression that he knew every American writer of consequence, from Emerson to Sinclair Lewis, with the exception of Herman Melville (who was then nearly invisible as a writer) and Emily Dickinson (whose life might have been altered had she written to Howells rather than T. W. Higginson). Howells' memory of Mark Twain stays green in these letters, and his praise of Henry James is discriminating but unstinted. James' tribute to Howells on the occasion of his seventy-fifth birthday may well be the finest tribute ever paid him, but the younger man's letters sometimes carry a faint aroma of malice, even hypocrisy, in speaking of his old friend and of Elinor and Mildred— an attitude that is nearly inconceivable in Howells himself, who always acknowledged James his senior in the art of fiction. In these late years, however, Howells clearly depended most often and most heavily on Thomas Sergeant Perry, Hamlin Garland, Booth Tarkington, and Frederick A. Duneka for every sort of friendly office. Garland's *Son of the Middle Border* pleased Howells immensely, and Garland stage-managed an eightieth birthday celebration in honor of his mentor, who wrote for the occasion but did not come. Tarkington's *The Turmoil* and *The Magnificent Ambersons* made Howells "tremble" for him because they showed that Tarkington might almost choose between popularity and greatness.[6] T. S. Perry had read more than anyone in all the European languages, but he also had "a genius [for] friendship,"[7] which Howells delighted in during long talks and joint visits to plays or movies. With Duneka, the Harper editor, Howells maintained the most complex relationship of his late years, hinted at in the closing of one letter, "Sincerely, almost affectionately, yours" (a deadly barb) and in the comment that their relationship was one of "touch and go-ments mostly."[8] Duneka faced the exceedingly difficult task of keeping happy an aging author with a high reputation, and Howells had to endure editorial cutting and delays in publication and changing contractual arrangements with Harper & Brothers. There can be no doubt of Duneka's regard for "his" author, or of Howells' affection for Duneka in the end, when the editor suffered from a painful growing paralysis. But Duneka's flat refusal to pay Howells a large fee for a long essay on James suggests some of the tensions in the relationship between author and editor, although the decision may have been forced on Duneka from above.

Surely a major impression the reader must receive from these late letters is Howells' undying curiosity about new writers, and his willing-

---

6. Howells to Booth Tarkington, 9 January 1915.
7. Howells to Thomas S. Perry, 28 February 1917.
8. Howells to Frederick A. Duneka, 23 March 1916 and 20 September 1917.

ness to change his mind on reexperiencing a work he had read many years before. Hence he insisted that every reader ought to have a second life in which to correct the errors of the first. Despite his reservations about free verse, he explored the new poets Amy Lowell, E. L. Masters, Robert Frost, Conrad Aiken, James Oppenheim, J. G. Fletcher, and a number of others in the "Editor's Easy Chair" in 1915.[9] He praised the tragic account of a mulatto returning from Canada to his birthplace in the South, Paul Kester's *His Own Country*. Himself the "inventor" of the "modern travel," he turned back to J. L. Stephens' *Travels in Yuca- tán* of the early 1840s and its revelation of Inca civilization in Central America. He discovered the "noise-poet," Vachel Lindsay, through H. B. Fuller.[10] He read Goethe, Eckermann, Brieux, Palacio Valdés, Tacitus, Bjornson, Cellini, Alfieri, Goldoni, Tennyson, Gilbert's opera texts, Browning, George Eliot, George Ade, Garland, Ernest Poole, Paul Kes- ter, Abraham Cahan, Keats, Whitman, and Froissart. He changed his mind, largely, about certain Dickens and Thackeray titles, finding *Great Expectations* especially a great novel, "an amazingly meaty book," that he had incomprehensibly read and dismissed many years before.[11] Some of this reading, of new or contemporary writers, became of course grist for comment or review in the "Editor's Easy Chair" mill, a department which he turned out every month from 1900 to 1920. But the openness to experience in literature extended from a love of the stage to a fascina- tion with the "movy," in Howells' late years. He followed Garland's "scenario" writing; thought a fine film might be made from the life of Coronado as well as from *The Leatherwood God*; planned to incor- porate some of the local film-makers he encountered in St. Augustine into a new novel, *The Home-Towners*; and often spent his afternoon at the movies.

The "shock of recognition" of talent or genius was, then, the kind of experience Howells lived for and lived in. He was able to create that shock for his own readers, from his own writing, less frequently than he found it in others, and he frankly recognized the fact of his lessening reputation. Writing to Henry James on 29 June 1915, Howells com- mented: ". . . I should say your worship was spreading among us. I am comparatively a dead cult with my statues cast down and the grass grow- ing over them in the pale moonlight." Yet there were new efforts. *New*

---

9. Even before Howells' comments on the new poets appeared in the September 1915 *Harper's Monthly*, Robert Frost had written to Edward Garnett, on 12 June 1915: "You seem to have made a friend for me in W. D. Howells. There is the best American, if you want to know the truth." (Lawrance Thompson, ed., *Selected Letters of Robert Frost* [New York: Holt, Rinehart and Winston, 1964], p. 179.)

10. Howells to Henry B. Fuller, 10 March 1914.

11. Howells to Frederick A. Duneka, 28 February 1918.

Leaf Mills: A Chronicle (1913) was Howells' attempt to embody his parents' character at the time of their venture into family communal living centered around a paper mill in Ohio. It was partly fictionalized and not very well received. *The Leatherwood God* (1916) was the continuation of a story Howells had begun fifty years earlier. It concerns an exhorter who half believes he is God, and who for a time persuades backwoods Ohioans, especially women, that he *is* God. The novel makes it dramatically plain that the source of the preacher's power is his stallion-like long black hair, snorting speech, and immanent sexuality. It is the best novel of Howells' old age and will stand with the dozen best of his lifetime.

Even though Howells believed with Tolstoy that "remembering is hell," he wrote the first portion of his autobiography, calling it *Years of My Youth* (1916), and planned a second volume, *Years of My Middle Life*. The writing was hard because he could depend on no one of an earlier generation in his family to talk to and ask questions of; but it was also difficult because he had to avoid repeating himself on phases of his life already treated in *A Boy's Town*, *My Literary Passions*, and other semi-autobiographical books. He managed, however, with a great deal of skill, and *Years of My Youth* is a striking memoir because in many aspects it displays an old man's candor. *Familiar Spanish Travel* (1913) reflects the last major travel effort in Europe and depicts Spanish cities and the Spanish countryside with the same talent for keen observation that had received critical praise ever since the first publication of *Venetian Life* thirty-six years earlier. The book at its best, in fact, limns Spanish national character, which Howells first discovered in *Don Quixote* as a boy struggling with his self-taught Spanish. A fantasy on Shakespeare and Bacon, *The Seen and Unseen at Stratford-on-Avon* (1914) and a collection of late sketches in prose and poetry, *The Daughter of the Storage* (1916) reveal that neither Howells' poetic imagination nor his interest in the fantastic had altogether subsided.

These books are largely of Howells' own making and choice; but as a Harper author and editor he performed certain chores for the house, such as introducing new editions of Artemus Ward, Maupassant, *Gulliver's Travels*, Garland's *They of the High Trails*, *Pride and Prejudice*, *Daisy Miller*, and books by Leonard Merrick and Blasco Ibañez. The most interesting editorial work that Howells undertook, however, was for Boni & Liveright: an anthology of *The Great Modern American Stories* (1920). It is a remarkable collection of short stories, including with tact and sensibility the stories that Howells himself thought first-rate along with stories that the readers of the *Atlantic* and *Harper's Monthly* had made popular. No Hawthorne or Irving or Poe or Melville was included because the collection was to be "modern." Stephen Crane was also left out, probably because Hamlin Garland answered Howells' request for "some best story of Stephen Crane's,"[12] with disapproving silence. But of the twenty-four tales in the anthology, eight are by women writers, and two of the women writers made the publishing negotiations the opportunity for speaking their minds to Howells. Charlotte Perkins Gilman wrote him that she was pleased and honored by his request for "The Yellow Wallpaper," explaining that she had come near lunacy at twenty-seven under Dr. S. Weir Mitchell's treatment of rest and minimal creative effort; that she then wrote the story and sent it to Mitchell; and that years later Mitchell told a friend, "I have altered my treatment of neuraesthenia since reading The Yellow Wallpaper."[13] And Edith Wharton recalled her first communication with Howells: "It must be nearly thirty years ago that a very shy young woman sent you a handful of worthless verse, & received the kindest of letters in reply. She is very glad to think that any work of hers ... may have partly liquidated her debt. I am proud to have 'Jane' included ... & especially proud that you should think she comes under the rubric of 'best.' "[14] The fact that Howells knew personally all the twenty-four writers in the anthology is a measure of his role in the history of American literature.

The failures of these late years are quite as interesting as the successes, and the question they raise is to what extent the responsibility rests with heirs and editors rather than with Howells himself. One was Howells' proposal to F. A. Duneka at James's death to write a long essay on the work of Henry James, an essay of the rounded, knowledgeable kind Howells had achieved in writing about Lowell and Holmes and Longfellow. Duneka unfortunately could not or would not meet Howells' price of $2,500, and thus the reader of Henry James is the poorer thereby, having only two fragments on which Howells was working when he died.[15] The second failure was Howells' paper recollecting the week he and Elinor had spent with President Rutherford B. Hayes and Mrs. Hayes in the White House in 1880. Webb Hayes, the president's son, protested some of Howells' facts, and F. A. Duneka protested *any* reminiscence at all of a president he, and—as he claimed—many others, still detested. So, caught between the two men's objections, Howells most uncharacteristically burned his manuscript, leaving us, the readers of his correspondence, to wonder whether the narrative might not have possessed peculiar historical value, errors or no.

---

12. Howells to Hamlin Garland, 16 October 1919.
13. Charlotte Perkins Gilman to Howells, 17 October 1919 (MH).
14. Edith Wharton to Howells, 5 November 1919 (MH).
15. See Howells to Frederick A. Duneka, 7 March 1916, and the letters following.

This volume, the last in the entire sequence covering so long and rich a period in the development of American literature, from 1852 to 1920, ought to end with Howells' own words—not those of his editors. For this reason and for its intrinsic refinement and depth we have chosen to conclude the correspondence with Howells' essay on old age, "Eighty Years and After."[16] It is a treatment of final things, closely wrought, full of wit and color, and in the direct style of Montaigne. It is the masterpiece of Howells' old age and his prayer that the devotee of art for humanity's sake may now depart in peace.

W. M. G.

---

16. The text in this edition is based on the manuscript (in the possession of William White Howells) and the first printing in *Harper's Monthly*, December 1919 (see Textual Record, pp. 212–13).

4 JANUARY 1912, NEW YORK, TO FREDERICK A. DUNEKA

130 West 57th st.,
January 4, 1912.

Dear Mr. Duneka:

Just what I said would happen when Johnson came last night and told me you had taken his Artemus Ward book![1] But I shall be delighted to do the introduction. I knew Browne personally in Columbus, New York and Boston, and always liked him. Let me have the stuff to go over, in good time. I think I can do something nice.[2]

Yours ever
W. D. Howells.

1. Clifton Johnson had interviewed Howells in 1894 and 1895 (*Outlook*, 31 March 1894 and 23 February 1895) and would illustrate with his photographs *Years of My Youth* in 1917. He selected *Artemus Ward's Best Stories* for Harper & Brothers; the book appeared in October. See U. Halfmann, ed., *Interviews with William Dean Howells* (Arlington: University of Texas, 1973), pp. 35–39, 46–50.

2. Howells' introduction treats Charles F. Browne's showman "Artemus Ward" in his relation to antislavery, Mormonism, spiritualism, and woman suffrage. Though neither so inventive nor so humane as Mark Twain, Ward at his best was "delicious," Howells observes, striking the same note as in a letter to Joseph A. Howells, 9 January 1912 (MH): "You know I knew him personally.... The non-showman stuff is best; his own direct account of things is most amusing. His books bring back the civil war time, though they treat only of its ludicrous phases. He was always something of a proslavery man, and he had not Mark Twain's generous heartedness."

18 JANUARY 1912, NEW YORK, TO FREDERICK A. DUNEKA

130 West 57th st.,
Jan'y 18, 1912.

Dear Mr. Duneka:

I hope you understood that I did not expect you to use my Spanish stuff as I gave it you. I only wanted you to see the autobiographical framework which I proposed for the book. For the magazine I thought you might find two papers in what I gave you: one on San Sebastian and one on Burgos; cutting and coming again as you liked. In the stuff to follow there will be papers, easily detachable and reducible about Valladolid, 2Madrid, 3Toledo, 4Cordova, 5Seville, 6Granada, 7Ronda and 8Algeciras and Tarifa. The range is pretty representative, and you could use any or all of the papers.[1] I would cut them for you; or any one else might do it—say, one of the office-boys who always wants to know which gentleman I want to see when I come to Franklin Square. I am no longer proud.

Yours sincerely
W. D. Howells.

1. Duneka did not use the papers on San Sebastian, Ronda, or Algeciras and Tarifa: these three appeared only in *Familiar Spanish Travels*. All the others appeared first in *Harper's Monthly* or the *North American Review* between May 1912 and April 1913. See Gibson-Arms, *Bibliography*, p. 67, for particulars.

19 JANUARY 1912, NEW YORK, TO JOSEPH A. HOWELLS

... The Buckingham ...
New York. Jan'y 19, 1912.

Dear Joe:

I am enclosing some interesting letters from Annie, which I know you'll be glad to get, and I am sending by tomorrow's boat a box of goodies in glass, besides some tablets for making beef tea which our Dr. Ostrom particularly commends. He has had a most intelligent letter from your T.'s I. doctor, whose treatment he entirely approves. I think, therefore, you may feel yourself in good hands, and may hopefully advise with him about coming away at once or staying on through the quarter.[1] He speaks most affectionately of you both, and has you fully in mind.

Above all, don't feel that you are serving out a sentence at T.'s I. When you want to leave, leave; and I will meet you in Brooklyn with a taxicab and a fur coat, and tumble you into a warm bed in a steam-heated room with beef steaks and baked potatoes and hot coffee at hand till you feel able to travel on. What I mean is, don't gnaw your heart out with the notion that you are giving up everything in giving your place up. By the way if you decide to come soon, better cable me—I'll pay you back—to the address Stockwells, New York. That is John's address,[2] and I shall get your message.

I know you are afflicted, but try to feel free about your staying or coming. Don't give way to gloomy fears, but act as you judge best and desire most to do. Neither your doctor nor mine regards your case as alarming, and I hope you will join them in their cheerfuller view.

Pilla and I are in this hotel till February; but we have at last found a furnished flat, and I hope soon to be sitting at my own table, after nearly a year of public tables.

Billy is getting on famously; he goes into the Park with a snow-shovel and digs holes in the drifts till he gets as red as fire. Then he starts home with a "train for Scoatland"—his nurse is Scotch, and is ready for a hot supper at six o'clock.

I am working away at my Spanish stuff,[3] while keeping a mental eye on New Leaf Mills. Pilla joins in love to you both

Your aff'te brother
Will.

1. For Howells' earlier concern with his brother's health and future plans, see Howells to Eliza Howells, 9 December 1911. Joe's health remained extremely precarious, and at this time Howells corresponded frequently with Joe's son and daughter-in-law, Willy and Ally, to make arrangements for moving Joe to Florida, expressing his willingness to bear the expense of Willy's visit to Turks Island and of making changes in Willy's house so as to accommodate Joe and Eliza. Willy and his parents arrived in New York early in February and immediately proceeded to Florida by train. See Howells to Joseph A. Howells, 10 February 1912 (MH).

2. The firm of Stokes and Howells.

3. The papers that were eventually collected in *Familiar Spanish Travels*.

29 FEBRUARY 1912, NEW YORK, TO SYLVESTER BAXTER

12 East 58th street,
Feb'y 29, 1912.

Dear Old Baxter:

Nobody's good wishes could be sweeter to me than yours.[1]

Here is a letter from Valdés which you can return when you like.[2] He is all that his books have painted him, and I hope no worse for growing a better Catholic. He made me want to crook the knee with him to the high altar of a church we visited, but I stood firm—and ashamed. He is very sweet but dignified, as all the Spaniards are. His wife is younger, and I fancy devouter. I said I liked his coming back to the notion of life hereafter. "Yes," he said and he touched his gray hairs, "one must do that when one comes to these." We had several visits back, and forth, and a long morning's drive and walk. We talked of you and I told him you were a buon diavolo (I spoke Italian and he Spanish) but I thought that not enough, and I gave him a full account of you which pleased him.[3] He showed me the flat-house where he and "Maximina" lived.[4] He is our height, well fleshed, and blue eyed, a Northern type.

The Spaniards are a great people, and we love them, Pilla and I, the more we think of them.

Yours ever
W. D. Howells.

P.S. I enclose several of V.'s letters. He asked me to write an introduction to a book of selections from him; but I could not.

1. Apparently Baxter had written Howells a letter of congratulations on the occasion of his seventy-fifth birthday.

2. See n. 1 of the following letter to Palacio Valdés; for Baxter's role in Howells' interest in the Spanish writer, see Howells to Palacio Valdés, 10 September 1911, n. 3.

3. For Howells' meeting with Palacio Valdés, see Howells to Abby Howells, 14 October 1911, n. 4.

4. According to Mildred Howells, the character of "Maximina" was drawn from Palacio Valdés' first wife, who died "a short time after their marriage." See *Life in Letters*, II, 313.

FEBRUARY 1912, NEW YORK, TO ARMANDO PALACIO VALDÉS

February, 1912.

Dear Friend:

I received your letter of the last month, but I have not replied because I felt a certain embarrassment concerning your suggestion that I should write an introduction for your collected work.[1] You can well believe that I feel most deeply the honor done me by your request: but the idea of making myself known to the Spanish people by means of a biographical notice before speaking of a person as well known as you, does not appeal to me. I am afraid it would occasion sarcastic, if not ill-natured, observations. Very willingly would I join my name with yours, and I hope that it will not be forgotten that I have always expressed my admiration for your writing. I have the pleasure of enclosing here a proof of this from the latest Easy Chair of *Harper's Magazine*.[2]

My daughter sends with me cordial greetings to the amiable Signora Valdés.

Your affectionate friend,
W. D. Howells.

1. The January letter, no longer extant, presumably asked Howells for an introduction to a volume of selections by Palacio Valdés and a brief biography of the introducer. Howells had interpreted and praised the work of the Spanish novelist since his review of *Marta y Maria* in the "Editor's Study," *Harper's Monthly*, April 1886. In his reply to this letter, dated 13 February 1912 (MH), Palacio Valdés wrote: "Comprendo su embarazo y sus escrúpulos para poner un prólogo á mis *Páginas escogidas*, y los respeto. Era un poco de egoismo por mi parte el desear que estas páginas fuesen amparadas por una autoridad tan reconocida como la suya" ["I understand your embarrassment and scruple to write a prologue to my *Paginas Escogidas* (Chosen Pages) and I respect them. It was a little selfish on my part to wish that these pages should be favored by an authority as well known as yours"]. See *Life in Letters*, II, 312.

2. In the "Editor's Easy Chair," *Harper's Monthly*, February 1912, Howells created a "genial cynic" to debate women's rights with the occupant of the chair, women now having the vote in California. The debate concludes with a demonstration by Carmen Salazar, a poet and Palacio Valdés' spokesman in *The Papers of Dr. Angélico*, that women are at their strongest in politics because they possess a higher sense of justice than men. Palacio Valdés liked Howells' piece on women, replying: "He leído con placer (¡ay y con dificultad!) el artículo que U. me envió. Mucho celebro que nos hallemos de acuerdo en cuanto á las dotes políticas de las mujeres. Estoy persuadido que dentro doscientos años el poder y la justicia habrá caído en sus manos. La objección del Cínico de que es un hombre quien lo demuestra ó lo hace constar no tiene mucho valor porque durante miles de años hemos mantenido á las mujeres alejadas de esa idea como si fuese una monstrosidad, un sacrilegio. En cambio, las hemos hecho creer que servían para el Arte" ["I have read with pleasure (oh, and with difficulty!) the article you sent me. I welcome very much what we have discovered about the political gifts of women. I am convinced that within two hundred years power and justice will be theirs. The cynic's objection, that only a man is capable of exercising it, does not have much value because over thousands of years we have kept women from it, as if it were a monstrosity, a sacrilege. On the other hand, we have made them believe that they are handmaidens to Art"].

16 MARCH 1912, NEW YORK, TO WILLIAM H. TAFT

12 East 58th Street,
March 16, 1912.

Dear Mr President:

In the rush of civic events you may well have forgotten the literary dinner of a fortnight ago to which your presence lent the dignity of the highest office in the world.[1] But for the ostensible occasion of that dinner it has still gone on. Ever since the first night of it I have been trying for some form of acknowledging your presence which should have the quality of the fact; but the grace of it, the kindness of it, is quite beyond any words of mine; I shall never be able to say how great and good of you I felt your coming to be. With all my heart I beg you to believe that no slightest circumstance or significance of it was lost upon me; and that the sense of my debt to you, which I cannot hope to discharge, will remain sole among the most precious experiences of my life.

Yours sincerely,
W. D. Howells.

Wm. H. Taft,
President.

1. Colonel George Harvey, always expert in public relations, arranged Howells' seventy-fifth birthday dinner at Sherry's on 2 March, with four hundred notables present, including President Taft, and "A Tribute to William Dean Howells" in a

special section of *Harper's Weekly*, 9 March 1912, reporting speeches made and letters received with names and photographs. Harvey reported to Howells that "it was the first public dinner in New York that Taft had ever sat through" (*Life in Letters*, II, 315). On being introduced by Harvey, the president responded that he took delight in "doing honor where it was due" and hoped to see American literature grow—that literature which Howells had "done so much to foster and make better" (Taft to Howells, 22 March 1912; MH). Perhaps Howells' most striking comment in his own speech concerned Mark Twain: "If I had been witness to no other surpassing things of American growth in my fifty years of observation, I should think it glory enough to have lived in the same time and in the same land with the man whose name must always embody American humor to human remembrance. What has been my own influence on that time in that land I should like so much to say, so much to say!" But, Howells concluded, he would not impose on the patience of the audience. Others did, at length; but many letters from writers in Europe and America were printed in the *Weekly* supplement rather than read aloud at the dinner. Henry James's remarkable letter, however, was too long even for publication in the *Weekly* and eventually appeared in the April *North American Review* under the title, "A Letter to Mr. Howells"; it was accompanied by a contribution from Franklin B. Sanborn and Howells' own response to the occasion.

17 MARCH 1912, NEW YORK, TO HENRY JAMES

12 East 58th street,
March 17, 1912.

My dear James:

I owe you an answer for two letters,[1] or two answers. The first, the public one, I do not know how to acknowledge. It almost convinced me that I had really been some help or service to you; at any rate, I am going to believe it as a pleasure to which I can turn in the night when I wake to the sense of what a toad I am and always have been. Your letter, so fully, so beautifully kind, will help to take away some of those dreadful moments of self-blame, and I can think, "Well, there must have been something in it; James would not abuse my dotage with flattery; I was probably not always such a worm of the earth as I feel myself at present." Your letter, meant for the public eye, brought before mine the vision of those days and nights in Sacramento street, "when my bosom was young,"[2] and swelled with pride in your friendship and joy in sharing your literary ambition, as if it were the "communion of saints?" I do thank you for it, and I am eager for all men to read it in *The North American* to which, as alone worthy of reporting it, it has been transferred from the *Weekly*.[3] I was rather glad it was not in our host's scheme to read it at the dinner, where the best, the finest effect of it would have been lost. No letters were read, but all will be printed in the Review—quaintly enough, as I feel, since they were some of them personally addressed to me, who may be supposed to smuggle them into print for the gratification of my vanity. But I believe it is the convention to ignore that sort of ostensibility; at any rate, I found the matter past my control. It is at the worst, part of the divine madness of an affair in which I still struggle to identify my accustomed self. It was really something extraordinary. Four hundred notables swarmed about a hundred tables on the floor, and we elect sat at a long board on a dais. Mrs. Clifford was among us,[4] two elbows from the President of the United States, and she can tell you better about it than I, who remained for the whole time in a daze from which I wrenched myself for twenty minutes to read my farrago of *spropositi*;[5] it was all, all wrong and unfit; but nobody apparently knew it, not even I till that ghastly waking hour of the night when hell opens to us.

I leave myself little room to say I am sorry you are not feeling so well as you promised to be; I hope by now you are trying to keep your promise. Your nephew and name-sake writes me from Cambridge that you have been sitting on an anti-suffrage platform;[6] we shall all be marching in the suffrage procession in May: John's *two* boys, their two grandfathers, John and his wife, the two White girls and Pilla, shouting the battle cry of female freedom.[7] Nothing but distance will save the windows of Rye House.—John's new boy is a beauty,[8] and Billy remains as divine as ever. He now has a feverish passion for Indians.

Pilla sends her love with mine. We are off to Atlantic City tomorrow for the week.

Yours ever
W. D. Howells.

1. On 19 February 1912 James wrote both a public letter for Howells' seventy-fifth birthday dinner (Percy Lubbock, ed., *The Letters of Henry James* [1920; reprint ed., New York: Octagon Books, 1970], II, 221–26) and a private one (MH). In the latter James wrote: "hearing from 45 Albemarle Street of the birthday banquet to be so gracefully offered you on March 1st., and that 'letters' contributive to this grace are in order for the occasion, I have wanted greatly to toss my little nosegay into the pile. But I have only been able to do this by a letter addressed to yourself—not to the 'Firm'; jamais de la vie!"

2. See W. S. Gilbert, *Trial by Jury*: "When first my old, old love I knew, / My bosom welled with joy; / My riches at her feet I threw— / I was a love-sick boy!" (*Plays and Poems of W. S. Gilbert* [New York: Random House, 1932], p. 45.)

3. See Howells to Taft, 16 March 1912, n. 1. In his reply of 27 March 1912 (MH), James expressed his disappointment about the decision not to read his letter at the dinner: "I confess I am sorry that the letter I contributed was not read out—as it was particularly & altogether 'built' to be; I wanted to testify publicly to you, & to be thereby present & participant; & it never occurred to me that these wouldn't be a rendering on the part of the managers . . . ."

4. Lucy Lane Clifford, Mrs. W. K. Clifford (d. 1929), was an English novelist and playwright whom Howells had met in the spring of 1904 as a friend of Henry James. See *Life in Letters*, II, 199.

5. Italian for "blunders, follies, absurdities."

6. James replied on 27 March that Howells had been misinformed about his "having sat on an anti-suffrage platform. Mrs. Humphrey Ward wrote & asked me if I would do so with her & I replied that I would go to her meeting with pleasure, out of cold-blooded curiosity, if she would understand that shld. Mrs. Pankhurst ask me the next week I would hold myself free to do exactly as much. She freely assented, but when the time came I hated even to appear to put myself in a false position (for I am utterly detached & uncommitted on the subject, which leaves me of a cold—!) & therefore went sneakingly in a box, as I might have gone to the Opera or the Hippodrome. The question simply overwhelmingly bores me—& I resent being hustled into concluding about it at all. Somehow, strangely, rather, I don't find it, even in its acute phase here, *interesting*—it is various other things but isn't that. One would have thought *apriori* that it *would* be—everything *else* about women is; but this is, to me, mortally tedious . . . ."

7. A large woman's suffrage procession took place in New York on 4 May 1912, but the New York *Times* of the following day, though naming some of the approximately 1,000 men who participated in the march, does not mention either Howells or Horace White.

8. John Noyes Mead Howells, the second child of John Mead and Abby White Howells, was born 11 March 1912.

25 MARCH 1912, NEW YORK, TO THOMAS HARDY

12 East 58th street,
March 25, 1912.

Dear Mr. Hardy:

Your letter about my birthday gives me the privilege of writing to you and the pleasure of thanking you. I wish it could give me the little more time I wanted when we met two years ago,[1] for trying to tell you how much I have loved your work both in verse and prose; how I have read it, and read it again. Now that you have stopped writing prose, I am not sure but I love your verse best. No, I will not say that, on second thought; but when I read your lovely rhyme, I forget how beautiful your prose is.[2] Certain things of yours haunt my ear with their matchless music; your poetry has a go of its own, the run of wild pretty girls, the stumble of maids forlorn.

Write some more of it, and I will give you a whole Easy Chair of praise.[3] But also, write me yet one more novel, to read and read again. I make the claim of one of your earliest and faithfullest lovers.

Yours sincerely
W. D. Howells.

1. Hardy's letter of 16 February 1912 (MH) mentions Howells' coming "to see me at my London flat about a year & half ago," a visit that "revived a friendship of I should think 30 years' standing . . . ." Howells actually first met Hardy at a dinner in the summer of 1883, made memorable by Hardy's praise of Mark Twain's *Life on the Mississippi*. See *Twain-Howells*, p. 434; also Howells to Gosse, 26 June 1883.

2. Hardy's birthday letter also praised Howells for his "many labours in the field of American literature." It then continues: "You have, too, always beheld the truth that poetry is the heart of literature, & done much to counteract the suicidal opinion held, I am told, by young contemporary journalists, that the times have so advanced as to render poetry nowadays a negligible tract of letters!"

3. Howells never wrote the "Easy Chair," but he read Hardy early and late and regarded him as a powerful ally in the war for realism.

25 MARCH 1912, NEW YORK, TO EDEN PHILLPOTTS

> 12 East 58th Street,
> N. Y., March 25th, 1912.

My dear Phillpotts:

So great a man as you and so good a friend will not mind my sending him a typewritten letter. I am sure it will carry my gratitude as if it were in my own hand.

I wish very much you could have been with me on the night of the second of March, which we made my birthday in order to convenience the President. I think you would have enjoyed looking at four hundred Americans all immersed in their meat and drink and hoping the speaking would not begin just yet. We really had a wonderfully good time, although I hated the notion of it with all my heart. Those things are not so bad in experience as in anticipation, as you will find if you live to have a seventy-fifth birthday. You must come over and have it here, and bring Mrs. Phillpotts, and that dear little girl of yours, and your delightful boy who so much preferred going motoring with my daughter and me to obeying his parents and staying at home to be measured for his clothes.

We are always recurring to our happy day or two at Torquay[1] and hoping we may have it again within easier reach; not but what I think Devonshire is the delightfulest country in the world, or one of the delightfulest. The name is so dear to me that I almost bought a tract of twelve acres in Bermuda last winter because it lay in the parish called Devonshire. It was clothed with palms and bananas and the kind government would have sold it to me for far less than it was worth. Come over and we will settle down on it and build us two Bermudian houses out of the coral, with a chimney at each gable of them. The thing is worth thinking of.

With my affectionate regards and my daughter's to all your family,

> Yours sincerely,
> W. D. Howells.

Eden Phillpotts, Esq.,
Torquay,
Devonshire.

1. Howells visited Phillpotts in September 1909. See Howells to Elinor Howells, 17 September 1909.

22 June 1912, Kittery Point, to Joseph A. Howells

Kittery Point, June 22, 1912.

Dear Joe:

John left an order with his druggist for your Frame Food, and I have done the same with mine in Portsmouth, and I hope we may get it, between us.

I want next to congratulate Ally and Willy on the prosperity of their children, especially their daughters'; their son's was to be expected. They have reason to be proud of their family, or, rather, glad of them, for they all seem good. John was speaking very admiringly of William, whom he values for his quiet good sense and good manners. The boy has just sent me a short story, very well done.—McClure's has taken a story of Annie's[1] which I sent to them anonymously, and has asked her to send more.

I am rejoiced that you are so prettily and pleasantly placed, and I know you will get better and better.[2] I like so much to hear from you in all possible detail. Do you have mosquitoes? They are very bad here this year, but the place was never lovelier. No, we are not giving it up, or selling it. John will come here more and more unless we return, as we may if we don't like York Harbor. I have bought a very pretty place there, which will readily rent at a large price, if we want to leave it, and to come back. It is terribly strange here without Elinor.[3] I miss her more and more as time passes, and *realize* that I shall never see her again unless I somehow, somewhere go to her. She will not return to me. Death, which parted us, can alone unite us.

—I am longing to take up the story of *The Leatherwood God*, which you looked up the ground of 8 or 10 years ago. I found the beginning of it which I had made; I thought it very good, and I have been working it out so clearly in my mind that it wont be hard to write.[4] I have *New Leaf Mills* ready to print now, but I shall not have it put in type till Mr. Duneka, Harper's manager, returns from Europe, next month. I have written my Spanish stuff half up.[5]

Harper's are getting out a selection from Artemus Ward's letters and stories, and I am writing an introduction to it.[6] The funniest and best parts are the non-Ward parts, where Browne deals directly with the reader. Did you ever see him?

I visited John on Staten Island last week. Dear little Billy was lovelier than ever, and the second boy is beautiful. Billy is a most interesting creature, and grows in charm. He was a little sick while I was there, and my heart was wrung, but he is quite well again.

I don't know the book about authors which you speak of. Do you care for the Railroad Man's Magazine which I've been sending you?

With our love for all

Your aff'te brother
Will.

1. Annie Howells Fréchette's story, "His First-Born," *McClure's*, September 1912, deals with a white father's reclaiming his ten-year-old half Indian son.

2. See Howells to Joseph A. Howells, 19 January 1912, n. 1.

3. See Howells to Duneka, 13 August 1912, n. 1.

4. In the next weeks Howells worked sustainedly and effectively on the tale he had begun to write in the early 1860s, for on 30 July 1912 (MWA) he wrote F. A. Duneka that he was sending him by express a novel begun fifty years earlier and finished in the past two years. He acknowledged taking the "historical outline" for *The Leatherwood God* from a narrative by Judge R. H. Taneyhill, but insisted that the characters and the vital incidents were his own inventions. See also Howells to Joseph A. Howells, 18 August 1911, n. 6, and *The Leatherwood God*, HE, pp. xi–xxiii.

5. The "Spanish stuff" became *Familiar Spanish Travels*, published in October.

6. For Howells' introduction to *Artemus Ward's Best Stories*, see Howells to Duneka, 4 January 1912, n. 2.

27 JUNE 1912, KITTERY POINT, TO ELIZABETH JORDAN

Kittery Point, June 27, 1912.

Dear Miss Jordan:

What I had madly imagined giving you was a series of social studies in the form of Twelve Distinctive Dinners, through which I should carry the hero and heroine in the character of observers or witnesses. The dinners should range from the first simple homelike meal of their childhood at noon to some final half-past eight o'clock gorge in the highest life possible. The diners should be of all types, children, young people, young married people, laboring men, bohemeans, public diners, commercial diners, professional diners, etc. You see how fruitful the theme might prove, and how it might well involve a story.

But—I have not the nerve for it now, and may never have. Besides with half my Spanish stuff to write out (alas for you that you can go to

Spain only in my shoes!) I have not the time.[1] So you can announce the grand daughters letters if you like; but don't promise any specific number of them.[2] I thought I might imagine her defending the present against the past in fashion, amusements, tastes, manners and customs, even morals. You know I am such a believer in the future that I *must* like the present a little.

Yours sincerely
W. D. Howells.

1. Still at work on his Spanish travel sketches, which were collected in *Familiar Spanish Travels*, Howells did not take up the projected "series of social studies" and never returned to it.

2. This project also never succeeded. Howells had first proposed it to Elizabeth Jordan on 30 May 1912 (NN): "I should like very much to write for the Bazar next year, say three or four papers, but as yet I don't know what about, quite. My daughter and I both think I oughtn't to be *instructive*; that women are lectured too much. How would it do to have a young woman lecture an old man? That might be fun. Say, *Letters to a Grandfather*. One could get in a good many digs both at youth and age." Howells had a novelist's longstanding preoccupation with difference and conflict between generations, as for example in "Reading for a Grandfather," *Harper's Bazar*, December 1903, and in dramatic dispute at the dinner table, as in *The Rise of Silas Lapham* (chapter 14) and *A Hazard of New Fortunes* (Part Fourth, chapter 6).

13 AUGUST 1912, YORK HARBOR, TO FREDERICK A. DUNEKA

York Harbor, Aug. 13, 1912.[1]

Dear Mr. Duneka:

It was stupid of me not to remember what you said of your printers' preoccupation.[2] I have had my own with the sickness and now the death of my oldest brother, who was very dear to me.[3] He died in Florida where we got him home from his consulate in the Bahamas, after his creeping paralysis had begun. He was very intelligent and interested to the end— and he especially wished to see *New Leaf Mills* in print, because it is almost entirely a family chronicle, and he gave me much material for it.

Yours ever
W. D. Howells.

1. Howells had recently purchased the York Harbor cottage, surrounded by hickory trees, where he had stayed in the summer of 1901. See Howells to Garland, 27 June 1901, and Howells to J. A. Howells, 22 June 1912. As the house was being painted, Howells had written to his brother Joe from Kittery Point, 5 May 1912 (MH): "It is hard to know whether it hurts more to stay here or go. Elinor's hand has passed over the whole place, and the house is full of her." Another reason for the move was that John

Howells and his family were beginning to use the Kittery Point house more frequently.

2. Howells had asked Duneka on 9 August 1912 (MWA) to put one hundred pages of his "Spanish stuff" into print, forgetting apparently that the printers were currently filled up with work, especially since two weeks earlier Howells had mailed Duneka the manuscript of *New Leaf Mills* for typesetting.

3. Joe had asked his brother to mark his grave with the stone on which as a printer he had composed the type of the Hamilton *Intelligencer*, the Dayton *Transcript*, and the Ashtabula *Sentinel*. Howells wrote and had cut into the stone this epitaph (manuscript at OFH; final version in *Life in Letters*, II, 323):

> Stone, upon which with hands of boy and man
> He framed the history of his time until,
> Week after week the varying record ran
> To its half-centuried tale of well and ill.
>
> Remember now how true through all those days
> He was: friend, brother, husband, father, son;
> Fill the whole limit of your space with praise;
> There needs no room for blame: blame there was none.
>   W. D. H.

15 SEPTEMBER 1912, YORK HARBOR, TO EDITH WYATT

York Harbor, Sept. 15, 1912.

Dear Miss Wyatt:

Ever since I read your generous words about my work in the North American Review,[1] I have been holding back my gratitude with both hands, loth to let it go to you, lest it should lose in going some sense of the very great kindness I felt you had done me, and come faint and halt to your feet. The kindness was so unexpected, so preciously surprising; and I cannot understand yet what moved you to it. You said things of me that I could have wished said above all others, and so intimately desired that I wonder still whether I have not rather written than read them.

Your praise is dearer to me in my age than it could have been earlier. When I was young many praised me; then came scornings and buffetings from every side, which now you have turned into sweetness. I did not think this would happen, but it has happened, and I am, with all my heart,

Yours sincerely
W. D. Howells.

1. "A National Contribution," *North American Review*, September 1912. Wyatt claims for Howells, whom she calls a "truth-teller," the "social sympathy" and "genuine understanding" that are the "great end of all letters."

6 October 1912, York Harbor, to Albert B. Paine

York Harbor, Oct. 6, 1912.

Dear Mr. Paine:[1]

I like your book more than I can say.[2] The first volume I have read nearly through, and the third, great part, and I have lived it all with sorrow as once I lived it all with joy; for I knew from Clemens whatever he had lived before I knew him at Hartford.

I could praise and blame many things in your book. It will remain one of the great biographies. Your postscript is *fine* and the spirit of all is frank and brave as the story should be of a man so frank and brave as he. It ought to have been perfect in diction, but it is not. At times it grovels in mere newspaper parlance. *How* can you bear to write "as does"? What do you mean by an "ill man"? I suppose, a sick man; but an "ill man" is a bad man.[3] Your book ought to be all proof-read* for a permanent edition.

These are the wounds of a friend[4] who loves you for what you have done, but not all you have done.

Yours affectionately
W. D. Howells.

* as I used to read the great M. T. himself.

1. Albert Bigelow Paine (1861–1937), journalist, novelist, writer of children's stories, biographer.
2. Harper & Brothers published Paine's *Mark Twain: A Biography* (1912) in three volumes. Howells devoted the "Editor's Easy Chair," *Harper's Monthly*, January 1913, to the biography. Not so much a review of the book, the essay is an effort to define Clemens' character, his "noble humanity," with the constant aid of hints and leads from the biographer.
3. In a note attached to the MS. of this letter, Paine commented: "I was very proud of this letter, even of its criticism–proud that he thought it worth while. He had his pet aversions as to the use of words & phrases and I had sinned sorely."
4. "Faithful are the wounds of a friend; but the kisses of an enemy are deceitful" (Proverbs 27:6–7).

14 October 1912, New York, to Frederick A. Duneka

Murray Hill Hotel....
New York Oct. 14, 1912.

Dear Mr. Duneka:

Brander Matthews closes his review of the Clemens biography with the suggestion that Clemens letters to me might well be published in full.[1] I think so too; they are wonderful; and if mine were printed with them perhaps it would not hurt.

Among your little fifty cent stories printed this fall, did you think of reprinting *The Daughter of the Storage* by W. D. H.?[2] Some people liked it.

Yours sincerely
W. D. Howells.

1. Matthews reviewed Paine's *Mark Twain: A Biography* in the New York *Times*, 13 October 1912. He compared "Mr. Howells and Mark" to Goethe and Schiller, Molière and Boileau, and suggested that their letters, only excerpted by the biographer, might some day "be printed in full for the delight of all lovers of good writing and good humor, good thinking and good fellowship." His suggestion remained unrealized until the publication of H. N. Smith and W. M. Gibson, ed., *Mark Twain-Howells Letters*, 2 vols. (Cambridge, Mass.: Harvard University Press, Belknap Press, 1960).

2. "The Daughter of the Storage" had appeared in *Harper's Monthly*, September 1911, but was not reprinted until *The Daughter of the Storage and Other Things in Prose and Verse* (1916). Duneka replied on 15 October 1912 (copy at MWA): "I am sorry I did not think of asking you to let us make a fifty cent book of your delightful story . . . . It is too late, of course, this year because the booksellers buy no new books after the end of this month. But next year we can do it."

23 OCTOBER 1912, KITTERY POINT, TO FREDERICK A. DUNEKA

Kittery Point, Oct. 23, 1912.

Dear Mr. Duneka:

I get such letters as this rather often, but I don't like to flourish them at you. Many people seem to read my books, but few buy them. Don't trouble to return this.[1]

Paines life of Clemens has almost been the death of me, for it is my life, too, in memories that are now all sorrows. It is really a wonderfully able and interesting book, worthy to rank with the great biographies, but because it is so modest and simple-hearted, few will have the courage to do it justice. I doubt if even I, the hero of so many forlorn hopes in literature, will have the courage.[2] But it is beautiful and wholly adequate; and enough to make Clemens's ghost swear at the "damned human race" which will not own it.

I am here with my grandson for company while my son, daughter and daughter-in-law are in Boston. This morning I took Billy to the house of the neighborhood Boss to see the President, who paid us a flying visit. He shook Billys tiny hand as a giant might a fairy's, and I loved him more than ever—great, kind, cheerful, hopeless man.[3]

Yours ever
W. D. Howells.

1. The letter from one of Howells' literary admirers is no longer extant.

2. See Howells to Paine, 6 October 1912, n. 2.

3. Presumably William Howard Taft was "hopeless" of reelection, in the face of the split in the Republican party created by Theodore Roosevelt's Bull Moose reform faction. On 4 August 1912 (Avon County Reference Library, Bristol) Howells had commented on the political situation in a letter to his English friend William A. Gill: "We are here in a very strange three cornered political fight over the presidency, with an even chance for Roosevelt against Wilson, and none for Taft, whom personally, I love. Under the strange local law, I am disfranchised in New York because I left my apartment in May, and have taken up no other residence, so that I shall not be obliged to choose between them, or to vote my socialist principles for [Eugene] Debs. But Roosevelt has come largely to socialist ground, only there is always the danger that he may cut it from under socialist feet. He is boldly and outrightly suffragist, and yet Pilla will not vote for him." For the relation between Howells and Roosevelt, see William M. Gibson, *Theodore Roosevelt Among the Humorists* (Knoxville: University of Tennessee Press, 1980).

17 NOVEMBER 1912, NEW YORK, TO FREDERICK A. DUNEKA

Hotel Wellington ...
New York ... Nov. 17, 1912.

Dear Mr. Duneka:

I am returning my story without either the prologue or epilogue which we desired.[1] The fact is, I could not think of anything to say, that would help out the tale. I am sorry, for I feel, unresentfully enough, heaven knows, that you do not like it, much, if any. Indeed I do not altogether like it myself, and if you were minded to kill it, I would willingly join in the murder. But perhaps you think you have imbrued enough in the blood of my fledglings. This one has little gayety in its flight, yet it is not altogether a bird of gloomy note. It is tragical,[2] yes, but it has moments of comedy, and I think it keeps fairly well the level of life as life is lived. As my poor brother[3] used to say of my work generally, it is as natural as the toothache; and I have suffered through it accordingly. There was the making of a high tragedy in it, but not in me, and I have left it a sad but not quite a hapless thing. I do not cherish the vain hope that it will sell, and as I say, if you wish to kill it—

Yours sincerely
W. D. Howells.

1. Howells and Duneka had earlier considered the need for a "prefatory paragraph" to *New Leaf Mills*, presumably to explain the mingling of fictional and autobiographical elements in it. See Howells to F. A. Duneka, 9 October 1912 (MWA). Howells actually wrote a brief note, had it set in type, but finally decided against its inclusion in the book on the ground that "The note 'pleads the baby-act,' which at

my age is not fitting." See Howells to J. W. Harper, 29 November 1912 (ViU), and Howells to F. A. Duneka, 5 December 1912 (MWA).

2. One of the tragic elements is the luring away from the Owen family of a pretty young housekeeper by her drunken bawd of a mother. Howells was to write of the episode again, briefly, in *Years of My Youth*, HE, pp. 36–37.

3. Most likely a reference to Joe, who had died three months earlier.

10 DECEMBER 1912, NEW YORK, TO FREDERICK A. DUNEKA

37 Madison Square,
Dec. 10, 1912.

Dear Mr. Duneka:

I had hoped to report at Franklin Square this morning, and account for all my ways, but I am going out to Plainfield this afternoon, and so must explain by letter. It seems that my daughter's nervous breaking down will require absolute rest at present,[1] (for 2 weeks) and then a building up somewhere out of town. She is now here, and I am not to see her except for a few minutes each day, and better not at all. She has a nurse but I have nobody, and am drolly, (or sadly) homeless. I can manage by day, but the nights are dreadful for the man of 75. So perhaps I may be forced for both our sakes to go to Europe with my son, to whom the outing is essential. My sister in law Mrs. Shepard takes me in for the present,[2] and then I shall come back to this hotel, or go to my son at Kittery Point till he sails. Then, heaven will provide—*I suppose!*

So much seems due to kind Franklin Square; but kindly keep it all to yourself. The Easy Chairs will follow each other as usual, and you are choked with Spanish stuff.[3] So I do not worry about copy. If Miss Cutting wants any of the papers you will gladly divide with her, of course.[4]

My address for letters and telegrams is A. D. Shepard, Fanwood, New Jersey. *Telephones, 1219 Fanwood.*

I will let my letters from the office come here, and they will be forwarded.

Yours ever
W. D. Howells.

1. The exact nature and cause of Mildred Howells' "nervous breaking down" are not known, except that on 30 December 1912 (MWA) Howells wrote to Duneka: "My daughter is in bed where she has been for a month, trying to get rested enough to get well of her nervous breakdown."

2. For Augustus D. and Joanna Mead Shepard, see Howells to Elinor Howells, 14 September 1865, n. 3.

3. The travel sketches that eventually were collected in *Familiar Spanish Travels*.

4. Elizabeth Cutting had become associate editor of the *North American Review* in 1910; between 1921 and 1924, during George Harvey's tenure as American ambassador to Great Britain, she served as editor. Only "To and in Granada" appeared in the *Review*, April 1913, subsequent to this letter.

17 JANUARY 1913, CAMBRIDGE, TO ANNE H. FRÉCHETTE

17 Buckingham Street,
Cambridge, Jan'y 17, 1913.

Dear Annie:

I can never fitly answer your beautiful letters either in quantity or quality, but I am always ungratefully glad to get them. The last was one of the most interesting and it touched me most by the great good news it gave about our dear Vevie.[1] How happy you must all be. Here, Pilla and I rejoiced together, but our joy was only a pale reflex of yours. Now life can begin again with you. But Annie, why do you think of that long, tiring journey home? Surely, Howells can see to selling *all* your possessions, or any of them; at the worst he could put a match to them. Don't let them become *ob*sessions; dont let them force you to something that at your age will overtask you. Do let me persuade you against coming.[2] Vevie will need you now more than ever, to be glad with her.—I have just got a letter from John who is settled for the winter with his family in Paris. He changed from Rome, and Abby eagerly with him, while we staid in New York, till Pilla finished her overdone rest-cure. Then we came on here together, where in the house of our old friend Mrs. Scudder,[3] we are as much at home as we can be out of our own. It is scarcely three minutes from here to the house on Concord Avenue, which Elinor and I built forty years ago to "live in always". It is sad, but it isn't so terrible as you would think, and Cambridge is not so ghostly.[4] Life can never be what it was, yet it is still life, and I am old and forget much more than I dared hope I could.— Pilla seems as well as ever, but she tires easily, and I must not put so much upon her as I have.—Are you writing something? It was shabby of McClure to get you to do that sequel and then refuse it.[5] If you will send me some story I will try it for you with the American Magazine. I will have it out with McClure, sometime. What about that old Canadian story? But perhaps it might make trouble for you. Dearest love from both to Vevie and to you all. Aurelia must take this for her letter for the present. I'll write to her soon.

Aff'tly,
Will.

1. Marie Marguerite Fréchette appears to have been stricken by a protracted illness. Howells commented on "the good report the doctor has given you" in his letter to Vevie of 19 January 1913 (MH), but later in the year he referred to Vevie as "Annie's invalid daughter." See Howells to Popenoe, 3 May 1913.

2. Annie, now living in Lausanne with her husband, daughter, and sister, did not follow Howells' advice. Later that year she traveled to North America, presumably to make arrangements for a permanent retirement in Switzerland and to visit her son, Howells, then employed in the Department of Mines at Ottawa. See James Doyle, *Annie Howells and Achille Fréchette* (Toronto: University of Toronto Press, 1979), p. 107.

3. Grace Owen (Mrs. Horace E.) Scudder was the widow of a longtime friend and associate of Howells on the *Atlantic*.

4. Actually the Howellses lived at 37 Concord Avenue for only five years in the 1870s. One reason why Howells felt the sadness of revisiting this scene of his earlier life with Elinor may have been his decision to sell the property in February 1912. It went for $7,000 to a Mr. Bazirgan. See Charles H. Fiske to Howells, 14 February 1912 (MH), and a bill issued by Perley Putnam, real estate broker at York Harbor, 19 February 1912 (MH).

5. Annie's earlier story was "His First-Born," *McClure's*, September 1912; no further story by her appeared in either *McClure's* or the *American Magazine*.

5 FEBRUARY 1913, CAMBRIDGE, TO JAMES F. RHODES

17 Buckingham Street,
Feb'y 5, 1913.

My dear Rhodes:[1]

I have beaten you, who only *expect* to be much pleased by My Mark Twain. I have already been much pleased by Your Civil War: really a fine, clear, calm, just piece of work. I finished the last chapter this morning between 3 and 4. Such is the ardor of study in the man of near-76. But I had lived and sorrowed through it all when it happened.

Yes, I hope to be at the Club,[2] though I had forgotten all about it. Where? Just when?

With best regards to Mrs. Rhodes,

Yours ever
W. D. Howells.

1. James Ford Rhodes (1848–1927), Ohio-born, retired in middle life from the coal and iron business to write history, notably *A History of the United States*, covering the years 1850–1877 (7 volumes, 1893–1906), and *Lectures on the American Civil War* (1913).

2. The Club, as it was known, was an informal organization for monthly dinners and conversation, established in the late 1860s by a group of congenial men, among them Henry and William James, Howells, A. G. Sedgwick, Henry Adams, O. W. Holmes, Jr., John Fiske, John T. Morse, Jr., John R. Dennett, and T. S. Perry. In its later years the membership of The Club included Rhodes and Alexander Agassiz. See

Virginia Harlow, *Thomas Sergeant Perry: A Biography* (Durham, N.C.: Duke University Press, 1950), pp. 46–47.

8 FEBRUARY 1913, CAMBRIDGE, TO HENRY JAMES

17 Buckingham Street,
Cambridge, Feb'y 8, 1913.

My dear James:

If I began owning my sins of omission against you, there would be no end. Forget that it is almost a year that I have owed you a letter. I am writing this chiefly in the hope of another from you.

Pilla and I have been here nearly a month, though she has now been some weeks in Boston to be the nearer to her dentist. She has had the national nervous break-down, and is now resting from a wretched rest-cure in New York, and her health promises to reestablish itself.— The strangeness of being again in Cambridge is very strange indeed. I am boarding here with the widow of my old friend and Atlantic successor Scudder,[1] in great comfort and greater quiet than New York would let me imagine was to be found anywhere in the world. The days come and go as silently as if they wore rubbers like the rest of us; it has been all January abnormally warm, but February so far has offered us the cold of other years, while I still lived, three minutes walk away in the house we built on Concord Avenue to "live in always."[2]—I know you abhor Cambridge too much to believe I can like it, but I do in a sort. My children are children still here, and I am a man of 28–38, instead of 76. But the other people are horribly old; every now and then I hear that some woman is ninety whom I thought my contemporary. The lines of my Cambridge are here, but swollen to bursting with strange new dwellings.

Last Sunday we were at Mrs. William James's (a white haired angel, she)[3] and had much talk of you, and of your being in Chelsea, and suffering from the "shingles" which is really being something like the "roof" if not "the crown of things."[4] But they said you were well again, and I am glad of that.—It's not impossible you may be run in upon by us before the spring is over. John with his wife and two boys and their two nurses is in Paris for the winter, and we may go over to come home with them.—Grace Norton has narrowly escaped pneumonia, but is now mending. I have seen her, and nearly every one I ever or never knew here. As usual I am writing a novel,[5] which someday you may see; I seem to have more muscle than for some years past, for that sort of work. Also I have done a book of Spanish travel, to come out next fall.[6]

I wish I could hope to hear of your doings. Do you see Miss Allen?[7] If you do give our love to her; after you she is best worth seeing of any person in England.

Yours ever
W. D. Howells.

Of course I see Perry much, and we always talk of you. Mrs. P. has done my picture.[8]

1. See Howells to A. H. Fréchette, 17 January 1913, n. 3.
2. See Howells to A. H. Fréchette, 17 January 1913, n. 4.
3. Alice James, Henry James's sister-in-law.
4. Possibly a wry reference to Tennyson's paraphrase of Dante, that "a sorrow's crown of sorrow is remembering happier things" (*Locksley Hall*, I, 75). James replied on 19 February 1913 (MH), explaining that he had been struggling with various illnesses for some months, but "What is of course *most* overwhelming is the repeated blight of work for so long; that almost breaks my heart . . . ."
5. *The Leatherwood God.*
6. *Familiar Spanish Travels.*
7. Elizabeth Jessie Jane Allen, a gossipy, generous English woman, "always on the move," and a friend of James for a long time. See Leon Edel, *Henry James, The Master, 1901–1916* (Philadelphia: J. B. Lippincott, 1972), pp. 150–56. James replied: "She has fallen upon evil days, alas—from having spent herself in the service of humanity: graveish heart-trouble & chronic failure of voice."
8. See Howells to Lilla C. Perry, 31 March 1913, n. 1.

23 FEBRUARY 1913, CAMBRIDGE, TO AURELIA H. HOWELLS

17 Buckingham Street,
Cambridge, Feb. 23, 1913.

Dear Aurelia:

I was greatly interested in what you wrote about those Welsh pepole, and their singing you the Welsh songs. I hope Annie and you will be able to stop at Hay on your way home. I ought to have called at the Castle when I was there last; but you know I hate bothering people, and I had no idea that Lady Glemesk was related to Canon Bevan whom I knew there in 1883;[1] the printer in our great grandfather's mill spoke only a lady living in the Castle.—Pilla talks of going over to be the paying-guest of some ladies at Torquay this summer, and perhaps she may see the Pritchards in South Devon.[2] She knows that country well.

I am sending you a copy of *New Leaf Mills* which has just been published. The great—the only—merit of it is the presentation of father's and mother's characters. I could not get the grip of the whole situation which I tried for. Still, considering what novels now are, I need not be so much ashamed of it. But I know that I am now an old man, and my best work is done. I am trying to do The Leatherwood God, but I work feebly. I ought to have done it thirty years ago. (It's the story, you know, of the imposter who passed himself off for the Deity in Eastern Ohio in 1828.)

We are drawing near the end of our stay here; Pilla's dentistry is practically done. We shall go to New York, and we may possibly sail together by the middle of March, I to join John's family in Paris, and she to go Torquay. But it is all very uncertain.—Abby has been three weeks in bed with the grippe, but is now quite well and the boys are fine; so is John.

I go about rather a good deal here and in Boston; and the thing is bright at the time, but it quickly turns gray. I am not unhappy, but the motive of life is half gone.—I hope all goes well with Vevie, still, and that Annie is well; I am sorry Achille is poorly.

My love to all.

Your aff'te brother
Will.

Sam wrote the other day quite cheerfully.

1. For Howells' first visit to and report from Hay, see Howells to W. C. Howells, 21 June 1883, where he also mentions William L. Bevan. "Lady Glemesk" probably was Alice Lister, who married Algernon Borthwick, Baron Glenesk (1830–1908).

2. The Pritchards have not been identified. Mildred Howells stayed with her father in Torquay in September 1909 to visit the novelist Eden Phillpotts.

2 MARCH 1913, CAMBRIDGE, TO FREDERICK A. DUNEKA

Cambridge, March 2, 1913.

My dear Duneka:

There *is* some use in being 76 years old, if your birthday brings you such a letter as I got from you yesterday.[1] I consider that in all decency I ought not to lagged on after that glorious celebration last year, and perhaps I really am dead. In that case it is the voice of posterity hailing me from Franklin Square and giving me a sense of posthumous glory. Love to you and to all of you.

Yours sincerely
W. D. Howells.

1. Duneka's letter of felicitation of 28 February 1913 (MH) laments his inability to write Howells "a proper roundelay" to honor "the Great Day," since he (Duneka) is only "a man of plain prose" rather than a poet.

29 MARCH 1913, CAMBRIDGE, TO FREDERICK A. DUNEKA

17 Buckingham Street,
Cambridge, March 29, 1913.

Dear Mr. Duneka:

I oughtn't to promise the beginning of my autobiog. for next Feb'y; for that would mean your having the copy in November. Six months later seems the very best I could do, and until my daughter and I are somehow settled for the summer, I must not promise *anything*. She is still far from well, and her discouragement re-acts on me, so that I can't clear my mind for work. With patience all will come right, and I will try to meet your wishes. I feel your kindness deeply, and value your faith in my work. The book might be called, "My Times and Places: An Autobiography."[1]

I enclose a very intelligent notice of "N. L. Mills" from the Manchester Guardian; I have heard of a still better one in the London Times.[2]

I liked your last advertisement.

Yours sincerely
W. D. Howells.

1. Howells loved reading the autobiographies of others—he edited a series of memoirs for J. R. Osgood in 1877–1878—but like Tolstoy he found writing his own autobiography thoroughly painful. His outline, "My Times and Places, An Autobiography," in twelve parts, begins with his ancestry in Wales and Pennsylvania, and closes with his travel years 1908 to 1912. He actually completed the record of his life up to his departure for Washington, D.C., in 1861, in *Years of My Youth* (1916), but only planned "Years of My Middle Life," from the Venetian experience through the Cambridge years on to his European residence and the move to Boston in the early 1880s. See *Years of My Youth*, HE, pp. 253–58.

2. The critic for the *Times Literary Supplement*, 27 February 1913, wrote that when the future observer comes to interpret the United States, "that gigantic jumble of ideas and activities," he will perhaps "find a greater importance in such dreamy beliefs and vain efforts as those of the Powells and their kind than in all the mines and manufactories." Edward Garnett in the Manchester *Guardian*, 12 March 1913, writing of "Howells's New Novel," observed that his style is "classical in its restraint, breadth, and serenity"; he has the secret of "spacing," of keeping parts in relation to the whole. Garnett concluded that because of its spiritual depth and artistic fineness, *New Leaf Mills* is "a book that good Americans should be proud of."

31 March 1913, Cambridge, to Lilla C. Perry

17 Buckingham Street,
Cambridge, March 31, 1913.

Dear Mrs. Perry:

Impossible—impossible! The shattered prose of my being could never rise to the poetry of your most hospitable, most lovable wish to have me your guest! I must stay where I can be shy and glum when I will, or want. Indeed, I could not come to your friendly house at this time, except some day to bring my silver gray coat, and offer you my hand for a postultimate sitting.[1] But I thank you, I thank you.

What a mercy that scandalous attempt on poor James's delicacy was so promptly defeated! I look back on it with horror, blessing God that I had no part in it.[2]

His—J.'s—new book has just come, and I have tasted it already.[3] Delicious.

Yours sincerely,
W. D. Howells.

1. Some time earlier, Lilla Perry had begun to paint Howells' portrait, while her husband, Thomas S. Perry, read aloud to Howells from Samuel Butler's notebooks and other books he was currently reading. See Virginia Harlow, *Thomas Sergeant Perry: A Biography* (Durham, N.C.: Duke University Press, 1950), pp. 204–5. The portrait now hangs in the library of Colby College.

2. A well meant but misconceived effort to solicit a fund for Henry James. Perry and Howells, who both "knew how little James would have liked such a fund," scotched the proposal. See *Life in Letters*, II, 327. Edith Wharton managed, however, to help James financially, in secret, through his publisher.

3. *A Small Boy and Others.* To Perry, Howells wrote on 4 April 1913 (MeWC): "James's book is a cloudy glory, but it is a glory."

22 April 1913, Cambridge, to John J. Chapman

17 Buckingham Street,
Cambridge, April 22, 1913.

My dear Chapman:

That is a very right and good thing you have written about "Fanny's First Play."[1] It makes me sorry that in my general Easy Chair paper about the winter's plays I did not express fully my sense of the abomination.[2] But all through I stood shoulder to shoulder with you. It *is* abominable that we should be forbidden to hope for a way out of our evils—even so gross an evil as hypocrisy. Some of Shaw's plays, like "Arms and the Man" and "Mrs. Warren's Professor"[3] are true and good; but "Fannys First Play" was an insolent and mischeavous lie.

Yours ever,
W. D. Howells.

1. Chapman's review of George Bernard Shaw's *Fanny's First Play*, in *Harper's Weekly*, 19 April 1913, noted references to adultery, which roused self-conscious laughter from a group of school girls attending the performance.

2. Howells had just commented on *Fanny's First Play* and other current drama in New York in the "Editor's Easy Chair," *Harper's Monthly*, May 1913. He found the sources of some of the laughter in the play regrettable, but thought the playing of it was even, equal, perfect.

3. Howells had praised *Arms and the Man* in *Harper's Weekly*, 30 March 1895, and followed Shaw thereafter on the stage and in print with critical comprehension and sympathy. Howells' use of "Professor" rather than "Profession" in the second title is probably a mere slip of the pen rather than an intentional pun.

22 APRIL 1913, CAMBRIDGE, TO MILDRED HOWELLS

17 Buck. st.,
April 22, 1913.

Dear Pilla:

No letter from you today, which I hope does not mean mounting snuffles with you.[1] I am expecting to hear momently of the Johnabbies arrival,[2] which they may telegraph. I have sent John my power of attorney to close up the 130 W. 57 business,[3] and I may not have to go on to New York, but whether I go or not I am likely to visit you soon.

I had a very pleasant lunch at Mrs. James's, and much Swedenborgian talk; her mother was there, and Peggy who is a dawning socialist and reading my Altrurian books.[4]

It is very warm, and I found poor Theodora Sedgwick on her porch; she was pathetically glad to see me, though she could scarcely say so.

The readings began again last night, and Mrs. H.[5] listened with voracity to 75 pages of Hazard of New Fortunes.

Poppy.

Little Sylvia[6] just now fell up stairs with your yesterday's letter. She cried, but gladdened enough to beat me at parting. I'm sorry for the cold, if its bad enough to mean rhinitis. The euonymus tree is not synonymous with the euonymus vine; that flourishes in the James house, with 18 inches of new wood this spring. It would be nice on your garden fence; but I wont put it without leave. I can't understand about no letters—I sent two on two days from K. P.

1. Mildred was recuperating from a "nervous breakdown" at Pomfret Center, Connecticut, after having at the last minute given up a voyage to Bermuda because Howells "from pure homesickness could not let her go . . . ." See Howells to Aurelia Howells, 30 March 1913 (MH).
2. John and Abby Howells with their children had spent the winter in Paris.
3. Howells was trying to sell his New York apartment.
4. Mrs. William James; her mother, Elizabeth Putnam Webb Gibbons; and her daughter Mary Margaret James.
5. Probably Mrs. Hillhouse, a boarder at Grace Owen Scudder's comfortable boarding house, where Howells mostly stayed when in Cambridge.
6. The daughter of Sylvia Scudder, Mildred Howells' longtime friend.

3 MAY 1913, KITTERY POINT, TO PERRY D. POPENOE

Kittery Point, Me., May 3, 1913.

My dear Perry Popenoe:[1]

It was delightful to get your bit of biography from the Los Angeles Examiner, and to realize that you were alive and well. It made me proud of my old boyhood friend.[2]

Since I last heard from you, I have lost my dear wife. My brother Joseph died last year; Sam is in the Government Printing Office at Washington; my sisters are living in Switzerland in the care of my sister Annie's invalid daughter. I am much alone in the world, but fortune has been friendly to me, and with one daughter living I cannot complain, especially as my son and his wife and their two little boys let me make my home with them when we are not housekeeping.

My heart turns kindly to old days, where I find myself young with you, in a world utterly vanished.

Yours affectionately,
W. D. Howells.

1. Perry D. Popenoe, according to Mildred Howells' note (MH), "fought through the Civil War on the Northern side, and was forty-three years in the railway Postal Service . . . . He and Howells were boys together at Eureka . . . ."
2. A careful search of the Los Angeles *Examiner* has failed to turn up the "bit of biography" referred to here.

3 May 1913, Kittery Point, to Annie A. Fields

Kittery Point, Me., May 3, 1913.

Dear Mrs. Fields:

I should be proud and glad to be on any committee (that required no work) with you; if you think a homeless ex-New Yorker can fitly represent Utopia among your great Bostonians, do count me with them.[1] The notion of a large, stone I suppose, and granite I hope, seems to me the right memorial to the scholarliness of the Doctor, and if it is put behind his house, I will always be coming out of the back gate 302 Beacon street,[2] two doors away, and begging his divine shade for a place on it beside him. Our library windows used to look upon the very same open water where the wild ducks swam till the winter almost seized their webs in its icy fingers. What memories the thought of his kind neighborliness calls up!

Yours affectionately
W. D. Howells.

1. Evidently Mrs. Fields was establishing a committee to plan a memorial to Dr. Oliver Wendell Holmes.
2. Howells' residence in Boston from 1884 to 1887.

23 May 1913, Kittery Point, to Waldo R. Browne

Kittery Point, May 23, 1913.

Dear Mr. Browne:[1]

I thank you for sending me that rarely interesting and beautiful picture of your father and his friends. None of them was more truly and proudly his friend than I, or could have valued him more for those spiritual, intellectual and moral qualities which in their peculiar concord rendered him unique in his time and place.

Yours sincerely
W. D. Howells.

1. Almost certainly Waldo R. Browne, son of Francis F. Browne, with whom Howells corresponded in 1887 about the Chicago anarchists' trial. See Howells to F. F. Browne, 11 November 1887; also Howells to W. R. Browne, 16 June 1916.

15 JUNE 1913, KITTERY POINT, TO WILLIAM A. GILL

Kittery Point, June 15, 1913.

My dear Gill:

I wish you were here this most Kittery Pointish day, with its high, dry sky, and its keen breath from the sea; I am sure you would intimately feel its quality. My daughter-in-law and I are going presently for a call on some ladies in a bungalow on the hill behind the estuary where you once paddled in John's canoe.—I am here for the present with her and her baby boys, while he is in New York, hard at his architecture. My daughter is with her friends the Fiskes in York Harbor, and early in July we are going over to England for two months. She has had a nervous breakdown, and it became clear that we should not keep house this summer, early in the winter, which we spent she in Boston and I in Cambridge where I took up the raveled threads of my young life again. It was very curious; not so much painful as bewildering. I boarded with a family friend easily in sight of the house which my dear wife and I built "to live in always."—I find all life rather bewildering; for the first time, I do not care to write; but I hope the will for that will come back with the two months' rest I am promising myself: my head *feels tired.* I must thank you, tardily enough, for the Falstaff book, the best part of which I found your introduction.[1] I wish you would now write a book of your own.

I suppose we shall be in London before we come home, and I am glad to have your Hampstead address, for I want to see you, to say nothing of Mrs Gill.

I shall look eagerly for your Atlantic articles.[2] I think Sedgwick is making about the best of the magazines.[3]

"New Leaf Mills" has found more intelligent acceptance in England than here. It was queered for our public by the Harpers' announcement of it as a study of backwoods life; I supposed it was rather a tragical study of peculiar psychological facts and of character in gentle kindly people unhappily and disappointingly conditioned. Ma come si fà![4]

With best regards to you both,

Yours affectionately
W. D. Howells.

1. Maurice Morgann's *Dramatic Character of Sir John Falstaff* (1912), with an introduction by Gill.
2. "Some Novelists and the Business Man," part 1, "In England," *Atlantic*, September 1913; part 2, "In America," *Atlantic*, October 1913. In the second part Gill discussed *The Rise of Silas Lapham* among other contemporary novels.

3. Ellery Sedgwick (1872–1960), one of Howells' successors as editor of the *Atlantic* (1908–1938), wrote a biography of Thomas Paine (1899).

4. Italian for "But how is this to be done?" or "How can you make this clear?"

17 JUNE 1913, KITTERY POINT, TO JOHN M. HOWELLS

K. P., June 17, 1913.

Dear John:

I have supposed Abby to be writing you enough for the whole household, and so have joined Billy and wee Brother in their literary silence. Silent otherwise they are not, and they shout with voices so much alike that I know Billy only by his gentler, more modulated inflections. Last evening, a nice young fellow brought me a beautiful half cord of beech and birch dry wood, sawed twice, and I asked him if he thought he could pull that stranded dory up from our beach to the front, and he guessed so; and he took one horse from his wagon and hitched by the swingle-tree to the dory, and warped it over the grass like winking. It has been full of small boys all the morning, under the lowest-hanging apple-tree, and now Billy sits captain on the deep bale of sweet hay Albert and I put into it. Pil has come over from York and thinks it wonderful; it eclipses all the attractions of Shoerman's house.

I am writing doggedly away at a succession of Easy Chairs, and gradually getting the better of my weak-headedness.

After suffering many years for the sort of paper I used to get from 8 Milk Street, I have found this, which is even better.[1] Last night was hot, but to-day it is cool again, after joking round the compass about rain.

Papa.

Abby digs and waters incessantly; at night I read Hardy to her. I cannot close this without some explicit praise of Wee Brother. He is the best child imaginable, and says Thank you, and calls me Dada.

1. The enclosure being lost, the reference has not been identified.

9 AUGUST 1913, STRATFORD-ON-AVON, TO HENRY JAMES

> ...*Shakespeare Hotel,*
> *Stratford-on-Avon.* August 9, 1913.[1]

My dear James:

We gratefully spare you an immediate incursion, and when we do incur it will be to put the Mermaid between all of us and you. We have had what your Peggy's brother would probably call a hell of a time in failing to get lodgings in this town, and are staying meekly on in this pretty good hotel. It is the Shakespear month, and every house is packt from cellar to garret: such enthusiasm for the Swan of Avon must make the real author crisp with envy; but we are of the true faith, and care nothing for the sorrows of Bacon.[2]—We have had two hospitalities from your friend Marie Corelli, and I have carefully concealed that you are my friend. I have also concealed amidst her praises of my books that I have read none of hers. If it comes to the worst I can say I have read none of Stevenson's and only one of Meredith's; she seems vastly good natured.[3]

I *am* glad you are so distinctly better, and I hope that it is providentially decreed that we shall get to Rye. Of course we thank you, and I long for a longer talk that I had with you in Cheyne Walk. But as yet I cannot forecast anything; when I begin to prophesy it will be your right to say, Too late! We are both in love with your Peggy who is at least partly ours.[4]

> Yours ever
> W. D. Howells.

1. Howells and Mildred had left Boston on 8 July, on board the *Franconia*. They arrived in Liverpool on 16 July and spent about two weeks in London and Somerset.
2. This same day Howells wrote to his sister Annie (MH): "I have got a famous scheme for a Bacon-Shakespear story, something seriously fantastic . . . ." The scheme was for *The Seen and Unseen at Stratford-on-Avon,* published in the spring of 1914.
3. The passage is of course a tissue of ironies and exaggerations. Howells was apparently teasing James by enclosing a recent note, now lost, from Marie Corelli praising James as a "master." James reacted appropriately, writing on 26 August 1913 (MH): "Bless the dear lady, what a tremendous discovery she has made, how she has dashed aside my grimacing mask & laid bare the native truth. Really she *has,* & she strikes me as a person of exquisite taste & penetration. I thank you for her honeyed words, but don't wonder you wanted to get rid of them by shipment off: they must been hard to bear. Dear restless creature, raving over the works of one master to another master— even with the beautiful nature of the latter so well & notoriously attested: Yes, I will write to her—but since she has produced fictions I will write to her in ecstasy, about *you.* That will show her!" Howells had written about Corelli's fiction under the head-

ing "The Vulgarity of Wealth" eleven years earlier, *Harper's Weekly*, 27 December 1902.

4. James's niece, now visiting him, read Howells with particular pleasure.

15 AUGUST 1913, STRATFORD-ON-AVON, TO HENRY JAMES, JR.

>...*Shakespeare Hotel,*
>*Stratford-on-Avon.* Aug. 15, 1913.

Dear Mr. James:[1]

I am reading your father's book,[2] and constantly thanking his son for it, while I hear his rich voice, and see his smiling look in it. If I do not find the meaning and the moral of The Leatherwood God amidst its wonderful commonsense psychology, it will be my fault.

We are having a quiet, idle time here, and more and more the leisure and lustiness of England appeal to me from the perpetual singing and dancing and mumming. It is a very naked-minded country.

>Yours sincerely
>W. D. Howells.

1. Henry James, Jr. (1879–1947) was the novelist's nephew and the son of William James.

2. Presumably William James's *Some Problems of Philosophy* (1911), the unfinished, posthumously published volume for which his son wrote the "Prefatory Note." See Gay W. Allen, *William James: A Biography* (New York: Viking, 1967), pp. 515, 543.

24 SEPTEMBER 1913, YORK HARBOR, TO FREDERICK T. LEIGH

>York Harbor, Me., Sept. 24, 1913.

Dear Major Leigh:[1]

I have signed the enclosed agreement; but I regret to find that you are not bringing the book out "early in the fall," as Mr. Duneka made me hope you would.[2] It is not even included in the Chicago *Dial's* editorial announcements of fall books. It seems to me the most promising book in matter and treatment that I have done in many years, and I hope the house has not lost faith in it.

I had arranged with Mr. Duneka to bring out after the holidays my story of *The Daughter of the Storage* as one of your 75 ct. books; it seemed to have pleased a good many readers who at least abused my fondness with their praise; but so has *The Critical Bookstore*. I don't care which you reprint.

I trust it is going well with Duneka's son. My own son has come down in New York with typhoid fever: a mild case, but always typhoid. His wife has left Kittery Point to be with him, and we are to have their two little boys here.

Yours sincerely
W. D. Howells.

1. Frederick T. Leigh (1862–1914), or Major Leigh as he was called, became treasurer of Harper & Brothers when George Harvey became president in a thorough reorganization of the firm in 1900. See Eugene Exman, *The House of Harper* (New York: Harper & Row, 1967), p. 188.

2. *Familiar Spanish Travels* came out on 18 October; Howells' inquiry seems to have speeded up publication. He had signed an agreement with Harper & Brothers two days earlier for a twenty percent royalty (signed document, 22 September 1913, at MH).

28 September 1913, York Harbor, to Brand Whitlock

York Harbor, Me., September 28, 1913.

My dear Brand Whitlock:

I am sorry indeed for Toledo that you will no longer be mayor; but much as you owe the city which you have befriended, perhaps you owe more to the country and the time your fiction has honored and instructed. If you have decided to go abroad and have some work in mind, there is no better place, out of London and Paris, than Florence, though the climate of Rome is better, and Rome is—Rome. If you could get the Florentine consulate it would be more to your advantage than the Embassy at Rome where, as in Florence, you would spend more than your salary. In fact there is no diplomatic post of ours which I would take as a gracious gift except the ministry to Switzerland. The consulate at Genoa—a democratic republic down to about 1825—would be next best after that of Florence. Genoa is full of art and history; it is most beautiful, and it is a kinder climate than the Florentine.[1]

It stirs my blood to think of your going to Italy; I wish I could go with you! I wish I could help you to go, but with this administration I could be no of use; though if you can think of a way, I wont refuse to think of it. In that thin, clear Italian air you can see American things distinctly, and your new American novel will be as American as if you had written it in Ohio.

I am afraid I shall not be in New York before November. I had expected to go there before this, but now my son is sick there with typhoid fever[2] and his wife is with him, and my daughter and I must keep their children till it is safe for them to go to town. It is of course an anxious time. But if you were coming to Boston, and could run down here (two hours,) we should be so glad to see you both. Give me notice, and give my love to Mrs. Whitlock.

Yours ever
W. D. Howells.

1. Whitlock was appointed by President Wilson as United States minister to Belgium and later became ambassador, serving during the critical war years from 1913 to 1922. For an account of Howells' role in securing the diplomatic appointment for Whitlock, see *Life in Letters*, II, 339–41.

2. In his letter to Hamlin Garland, 18 October 1913 (CLSU), Howells explained the nature of John's illness more carefully, pointing out that "The case is very light, but it seems very long, and at times my heart is heavy, though I know there is no cause." By early December John had experienced a temporary recovery and a relapse, so that on 7 December 1913 (MeWC) Howells wrote to T. S. Perry: "What a cursed disease typhoid is! In romantic fiction it runs three weeks; in real life poor John has been ten weeks in bed with it."

16 OCTOBER 1913, BOSTON, TO SAMUEL S. McCLURE

Hotel Bellevue,...
Boston. Oct. 16, 1913.

My dear McClure:

I have been reading the very touching and beautiful story of your life. I cannot remember anything of more peculiar interest. As a self-study, temperamental and social, it must stand with the great auto-biographies.[1] It makes me love you better than ever.

Yours ever
W. D. Howells.

1. McClure's *Autobiography*, published in book form in 1914, was serialized in *McClure's*, October 1913–June 1914. Howells' enthusiasm, based on reading the first installment, was largely due to Willa Cather's expressive and interpretive skill, since she wrote the book from McClure's laconic oral account. See E. K. Brown, *Willa Cather: A Critical Biography* (New York: A. Knopf, 1953), p. 182. James Woodress calls McClure's *Autobiography* the "best ghost-written autobiography" ever; see *Willa Cather: Her Life and Art* (New York: Pegasus, 1970), pp. 160–61.

Laurel House,
Lakewood, Nov. 22, 1913.

My dear Mitchell:

Your letter found me by chance in New York the other day, and last night I read your very interesting little essay on *American History in Fiction*.[1] The points you make seem to me of great psychological importance, especially that of our restrictedness through the lack of the English class-labels; we are obliged to create characters, while the English can let themselves up with types. Also, what you say of a battle-witness strikes me as fresh as well as true. I don't know your own historical novels except that delightful study of manners which you dedicated to me,[2] and so I can only count *War and Peace* and The *Charteuse de Parme* as the best.—It is curious about the rejection by critics of your facts in *Westways*.[3]

I am here[4] with my daughter to help her get rid of a cold; then, oddly enough, we are going to spend the winter in Boston, where she is always well, while New York always attacks her throat.

I too lament that we do not meet; you are the only contemporary left whom I could talk with.

I wonder if a little psychological fact concerning the effect of veronal on me will interest you. Night before last a poor man coughing kept me awake (his heart, not his lungs, was wrong) till I could not sleep. Then I took 2½ grains of veronal, and all the forenoon I worked successfully; in the afternoon I was wild for a nap and took two naps. So it mostly happens with me from veronal; the first effect next day is as creative as that of morphene; the second, the sleep of the just.

Yours sincerely
W. D. Howells.

1. The essay seems never to have been printed.
2. Mitchell dedicated *The Red City* (1907) "To Wm Dean Howells / in payment of a debt long owed / to a master of fiction and to / a friend of many years."
3. *Westways, a Village Chronicle* (1913), a novel of the Civil War.
4. On the same day Howells wrote to F. A. Duneka (Arms), commenting about the Laurel House: "I let our landlord read what you said of his hotel (which I told him I agreed with; it's wonderful) and it did him so much good that he is giving us roast partridge for dinner in the teeth of the law. But poor old Lakewood, entrancingly pretty still is, I'm afraid, done for. Done for by the Jews, who think it is Jerusalem. There are not 25 people in this house, and this is the fullest in the place."

19 DECEMBER 1913, BOSTON, TO HAMLIN GARLAND

65 Mt. Vernon Street,
Boston, Dec. 19, 1913.

My dear Garland:

Yes, indeed, the Harpers sent me your letter and its enclosure,[1] and I acknowledged it to them, when I ought to have thanked you for the whole business, you dear, faithful friend. It is far more that you remember me than that others learn to know me, but it is sweet to me that they learn through you. Sometimes I think I am left aside by the rush of the new tide, but I take myself by the collar, and ask, "Here! Haven't you had your share?" and so try to behave.

Isn't it droll I am back in Boston, again? I suppose it is only for this winter, but the pestilential air of New York is so hostile to my daughter's throat that we are keeping a whole year out of it. Next winter we may be in Bermuda. I have my little pangs here when I retrace the upward steps that other feet took with mine; but if we live we must die, and if we outlive we must lose.—I am glad your little girl reads Shakespeare as well as you. Tell her that I spent all August in his sweet English home, and learned to know him as if he were still alive. I have done a queer book about it all,[2] which someday you may see.—How is Fuller?[3] Well enough to accept my love, I hope, which also I send with Pillas to you and all yours.

Affectionately, gratefully
W. D. Howells.

1. The enclosure is missing; presumably it was a manuscript essay by Garland on Howells.
2. *The Seen and the Unseen at Stratford-on-Avon* had been rejected by F. A. Duneka for publication in *Harper's Monthly* and by Colonel Harvey for the *North American Review*. On 22 November 1913 (Arms) Howells had written Duneka: "...I can understand why in these heated hours of fiction you would wish to serialize the whole thing. The fact is, I never had the monthly in view; but I hoped to abuse the innocence and inexperience of the Colonel and work it in on him for the N. A. Review. What I ask now is that you will not betray me to him; if he knew you had refused it, he would not take it."
3. Henry Blake Fuller.

19 December 1913, Boston, to Thomas S. Perry

65 Mt Vernon Street,
Dec. 19, 1913.

Dear Perry:

That notice of James is one of the best notices I have ever read, and your best piece of writing.[1] It is close, fine, simple, true.

I *don't* want to meet the Bs.,[2] either he or she; keep me for something else; I am old and scarce.

What is that confounded book I said I would buy you?

I will give you a box of this paper, if you are good.

Yours ever
W. D. Howells.

1. Perry's notice of James's *A Small Boy and Others* in the *Yale Review*, October 1913, comments on "this inner history of a human being" encountering a "ripe civilization"; and though he admits the author's sentences are often long and complex, he calls the work in sum "a delightful book."

2. Very probably Bernard Berenson (1865–1929) and his wife, Mary Logan Costelloe Berenson. Perry had aided Berenson as a student abroad in European art studies through a fund he raised among Boston friends. See Virginia Harlow, *Thomas Sergeant Perry: A Biography* (Durham, N.C.: Duke University Press, 1950), p. 109.

12 January 1914, Boston, to John M. Howells

65 Mt. Vernon Street,
Jan'y 12, 1914.

Dear John:

The anti-germ intelligence is the best news imaginable. Now, on to K. P.! Of course I don't mean at once, but when your applausive doctor cheers you off. If there is anything we can do about doubling the assurance of the working condition of the hot-water heating, you will let us know.[1] I shouldn't care to go down till this cold snap has unsnapped, but later, during the blandness promised next week, yes.

You mustn't suppose Nilsson ever had a chance at the Lincoln sig.[2] She only asked for one, and I have recurred to the possibility of my giving it her, and forgetting that I had done so, as one explanation. But it doesn't satisfy me. The name was cut out after the papers were bound up for you. We used to leave the book lying on our parlor table in Berkeley street. The Bret Harte boys had nothing to do with the loss, or their parents.[3] But the callers during their visit were not always our acquaintance, and anyone carrying scissors might have been tempted.

It's interesting to hear of Billy's modelling; and perhaps he managed that classic group with Donny[4] in the interest of plastic art. When I think of those boys I can hardly wait to see their parents.

I am working every day at the autobiog.,[5] with a general feeling that it is truck. I always supposed my Columbus life was most brilliant and joyous, but I can't seem to prove it, or that it was even important. I find largely that Tolstoy was right when in trying to furnish reminiscences for his biographer he declared that remembering was Hell:[6] with the little brave and good you recall so much bad and base. However, I shall push on and get it all down, and then cut, cut, cut, until I make myself a respectable figure—somebody that the boys won't want to ignore when people speak of him. At present I feel that they may wish to change their names, or their last name, unless Fafa White[7] makes out such a bad case for himself that mine shall seem better.— Did you know that since you "came down," I have written a rather largeish little book about Stratford-on-Avon which Harpers will publish in the spring?[8] It is a fantasy of the reconciliation of Bacon and Shakespeare, returning as materializations for the August memorials of Shakespeare. Pilla thinks it is pretty good. (Read this letter—all about me!)

With our best love,
Papa.

1. It appears that John Howells was at last recovering from his long but mild attack of typhoid fever and making plans to spend some time at the Kittery Point house, which had recently been equipped with a heating system.

2. According to Mildred Howells' note in *Life in Letters*, II, 330, Christine Nilsson was a singer, and "the Lincoln sig." refers to "one of Lincoln's signatures on Howells's Venetian consular papers, that had been cut out of them by some one after the papers were bound together in a book for John Howells."

3. The Howellses lived at 3 Berkeley Street, Cambridge, when Bret Harte and his family visited in March 1871. See Howells to W. C. Howells, 5 March 1871.

4. "Donny" is probably Howells' imitation of baby talk for "Johnny," Billy's brother.

5. *Years of My Youth.*

6. Tolstoy furnished his biographer Paul Birukoff with a number of reminiscences which appeared in *Leo Tolstoy: His Life and Work* (1911). Howells refers to one of these passages in the "Editor's Easy Chair," *Harper's Monthly*, October 1913: "Remembering the sins that we can't expiate with remorse, *that* is the worm that dieth not, *that* is the fire which is not quenched, *that*, as Tolstoy says, is hell."

7. Horace White, Billy and Johnny Howells' other grandfather.

8. *The Seen and the Unseen at Stratford-on-Avon.*

18 January 1914, Boston, to Bertha Howells

65 Mt. Vernon Street,
Jan'y 18, 1914.

Dear Miss Howells:[1]

I thank you for your kind letter with all the accompanying "litera-ture" and illustrations. You may be sure that they have very much inter-ested me, and that I am in full sympathy with you and your brother politically; perhaps I am in *more* than sympathy, if that is possible, for I do not stop short of the millenium as a civic ideal.

Of course the identity of our names has strongly appealed to me. Of my own family my father's "Life in Ohio—1813, 1840"[2] (Ohio Valley Series, Rob't Clarke Co. Cincinnati) will tell you all we know. At Llandrindod Wells, summer before last,[3] the kind rector of Merthyr-Tydfil tried to make me believe that I was descended from Prince Hywel (Howel) Dha, who codified the laws of Wales in the tenth century; but my father always said we derived from a remote blacksmith who was "a very good sort of ancestor." You may have the prince.

My father himself was born at Hay in Breconshire; we motored down to see the place from Llandrindod Wells along the lovely, laughing Wye. At Hay we bought things in the variety store which now occupies one of my great-grandfather's flannel mills.—After my daughter and I left Wales we traveled down through Spain, and very likely we saw you in the Alhambra and mistook you for a Moorish princess.[4] With my best regards to your brother and my high hopes of him,

Yours sincerely
W. D. Howells.

Lloyd-George told me the name was from the Kingdom of Powys; others that it was from South Wales.

1. Bertha Howells was a sister of Thomas J. Howells, of Pittsburgh, and thus only distantly related to Howells. Her letter, to which Howells is referring in the opening, has been lost.

2. W. C. Howells' *Recollections of Life in Ohio* was published in 1895.

3. Actually Howells and Mildred traveled through Wales and Spain in 1911, not 1912 as implied here.

4. Considering Howells' observations on his "countrywomen and their stranger be-havior in strange lands" (see Howells to James, 3 November 1911), this comment may be not entirely complimentary.

1 FEBRUARY 1914, BOSTON, TO LEE F. HARTMAN

65 Mt. Vernon Street,
Boston, Feb'y 1, 1914.

Dear Mr. Hartman:[1]

The people in your book[2] are so well done that I wish they were people of leisure, with no plot to work at; the spectacle of their industry fatigues me. Your girl is particularly good, and I am glad she is not bad, as so many girls in books are now; I cannot bear bad girls, or even baddish.[3] There are a lot of things I could say in your praise, but perhaps the best is that I somehow feel a future in you, whereas most of the fellows are hollow where they should have a future. There is so much reality in your book that I found myself putting it here and there where I had been, and it has freshness and force.

I was going to reproach you for writing "queried Poole, reflectively," and "quoted Evelyn in a stage whisper," and "protested the man," and the like; but reading over *Silas Lapham* just now I found that I had done the same thirty years ago. Still those inversions are not modern, and they were always ungainly.

Take care of the minor morals in literature and they will help the major to take care of themselves.

I hope for a novel from you with no more plot in it than you find in life.

Yours sincerely
W. D. Howells.

1. Lee Foster Hartman (1879–1941) joined the literary department of Harper & Brothers in 1904 and became an associate editor of *Harper's Monthly* in 1908. Eventually he became a vice-president of the firm.

2. *The White Sapphire: A Mystery Romance* (1914).

3. Howells had grown conservative in this respect. He had himself vividly depicted bad and baddish girls in *Mrs. Farrell* (1921; originally serialized as "Private Theatricals," in 1875–1876) and *The Landlord at Lion's Head* (1897).

3 FEBRUARY 1914, BOSTON, TO FREDERICK A. DUNEKA

65 Mt. Vernon Street,
Feb'y 3, 1914.

Dear Mr. Duneka:

I thought it might do you good to read this praise of me from the great soul of Kansas,[1] and perhaps "whet your almost blunted purpose"[2] of some time continuing my "complete works" before I am myself completed. After you have failed with the five volumes of travels "in a box," why not add another volume to them, and then add them all to the first six of the complete works, and issue a set of twelve?[3] The first six must be feeling very lonely by this time.

Since you have heard from me I have almost entirely finished the Columbus episode of my life,[4] a good long one, and full of weighty matter. It has almost killed me to do it, and many a time, if the thing had not been announced by you it would have been renounced by me. Tolstoy truly says that remembering is hell;[5] with me the experience was truly infernal; I could not describe it. The thing will not be ready to show you for fully a month yet. When you get it you will apologize to the public, reduce the Easy Chair to kindling wood and strike me from your list of authors.

It is queer being here in Boston. I should like to do a story called *Boston Revisited*, but I had better not. On Beacon Hill here it is quieter than Cambridge, and far quieter than the country.

With regards to all at Franklin Square,

Yours ever,
W. D. Howells.

1. William Allen White had praised Howells in a "lovely" letter no longer extant. See F. A. Duneka to Howells, 5 February 1914 (copy at MWA).

2. *Hamlet*, III, iv, 111.

3. Howells' suggestions for marketing his books are not entirely clear. The Library Edition of his works was first proposed by Harper & Brothers in 1902 and further discussed in 1904, 1905, and 1909. Eight titles were eventually published in six volumes on 26 July 1911, but since they did not sell well, no more were issued. See Robert W. Walts, "William Dean Howells and His 'Library Edition,'" *Publications of the Bibliophile Society of America* 102 (1958), 284–94. The boxed set of five travel books probably was an idea that Duneka never realized; the set, at any rate, is not listed in *Publishers Trade List Annual* for 1913 and 1914. However, *London Films* (1906), *Certain Delightful English Towns* (1906), *Roman Holidays* (1908), *Seven English Cities* (1909), and *Familiar Spanish Travels* (1913) were published in a uniform octavo size suitable for boxing. A puzzling aspect of Howells' suggestion, furthermore, is that *London Films* and *Certain Delightful English Towns* make up one of the volumes of the Library Edition and thus could not very well be added to it for a total of twelve volumes. Finally, it is unclear what Howells had in mind as a sixth volume added to the five travel books.

4. "In an Old-Time State Capital," *Harper's Monthly*, September–November 1914.

5. See Howells to J. M. Howells, 12 January 1914, n. 6.

9 FEBRUARY 1914, BOSTON, TO LAURA MITCHELL

65 Mt. Vernon Street,
Boston, Feb. 9, 1914.

My dear Laura:

I was thinking after I read your letter about Joanna,[1] with its touching appeal for knowledge that no one really has, or can ever have, that I would send you Swedenborg's *Heaven and Hell*, which would interest you at least as a stupendous piece of imagination if not as revelation. I do not quite accept it as that, any more, but I cannot help wondering at the realistic circumstantiality of his account of the spirit after its arrival in the other world, when the celestial angels come to rouse it to consciousness, and leave it to choose its companionship among the souls that it likes best. Then I opened a letter from my sister Aurelia (at Lausanne), which had come with yours, and I read this in it: "Do you know I do not feel or believe all of Swedenborg's doctrines of the life after death," she having been the most strenuous in her faith. "I sometimes feel as if they were almost as obsolete as the old orthodox wings, and palms, etc. I have a belief growing up in my heart that the future life will be just what we most want it to be: that is, at least, at first it will be a glorified earthly life; that the world of spirits will be a glorified earth, and our friends will be waiting within, and we shall live very much as we do here, only perfectly instead of imperfectly, and the characters will be sweeter and more charitable, and absolutely truthful." I think there is something in this, though of course it has the vagueness of all endeavor to imagine the future. What is so prodigious in Swedenborg is that he imagines everything in detail, and portrays it in line and not in color. There is something to grip. I wonder if you have read the book.

I try in vain to tell you something, but you know as much as I do. Now, there is something I should like you to tell me. I have finished my Columbus history, but I have not been able to say anything about meeting Elinor, the vastly most important thing in my whole life. I haven't brought myself even to mention her, or so much as to say that here I met the one who became my wife. What shall I do?[2] In his memoir my father barely noted the fact in regard to my mother, but they were most tenderly and beautifully attached, and from my own widowerhood, I know that he was always thinking of her. If I indulged my feeling, I should not say anything; that part of me is inexpressible. What do you think?

What was the battle which your John won, almost the last thing in the war, I think in North Carolina?[3]

We are happy in seeing your son John, so often, the sweetest, kindest, best fellow in the world. It is so good of him to come to us. We had him meet one of Perry's daughters at lunch, a girl who had admired him so much in the part he is playing.[4]

John Howells, up from his three (or four, rather) months typhoid, has at last got to Kittery Point with his dear wife and delightful children, and they are radiantly happy there, and we happy to have them so near. He called me up last night on the phone, to tell me how warm and glad they all are. We have had steam put into the house, and it is summer indoors while the shining snow lies all round outside, and carries the moonlight into the sea. Billy, after a bad sore-throat, went at once to a neighbor's and borrowed a sled.

This is a crazy, useless letter. Pilla joins me in love.

> Yours affectionately,
> W. D. Howells.

1. Laura Mitchell's letter is not extant; presumably Joanna was her daughter who had died.

2. It is likely that Mrs. Mitchell advised Howells simply to record his meeting Elinor Mead as a visitor in Columbus. The fact is he only spoke of "the raptures of the time" just before the Civil War "which was the most memorable of my whole life; for now I met her who was to be my wife. We were married the next year, and she became with her unerring artistic taste and conscience my constant impulse toward reality and sincerity in my work. She was the first to blame and the first to praise, as she was the first to read what I wrote. Forty-seven years we were together here, and then she died. But in that gravest time when we met it did not seem as if there could ever be an end of time for us, or any time less radiant." See *Years of My Youth*, HE, p. 194.

3. John G. Mitchell, Laura's husband, had distinguished himself in the battle of Bentonville, North Carolina, on 17 March 1865, and was breveted major general.

4. John Grant Mitchell was an actor on the New York stage. See *Life in Letters*, II, 184.

10 MARCH 1914, BOSTON, TO HENRY B. FULLER

> 65 Mt. Vernon Street,
> March 10, 1914.

Dear Mr. Fuller:

Yes, Boston is full of old friends, but not old enough, and it is largely the play of Hamlet with Hamlet left out. Living is all well enough, but out-living has its pains. It was not quite a voluntary thing our coming back; it was a choice between the two Bs, Boston and Bermuda, and we thought there might be more snow in Bermuda; but we were mistaken.

I am sorry indeed if what I said in criticism of Chatfield-Taylor seemed harsh; I meant it most amiably, but the things though usual were more than usually obvious, and I banned when I meant only blessing. His book was delightful; as what book about Goldoni could help being? He was worthy to write of him.[1]

I have never heard save from you of your Noise-Poet.[2] Is he in a book? One of his own? I used to hear of every new author; but one gets hard of hearing, with age; and the new authors are so many, you cannot make out any one in particular.

Yours affectionately,
W. D. Howells.

1. Howells reviewed H. C. Chatfield-Taylor's *Life of Goldoni* in the "Editor's Easy Chair," *Harper's Monthly*, March 1914. Although he had some reservations about the "manner of the work," the review was generally favorable.

2. Fuller's "Noise-Poet" was most likely Vachel Lindsay (1879–1931) whose fourth book, *Adventures while Preaching the Gospel of Beauty* (1914), Howells reviewed with the work of other new poets in the "Editor's Easy Chair," *Harper's Monthly*, September 1915. Fuller may have referred to such poems as "General William Booth Enters into Heaven" (1913) or "The Congo" (1914) as being noisy.

6 MAY 1914, YORK HARBOR, TO FREDERICK A. DUNEKA

York Harbor, May 6, 1914.

Dear Mr. Duneka:

I have the MS. back and have run over it in the light of Alden's and your own suggestions. With all my biddableness I confess that I am a little dismayed at the things you together want left out for the magazine.[1] You see the thing was "contrived a triple debt to pay."[2] It is my confession, it is a study of an old fashioned state capital, it is the echo of a period. If much of either interest is left out it will be a hollow thing indeed. I say this frankly, feeling that I may be quite wrong, but so it seems to me, and I am by nature both editor and author, you know. I can pinch and pare, but to cut out pounds of flesh nearest my heart! Very likely the whole thing is a mistake; I don't say it isn't; but without the carefully painted background of time and place, it will be a lifeless portrait of me!

You speak of "the book". Had you thought of publishing this apart from the rest of the autobiography, or don't you want any "rest"?

Of course I insist upon nothing. When must you have the copy? I will write to Alden.

Yours ever
W. D. Howells.

More in sorrow than in anger.

---

1. The manuscript was any of three papers entitled "In an Old-Time State Capital," *Harper's Monthly*, September–November 1914. Duneka responded the next day (copy, Arms) that he and H. M. Alden wanted every bit of the book that Howells could write, and had proposed deletions only because "no continuity of background" was possible in three separate issues of the magazine. He hoped Howells would acquit him of all faults save ignorance and stupidity.

2. See Oliver Goldsmith, "The Deserted Village": "The chest contriv'd a double debt to pay,— / A bed by night, a chest of drawers by day" (lines 227–28).

---

8 MAY 1914, YORK HARBOR, TO THOMAS S. PERRY

York Harbor, May 8, 1914.

My dear Perry:

I miss you greatly, but I am glad you are not here to share my pharyngitis. It was inevitable from the bitter weather which has welcomed us as with the slashing hatchet of a suffragette.—What a cruel shame to spoil one of the most beautiful portraits in the world! I think it must have the work of some capitalist in disguise.[1]

I hope your grandchildren have arrived in good case. Mine are devoted to Indian forays and the sandbox at K. P. For the moment they have no colds. But their father has one which has gone to his nose, and swelled it up twice the size of nature.

We have read the **Germania** and the **Agricola** of Tacitus—a pretty good writer.

Yours ever
W. D. Howells.

---

1. John Singer Sargent's portrait of Henry James, painted for the master's seventieth birthday in 1913, had been badly damaged early in May 1914. Mrs. Mary Woods, a militant suffragette, had shattered the glass fronting the exhibited portrait and had made three slashes in the canvas with a meat-cleaver. James wrote to Howells on 13 May 1914 (MH): "You will, I am sure, be glad to know that Sargent's extraordinarily fine portrait of me (as I didn't paint it myself I don't see why I shouldn't unreservedly admire it,) which was horribly gashed a while back by an idiotic suffragette, is under such successful treatment that it will probably be restored to effective life & bloom

again. That those ladies really outrage humanity, & the public patience has to me a
very imbecile side. Another of them has hacked with a chopper another picture today
(a Herkomer portrait;) & the work goes bravely on." See Leon Edel, *Henry James, the
Master, 1901–1916* (Philadelphia: J. B. Lippincott, 1972), pp. 487–91.

12 MAY 1914, YORK HARBOR, TO AURELIA H. HOWELLS

York Harbor, Maine, May 12, 1914.

Dear Aurelia:

I was glad finally to get a Roman letter from you with a local address;
but now I am afraid of a quick change, and so I will send this to Annie
and let her forward it to you. It will be too late to say that in your
place I would rather spend the time in Rome, and not take it for
Naples and Pompei, but if you have been there by the time this reaches
you, and are safely back in Flame Street, you will probably glad you
went. Remember that there is such a thing as tiring yourself to death,
though. That is to be considered at your age, and more at mine. I
capered very lightly over the ground at 72 but at 77 I don't caper.—I
am glad that you and Vevie like Italy, but of course you couldn't help
it. Truly to enjoy it, you ought to get my books out of the libraries:
Poole's in Rome, Goodban's or Viesseux's in Florence, and what used
to be Münster's in Venice; there are no books like them for Italy:
Venetian Life, Italian Journeys, Tuscan Cities, Roman Holidays; they
give historic outlines as well as impressions.—The Pages in Rome are
our summer neighbors here, and can be very nice if they will; but they
are very rich and may be trying to be fine. I don't know Mr. Coleman,
or generally any of our officials.[1] American society is not worth the time
you would take for it from the churches and monuments.—The Italians
are lovable people, and as trustworthy as any hateful people.—Victoria
went with father and me my first winter in Columbus (1856) and we
were all at the Goodale House together. I have finished my whole Columbus episode, and have gone back to pick up my childhood in Hamilton
and Dayton, of course making large skips over the ground covered by
A Boy's Town, etc.[2]

Our young Irish cook after putting us to the time and cost of bringing
her here has decided not to stay, and Pilla is up at Boston laying in an
elderly Scotch body; who probably wont stay, either. Unless they are
perfectly worthless they are not worth having.—Sam reports himself
better, and pesters me with reports about Ethel and her child; I suppose
they are dear to him, though.—John and family of course we see often.
Little Johnny is very winning, now; but he will never be Billy. They

have had rows of colds all winter; but John is well of his long sickness and getting fat.—Great news about Howells, isn't it?[3] I've hailed him on it without waiting to hear from him. With love to Vevie,

Afftely your brother
Will.

Annie, please forward this when youve read it.

1. Thomas Nelson Page, who had made his literary reputation as a local color writer of the South, was the American ambassador to Italy (1913–1919); Chapman Coleman was the American consul in Rome at the time of Aurelia's visit.

2. Howells was working on the papers that eventually became *Years of My Youth*.

3. Howells Fréchette was presumably engaged to Lena Van Derck, whom he married in December.

13 MAY 1914, YORK HARBOR, TO FREDERICK A. DUNEKA

York Harbor, May 13, 1914.

Dear Mr. Duneka:

I am writing out my "Hours of Childhood" very fully,[1] and I will send it when finished for you to chop as you must. Only this: Alden has intimated the hideous wish for pictures for my stuff, and I particularly *don't want* pictures, in it, at all. It seems to me that I write rather pictorially, and why not leave the rest to God, as the old pietists used to say? If you omit them, you can give me the more room, and not scant the hapless reader with a pitiful seven thousand words.[2]

Think this over; pray it over; and you will win the lasting esteem of

Yours sincerely
W. D. Howells.

P.S. Tell Alden I have no such portraits as he wants, and wouldn't let him have them if I had.

1. See Howells to Duneka, 9 February 1915, n. 2.

2. See Howells to A. H. Howells, 12 May 1914, n. 2, and Howells to Duneka, 9 February 1915, n. 2. Clifton Johnson took photographs of the towns and scenes of Howells' childhood and youth for a special illustrated edition of *Years of My Youth* (1917), but no photograph of Howells appears in the book.

15 JUNE 1914, YORK HARBOR, TO ANNIE A. FIELDS

York Harbor, June 15, 1914.

Dear Mrs. Fields:

I am so glad to hear from you, and just now Pilla and I have been promising ourselves to run down and up to see you. We think we can motor over from Salem, and make you a call that wont fatigue you. It makes me very sorry to hear that you have not been well since I saw you in Boston.

We have been here ever since the 4th of May preceding Mrs. Bell[1] by more than a month. But now she is here, as wonderful as ever, and we see each other every other day: she lives every other house from us, and our lights look at one another after dark, and we run the same risks of being motored down by day.

I had a letter from James, lately, and he seemed very cheerful; he's greatly pleased at the way the English have taken his book; and I don't wonder.[2]

Can it have been as bitter cold and cruel hot at Manchester as we have had it here, three or four times in the same day? Just now it's very dry, and our gardens are rather disconsolate.—I've been reading the "Ring and the Book" over forty or fifty years—a great poem;[3] and my daughter-in-laws sister having spent the winter in Guatemala we've been reading Stephens's travels (1839–40) aloud, for his account of the prehistoric cities she's been seeing.[4]

With Pilla's love,

Yours affectionately
W. D. Howells.

1. Mrs. Helen Choate Bell (1830–1918), daughter of Rufus Choate, was "a true lover of literature and famous for her wit," according to Mildred Howells. See *Life in Letters*, II, 335; also Paulina C. Drown, *Mrs. Bell* (Boston: Houghton Mifflin, 1931).

2. Henry James wrote Howells on 13 May 1914 (MH) that he had been "deeply touched by your expression of intimate interest in my late book. You are one [of] the very few individuals I dreamed at all of reaching as I wrote, & I had you so often in mind that I rejoice to know from you that my message didn't fall short. You express to me this in a way that much moves me; your image of your going over it all with T. S. P.[erry] is the most genial I could desire—so much of my meaning must have been at this time of day wasted & missed by the 'general' reader that I take comfort in your gathering it up, you two, together." His book was *Notes of a Son and Brother* (1914).

3. Robert Browning's *The Ring and the Book* (1868–1869).

4. See Howells to Perry, 23 June 1914, n. 1.

York Harbor, June 21, 1914.

Dear Aurelia:

Yesterday came your letter of the 6th from Milan, and by now I suppose you have been for a fortnight in Montreux.[1] Your happiness in your Italian travel has been a great happiness to me, and if we are to look forward to rewards and punishments in this world, I think you may fairly regard it as a partial compensation for your long years of devotion to Henry and father in the loneliness of Jefferson. I do not know whether I ever told you of Joe's speaking to me of what you had daily done for the afflicted brother left to your care. He realized this in his journey from Jefferson to Ottawa with you, when he shared for the little time in your constant self-sacrifice. He was not apt to speak of such things, and I hope you will like to know it. Late in life your bread cast upon the waters is returning to you.

I wish you might have gone to Venice, for that was most of all my Italy, and the great Venetian art cannot be adequately seen anywhere else. Perhaps the whole Fréchette family will go with you to spend the rest of their days in Italy, and then you will see Venice.

We are on the verge of summer here after the dryest and coldest spring I have ever known, almost. Today we have a fire in the furnace, and on the hearth in the parlor; yesterday I sat with my back close to the hearth here in my study.

After a long season of autobiography I have resumed my story of *The Leatherwood God*, that strange epsiode of Ohio history which has always fascinated me; but the dreadfulness and the mystery of the imposture rather distress me, and I wish I had some cheerfuller theme.—I find that there is a distinct flagging in my mental force, either from age, or from the constant work of fifty or sixty years. If I regard quantity, without regarding quality, what I have done is really immense, and if people care to remember me, the future must be amazed at the amount of my production.

Yesterday I went over to Kittery Point to see the children. Little Johnny, though so different from Billy has his increasing charm. He is a handsome little creature, and very sturdy, and wants to be noticed and applauded. He runs forward with his arms spread to give *"Fafa bic huc"* (big hug) and is incessantly on foot.—Billy is picking up strength after rather a poor winter; he grows dreamier, and a book of any sort lures him. We took him to the circus last week, and of course he is doing acts, now.

With love to you all,

Your aff'te brother
Will.

1. Aurelia was still staying in Switzerland with Achille and Annie Fréchette, who had recently moved from Lausanne to Montreux, where, as Howells wrote to Aurelia, 25 May 1914 (MH), "I was so often with Elinor and the children...."

23 JUNE 1914, YORK HARBOR, TO THOMAS S. PERRY

York Harbor, Me., June 23, 1914.

My dear Perry:

In returning this letter unopened, as a just punishment of my long neglect, I wish you would not fail to tell me from Mrs. Perry what or which Dr. Cabot it was who went to Central America with the traveler Stephens in the early eighteen forties.[1] Stephens and his friend Catherwood were unearthing those incredible prehistoric cities down there, and Dr. Cabot was shooting and stuffing the strange birds that flapped about in them.

There is not much progress to report in literature here. One aged author is slowly and painfully digging up his memories, and finding each more loathsome than the other.—We read together and separately a good many books, as Tacitus his Annals, Björnson's plays, R. Brownings Ring and the Book, Gilbert's opera texts, Tennyson's poems, Ade's sketches, Cellini's autobiog., Stephens's Travels (4 vols.) etc. Also, Herrick's capital new novel, Clark's Field.[2]

We see the wonderful Mrs. Bell much and often, thanks be. She lives the second house up the hill.[3] I call it Beacon Hill because it affects my legs in the same way as that bad eminence.[4] With love to all,

Yours ever
W. D. Howells.

1. Dr. Samuel Cabot, Jr. (1815–1885), Harvard M. D., naturalist and ornithologist, father of Lilla Cabot Perry, joined the American explorer John Lloyd Stephens and the English artist Frederick Catherwood on their second expedition to Yucatán in 1841–1842. He performed strabismus operations on the Yucatanese with great success; and he brought home hundreds of bird skins from Central America. By the time of the Civil War he had become a distinguished surgeon and a militant abolitionist. See Victor W. Von Hagen, *Maya Explorer, John Lloyd Stephens and the Lost Cities*

of Central America and Yucután (Norman: University of Oklahoma Press, 1948), pp. 205–11 and passim. Howells was reading Stephens' *Incidents of Travel in Yucután* (2 volumes, 1843), along with his *Incidents of Travel in Central America, Chiapas, and Yucután* (2 volumes, 1841). Although Howells once boasted, "I invented the modern travel, and can beat anybody else with one hand tied behind me," he read earlier travel books like Stephens' with zest. See Howells to Mildred Howells, 11 April 1913 (MH).

2. About *Clark's Field* (1914) Howells had written to Robert Herrick on 20 June 1914 (ICU): "Your book caught me, when I looked into it, not meaning to read it at once, and held me to the end. [¶] I should like to talk it over with you. It arrives, economically and morally, magnificently."

3. Helen Choate Bell.

4. Howells counted on the Bostonian Perry to be amused by his likening of Beacon Hill to Satan's throne on Pandemonium in Milton's *Paradise Lost*, book 2, lines 5–6.

12 JULY 1914, YORK HARBOR, TO THOMAS S. PERRY

York Harbor, July 12, 1914.

Dear Perry:

I hope you are well and happy. I should be so if it were not for the loathsomeness of my autobiographical papers, now beginning to come in proof, and needing to be cut for the magazine. It is the great error of a blundering, misspent life, to have written them.

Did you see that really abominable review of James's "Son and Brother" in the *Nation*? It made me sick with shame by its cruelty and perversity. I wonder who did it.[1]

It is a blessing to have Mrs. Bell so near.[2]

Yours ever
W. D. Howells.

1. The review in the *Nation*, 2 July 1914, is by Stuart P. Sherman; it ranges in tone from captious to severe. Sherman contrasts Henry and his brother William, finding Henry "too refined." Henry expresses the simplest thought on "heroic stilts," and his aestheticism is "tremendously high-bred." Sherman finds it "intolerable" that James should speak of the Civil War as "our national drama" or of the country as "this American scene."

2. Helen Choate Bell.

23 JULY 1914, YORK HARBOR, TO FRED L. PATTEE

York Harbor, Me., July 23, 1914.

Dear Mr. Pattee:

It *does* seem a little odd to me that you should ask me those questions, but since you ask them I do not mind saying that I thought it to my advantage to change from a Boston to a New York publisher, and it was finally natural that I should go to live in New York. Whatever were the effects on my fiction, I cannot see that these personal facts have properly anything to do with a literary study of the period, and I had no psychological motive in the affair.[1]

> Yours sincerely
> **W. D. Howells.**

1. Fred Lewis Pattee (1863–1950) had asked Howells why he moved from Boston to New York—a shift which he would soon equate, in his *A History of American Literature since 1870* (1915), with a new third period, scientific and ethical, of which the "classical" writers Howells and James were representative. Pattee printed Howells' response in *Penn State Yankee: The Autobiography of Fred Lewis Pattee* (State College: Pennsylvania State College Press, 1953) and commented, "William Dean Howells never liked my book ... shied away from it even before it was written" (p. 278).

28 AUGUST 1914, YORK HARBOR, TO BOOTH TARKINGTON

> York Harbor, Me., August 28, 1914.

Dear Mr. Tarkington:
I have read your first two numbers with great interest and pleasure. The stuff is good and new, and handled in a strong, strikingly fresh way, with fully justified courage.[1] I am curious to know more, mostly, of your peculiar find, Bibbs. I am sorry to have missed Mr. McCutcheon and yourself.[2]

> Yours sincerely
> **W. D. Howells.**

1. Howells was reading the first two installments of Tarkington's *The Turmoil*, *Harper's Monthly*, August and September 1914. The serial ended in March 1915.
2. Tarkington (1869–1946) and George Barr McCutcheon (1866–1928), another Indiana novelist, had called on Howells at York Harbor but had failed to find him in.

11 SEPTEMBER 1914, YORK HARBOR, TO BARRETT WENDELL

> York Harbor, Me., September 11, 1914.

Dear Mr. Wendell:[1]
Once I wrote of a book of yours which I did not like in a very abominable spirit.[2]

Your behavior to me since, as often as we have met, has made me wish to tell you that I was, when too late, immediately sorry for what I had done, and have always been ashamed.[3]

Yours sincerely
W. D. Howells.

1. Barrett Wendell (1855–1921) was professor of English at Harvard and wrote a biography of Cotton Mather.

2. Howells had written "Professor Barrett Wendell's Notions of American Literature," *North American Review*, April 1901. He had found *A Literary History of America* "priggish and patronizing" in tone, the language "without distinction" and the thought too often "without precision." The basic flaws of the work were that Wendell had written a history of literature in New England, not in America; and that he suffered a "radical disqualification" in his "absence of sympathy" for his subject. See also Howells to Fuller, 5 April 1901, n. 1.

3. Wendell's immediate response, 13 September 1914 (MH), expressed his wonder that Howells should have kept his review-attack in mind so long, and acknowledged how deeply touched he had been by Howells' "more than kind words." See *Life in Letters*, II, 337.

13 SEPTEMBER 1914, YORK HARBOR, TO ANNE H. FRÉCHETTE

York Harbor, Me., Sept. 13, 1914.

Dear Aurelia:[1]

It was like rain after long drouth to get your letter from Montreux, and then Aurelia's, apparently written before yours, and leaving me in doubt whether she ever got the money I sent, and whether it was the Sub-Treasury $200 or the cabled $200 which she failed to get at Vevey. I wish I could feel as little anxiety as she seems to feel about her income; but I have no brother to worry for me.[2] Even Sam doesn't worry for me. I had him here for a week's visit;[3] for I had reflected, with a very bad conscience, that I had never, in all my long housekeeping years, had him under my roof for a night. He staid a week, and we drove, ate, and talked together—even walked a little, or a good deal, for two fat old men. I found him physically like me, but perhaps 20 pounds heavier, and morally I think I should have been a good deal like him, if some dynamite had not been somehow got into me. I sent our English inside man up to Boston with him to see him safely off, and he wrote back to me back, that the journey to Washington was the worst he ever made. He said nothing about his visit, but I dunned him for some acknowledgment, and then he wrote that I had treated him "royally." But kings don't usually pay their guests' way to and fro, and recompense them for time lost from their jobs.—I found that the poor old fat victim worked—or rather sat round—365 days of the year; but I have put him up to taking off, if he can get it, every other Sunday. Now Sam is out of the story, as the Saga of Burnt Njal says.

Pilla and I are reading that Icelandic epic when we are not reading the war news. We have suffered many things because of the war, but it seems to be going right now. I never doubted that the Allies would win, but sometimes I shook in my shoes. We are all, all the Americans I know or hear of, pro-entente, for we feel that the Allies are fighting for humanity and democracy against the most abominable despotism; and while we pity the poor, kindly German people, we abhor their tyrant.[4]

The summer has slipped away, and our hickory trees are beginning to shrink with a feeling of autumn. It has been a very lunch-getting and lunch-giving summer, but now the summer folks are flitting. We hope to stay through October, partly because we have no settled plan for the winter. Naturally we should have gone to Bermuda, but somehow the war has burst that ideal, and we are now thinking of Panama, with excursions to all the South American republics. By the way I hope that when the German despotism is smashed, the bits will form a union of European republics, though I shouldn't mind a hereditary republic like G. Britain for one of them. How gloriously our old grandmother-country has behaved!

I have been working diligently all summer, and have finished *The Leatherwood God* which I began thirty years ago.[5] You know it is the story of that famous imposture in Eastern Ohio about 1830. Father used to tell of it, and I to talk of it, and of writing a story about it. Now I have done it; but some people will still think Tolstoy's *War and Peace* a greater book.

You seem to be all so safe and sound that I am afraid you will spurn my love and Pilla's. However we send it to each and all at a venture.

Your aff'te brother,
Will.

1. Although the salutation reads "Dear Aurelia," the letter is clearly meant for Annie Fréchette, as is evident from the content and Howells' remark in a letter of the same date (MH) to Aurelia Howells: "I wrote Annie a long . . . letter, this morning. . . ."

2. For many years Howells had been paying Aurelia a monthly allowance, and he administered some modest investments for her.

3. Samuel Howells had visited York Harbor in August, and Howells had already reported to Aurelia on 17 August 1914 (MH) that Sam "left me to take the trolley half an hour ago. He is not stupid, but powerfully inert, and is as affectionate and humble as can be." In his 13 September letter to Aurelia, Howells explained that he was still making substantial contributions to Sam's income, as he had been doing for many years: "I found him paying $30 a month for a three room flat [in Washington, D.C.], and I suggested his taking a better one at $20, and I am paying the rent! How long I can keep that up I don't know. . . ."

4. The intensity of Howells' feelings about Wilhelm II, emperor of Germany, is revealed in his letter to Thomas S. Perry, 23 September 1914 (MeWC): "The war has greatly troubled me, so greatly that I can scarcely read about it, any more. I suppose if the Germans won, God would still rule,—but under the Kaiser! What a loathsome beast, with his piety, the K. is!"

5. More than a month later, on 19 October 1914 (MeWC), Howells asked T. S. Perry to "tell me something about religious impostors and false prophets; so that I can give a learned look to the last chapter of my Leatherwood God? I mean, give me their names, so I can find them in the Encyc. Brit." Perry sent the requested information, but his letter is now lost.

23 SEPTEMBER 1914, YORK HARBOR, TO FREDERICK A. DUNEKA

York Harbor, Me., Sept. 23d, 1914.

Dear Mr. Duneka:

I am glad I could come to time with the second Easy Chair; though I had no such luck as with that in the spring. I am out of a subject for the Christmas number. Can you suggest anything?[1]

You have been getting out some more of these thin little books which excited my grudge last year; and I suppose it is now too late to join the band. Perhaps next autumn if any reader survives this war you will like doing *The Daughter of the Storage,* or *The Critical Bookstore.*[2]—I have finished a novel (historical, oddly enough) which I have thought of for forty years and got well started thirty years ago. It is called *The Leatherwood God,* and is the story of a religious imposture in Ohio about 1828. I think it rather well done, but there is no "love interest" of the merchantable sort, though there is the pathos of a grim woman's wrong, (*not* seduction.). The structure is almost wholly fact.[3]

I suppose our poor little dirigible of an autobiography has fallen fluttering dead from the belligerent fire over yonder.[4] Later I may want to talk of it.

Yours sincerely
W. D. Howells

1. Howells labored increasingly under the pressure of his monthly "Easy Chair" assignments. Finding something to write about was one problem, and writing in such a way that it would satisfy Duneka was yet another. It appears that Duneka did not like Howells' first submission for the November *Harper's Monthly* and had telegraphed his request for a new piece on short notice. Howells responded, expressing both his annoyance and his willingness in a letter to Duneka of 16 September 1914 (MWA): "I confess your telegram asking for a new E. C. shook me up. The copy for this one you have has been eight days in your office, and I have been busy ever since on a N. A. Review paper. However, I will set to work on another tomorrow, and perhaps I can get it out on Saturday, though as yet I have not the least notion what it will be about."

2. Two years earlier Howells had suggested to Duneka that *The Daughter of the Storage* be issued in a fifty-cent edition, and the following year he suggested a similar arrangement for *The Critical Bookstore*. See Howells to Duneka, 14 October 1912, and Howells to Leigh, 24 September 1913.

3. Two months later, on 5 December 1914 (Arms), Howells advised Duneka to delay publication of *The Leatherwood God*: "Unless the war is over by spring I think I would rather not waste The Leatherwood God on the slim chances of any sort of publication in 1915. I began it 25 years ago, and I can employ another year usefully on it.... [¶] Please keep the MS. of the L. G. carefully till I ask for it."

4. Dissatisfied with his autobiographical effort in "In an Old-Time State Capital," Howells feared that the war news would completely overshadow what little effect he may have hoped for.

6 NOVEMBER 1914, BOSTON, TO BRANDER MATTHEWS

Hotel Vendome,
Boston. Nov. 6, 1914.

Dear Matthews:

Thank for your letter. I've been reading Brieux's plays with fluctuations of opinion, but with my first mind that he is a great and glorious fellow.[1] I have got all his pieces and more, so don't be weighed down by my want of them. I have not the least notion of our procedure, and I am awaiting Johnson's instructions as to which strings shall be pulled in me to make me function.[2] Of myself I cannot get beyond the first syllable. (pun.) I will ask Baker for his article.[3]

Yours ever
W. D. Howells.

1. Eugène Brieux (1858–1932), French playwright and representative of the Académie Française, whom Howells as president was to introduce at a meeting of the American Academy of Arts and Letters on 19 November. R. U. Johnson was secretary of the Academy. Howells wrote at length on "The Plays of Eugène Brieux" in the *North American Review*, March 1915.

2. Nevertheless, Howells had some ideas of his own about what he would say or not say in his address, as he explained to R. U. Johnson in a letter of 5 November 1914 (NNAL): "Will you kindly let me say that I shall *not* 'strike the note of neutrality' in welcoming M. Brieux. I expect simply to speak in praise of his wonderful drama, and his most noble and generous country. If I tried to voice my 'neutrality' in the present attrocious war upon humanity, I should simply explode in the most violent denunciation of the German behavior throughout...." See Howells to Johnson, 8 November 1914, n. 2.

3. George Pierce Baker (1866–1935), a Harvard professor of dramatic literature, had presumably published an article on Brieux, possibly "The New Feminist Play by Brieux," *Review of Reviews* 47 (1913), 494–96.

8 NOVEMBER 1914, BOSTON, TO ROBERT U. JOHNSON

> Hotel Vendome,
> Nov. 8, 1914.

Dear Mr. Johnson:

Here is some one else bothering about an invitation. "My Lord Chief Justice, speak to this vain man," and tell him how and where he may be seated.[1]

Thank you for all your good will about the Brieux facts; I can get all I need without troubling you further.

As always you are most self-sacrificingly active on the Academy's behalf. But if anything is said about establishing the fact of our "neutrality," by any officer of our body, I shall publicly disavow him.[2] We are not a political body, and have nothing to do with the European situation. Also, if the Mayor[3] makes the *first* address of welcome, or ceremonially precedes me, as stated in this cutting, I will take no part in the affair, and will leave the stand. We are not a civic body, and as President, I will not let the city of New York patronize us; though I should be glad of the mayor's presence and of his speech of welcome *after* mine.—I wish you would present these points, which I make on behalf of the Academy and its dignity, to Mr. Sloan and Dr. Butler.[4] I am not well, and I am old; and I will not take the trouble of presiding in order to ask the Academy to a back seat in its own house.

I enclose a letter to M. Brieux which I will thank you to hand him, if he does not land sea-sick, as a true Frenchman ought.

> Yours sincerely
> W. D. Howells.

1. Apparently someone had requested an invitation for the forthcoming dinner of the American Academy of Arts and Letters in honor of Eugène Brieux. Howells paraphrases King Henry IV, speaking of Falstaff, in Shakespeare's *King Henry IV*, Part II, V, v, 48.

2. See Howells to Matthews, 6 November 1914, n. 2. Johnson had replied on 7 November 1914 (copy at NNAL): "I am so in sympathy with your point of view of the war,—occupying as our country does the position of 'boiling' neutrality, as I phrase it,—that I appreciate what you say of the danger of touching upon the subject. We need not apologize for having invited a member of the French Academy to take part in our meeting, but I was thinking that the occasion would be put upon its proper basis by stating that the arrangements were made before war was thought of."

3. John P. Mitchel (1879–1918), lawyer and Democrat, was the mayor of New York City (1914–1917).

4. William J. Sloane and Nicholas Murray Butler.

14 NOVEMBER 1914, BOSTON, TO WILLIAM R. THAYER

Hotel Vendome,
Nov. 14, 1914.

Dear Mr. Thayer:[1]

I have been troubled since I saw you the other day lest you should take anything I said in criticism of John Hay as the result of my studied own experience or observation. He was one of the earliest and oldest friends I ever had, and in our long acquaintance of nearly fifty years he never ceased to seek occasions to do me kindnesses, to offer me the promptest and most cordial recognition for anything worthy in what I wrote. My *knowledge* of him is that he was one of the truest men we have ever had in public life; he was our wisest and bravest statesman in imagining the right concerning China when all the rest of the world saw wrong. I sorrowed for his connection with the Panama business, but I condoned even that because as I said to myself, "Hay did it, and he must have had reasons I cannot see."[2] He loved the world which he so easily won and was so fit to shine in, but he never "stooped to conquer" it. He was almost painfully modest about his verse; but if he had only half-written that great life of Lincoln,[3] how truly he might have vaunted himself not last among our first historians.

As to poor, dear Clarence King, do not let his love of a marvellous tale wrong in your judgment one of the most generous, the most hero-ically honest and lovablest of human beings. What he did life long for others, others only could tell; he would not; to me he was ever sweetness and light.

Shall you be going on to the Brieux reception by the Academy and Institute?[4] I hope so. You will find me at the St. Hubert, 120 W. 57th.— We are off in the morning.

Yours sincerely.
W. D. Howells.

1. William Roscoe Thayer (1859–1923) was then writing his *Life and Letters of John Hay* (1915). In his reply of 16 November 1914 (MH), he wrote Howells that "a biographer hears–if he is fortunate–all the *pros* and *cons*, and, finally, makes up that resultant, or composite, which is his portrait of his subject. In the end, the character of the portrait depends on the biographer; and any squint or flaw in his vision is sure to be detected."

2. In his review of Thayer's biography, "Editor's Easy Chair," *Harper's Monthly*, January 1916, Howells comments on Hay's involvement in the "Open Door" policy in China (1899) and in American military support for the Panamanian revolution (1903). Referring to the latter, he concludes: "There is nothing more important in Mr. Thayer's book than the passages dealing with Hay's part in that affair [Panama], and

showing that he acted from the belief that he had to do with a corrupt political ring bent upon plunder rather than with a nation jealous of its sovereign integrity. To many the light thrown upon the fact will come, as we own it came to us, with relief from the uneasy sense that our government had played some such part as England and France might have played in instantly recognizing the independence of South Carolina when she seceded in 1861."

3. John G. Nicolay and John Hay, *Abraham Lincoln: A History* (10 volumes, 1890), which Howells reviewed in the "Editor's Study," *Harper's Monthly,* February 1891.

4. See Howells to Matthews, 6 November 1914, n. 1.

29 NOVEMBER 1914, NEW YORK, TO H. A. McCALEB

New York, Nov. 29, 1914.

Dear Mr. McCaleb:[1]

I can only thank you for the expression of a feeling very gratifying to me. I know that Clemens was one of the most truthful and honest of men, and that I have tried in my own way to keep my hands off my neighbor's ox and ass and ideas.

Thank you most cordially for your letter.

Yours sincerely
W. D. Howells.

1. Possibly McCaleb had written Howells about the originality and freshness of *My Mark Twain,* perhaps with a glance at Albert B. Paine's use of others' writings about Clemens in his *Mark Twain: A Biography* (3 volumes, 1912). Howells enclosed with this letter "An Impression of Albert Bigelow Paine by Booth Tarkington," a pencil drawing now missing. But this conjecture about Paine's use of sources *is* conjecture: Howells truly admired Paine's accomplishment in the Mark Twain biography, though not his style. See Howells to Paine, 6 October 1912.

29 NOVEMBER 1914, NEW YORK, TO WILLIAM E. DEAN

St. Hubert
One Twenty West Fifty Seventh Street
Nov. 29, 1914.

Dear Cousin:

Thank you for your very kind and welcome letter. Of course The Archangelic Censorship ought to have been better, or bitterer;[1] but perhaps it would help the Kaiser as it is, if he had time to read it. Poor wretch! What misery he has caused in the world! But perhaps it was well for us to know, even through all this bloodshed what devil's doctrine these Germans have come to believe in, so that somehow it could untaught them.

You so heap my work with praise that I hardly know how to disclaim it all. If I do not disclaim it wholly, it is because I love it.

Pilla is grateful on her part that you felt the thoughtfulness in her poem.[2] She and I are faltering here for a plunge southward after New Years. Is it too mad to think of going to New Orleans by boat from Cincinnati? *Are* there any boats?

I am only half in this world since my wife left it. I work still, but life is like a dream, and flows away shadowily.

With love to you all,

Your aff'te cousin
W. D. Howells.

I miss Joe, terribly. There is no one left now whom I can ask about the past.

1. Howells' "The Archangelic Censorship," *North American Review*, October 1914, is a wry, if not bitter, drama of the archangels' censorship and concealment of God's will, even though the Deity, it is clear, finds himself "tired of kings."

2. Mildred's poem, "If This Be All," was published in the *North American Review*, November 1914.

15 DECEMBER 1914, ASBURY PARK, NEW JERSEY, TO THOMAS S. PERRY

Asbury Park, Dec. 15, 1914.

My dear Perry:

You, who instructed my youth that nobody ever invented anything, to accuse my age of inventing tendentious—a straight translation of the Spanish *tendencioso*! But I shall not shoot you on sight. The only violents are your conservatives, who like poets are born, not made; who never reason, but always merely emotion. It is we extremists who have got to the length of our tether by reflection, by the logical exercise of our faculties.

The Fic. Com. of the B. P. L. must be Catholic, and scent heresy in the bland Marshall;[1] but do you read—or get Mrs. Perry to read Herrick— all whose books are good, except "Together,"[2] which is not bad aesthetically.

I always thought well of Lucas;[3] now I think better—on your say, for I have not seen his.

It is very cold in this tropic today. It is a good thing for them that the farmers washed in August.

> Yours ever
> W. D. Howells.

1. Archibald Marshall (1866–1934), was a Trollope-like American novelist, five of whose books Howells wrote about in "A Number of Interesting Novels," *North American Review*, December 1914, along with Robert Herrick's *Clark's Field* and the fiction of other new novelists. Apparently a committee of the Boston Public Library, an institution that Perry had served many years, found Marshall's fiction objectionable. Perry always stood with those officials of the library who considered themselves "servants of the general public rather than censors of their morals or manners...." See Virginia Harlow, *Thomas Sergeant Perry: A Biography* (Durham, N.C.: Duke University Press, 1950), pp. 98–99.

2. Robert Herrick's *Together*, a novel about modern marriage, was published in 1908.

3. Probably E. V. Lucas (1868–1938), English travel writer and critic, and master of an easy style.

6 JANUARY 1915, ASBURY PARK, NEW JERSEY, TO MILDRED HOWELLS

> Asbury Park, Jan'y 6, 1915.

Dear Pilla:

I got your letter about poor Mrs. Fields,[1] and wrote at once to Mr. Beal.[2] There was nothing else to do, for I have had no invitation to the funeral, and could not have gone if I had been able.

The news has been a blow to me; she was the last of the world I came into at Boston, for Mrs. Bell[3] was not in it for years later. It was to Mrs. Fields's liking me, Lowell insisted, that I owed my place on the Atlantic. Yes, I am glad we went to see her last summer; I wish I had gone oftener to see her in Boston; but we cannot treat people as if we expected them to die.—You have planned rightly in sending flowers, and in proposing to go with the Nortons.

I shall be so glad to see you, but sorry if you feel I have hurried you back. I have tried not to do so. My teeth seem quiet, now; but I must really have my eye looked after. It's the one that had the little lump on the lid. The oculist has gone from here to St. Augustine, but I shall see one in New York.

The weather is very mild. All well.

> Papa.

1. Mrs. Fields died on 5 January in her eightieth year; Howells had known her since his first days in Cambridge, nearly half a century earlier.

2. James H. Beal, a Boston businessman, was the husband of Annie Fields's young-est sister, Louisa Jane Adams Beal.

3. Helen Choate Bell.

9 JANUARY 1915, ASBURY PARK, NEW JERSEY, TO BOOTH TARKINGTON

Coleman House
Asbury Park N. J. . . . . January 9, 1915.

Dear Mr. Tarkington:

I have read four times over the great scenes of Mrs. Roscoe and the doctor, and of Sheridan and his son and the doctor.[1] I tremble a little for you. Now you must go on and be of the greatest, or you must retreat and be of the most popular as you have always been. Such power as you show in this story cannot endear you to such a public as ours, though it may make you "a great heir of fame."[2] As yet, I do not get the full effect of Bibbs except in his collisions with his father, though I know the fine, lovable Mid-Western type of him. Mary Vertress seems to be mark-ing time, after splendidly going forward. But the rest is great, *great*.

> **Yours sincerely**
> **W. D. Howells.**

1. The scenes and characters are all from the current serial chapters in *Harper's Monthly* of Tarkington's *The Turmoil* (1915). Howells reviewed Tarkington's novel in the "Editor's Easy Chair," *Harper's Monthly*, April 1915, and wrote to Duneka on 28 February 1915 (RPB) that all of Tarkington's women characters are done "wonder-fully" well.

2. "Dear son of memory, great heir of fame" is from Milton's "Epitaph on Shake-speare," which holds that Shakespeare's writing is all the monument he needs. In his reply of 16 January 1915 (MH), Tarkington wrote: "I share the opinion of all the writers I know—that you are the only critic who *knows*. We are afraid of no other (and yet you have always been the kindest) and we really *care* to please no other. My feeling is that 'The Turmoil' must have been a 'long stride' for me since you could write to me so heartily. Popularity, when I've had it, has been—or seemed—accidental: I've always tried for the other thing—and often got neither! But I have got some of 'the other thing' this time, since you say so."

9 JANUARY 1915, ASBURY PARK, NEW JERSEY, TO FREDERICK A. DUNEKA

Asbury Park, N. J., January 9, 1915.

Dear Mr. Duneka:

I would like to do what you ask, or scarcely ask, and of course I admire Maupassant's wonderful skill. But I would not like my name to go to our public with a volume[1] containing the stories *Tony, My Wife, An Evening,* and *The Log,* without saying frankly that the first was bestial, and the other three such stories as men tell after dinner when they are not quite drunk enough to keep decently silent. I don't suppose you would like me to say this, especially as I should have to add that I thought these stories without scientific or artistic excuse, cynical and false. If by any most improbable chance you *should* like it, I should have great pleasure in freeing my mind about *one* master who was also a blackguard. I shall wait your answer before sending the sheets back.

Yours ever,
W. D. Howells.

P. S. Both of the packages have come; sorry I bothered about the delay of the first. Tarkington's last number is tremendous.[2] I have read the two great scenes four times over. The other stories are wonderfully good, mostly.

1. Howells did write an introduction to *The Second Odd Number: Thirteen Tales* (which Harper & Brothers published in May 1917), when he read on the cover of the first Maupassant volume, edited by Henry James, that he was "promised to introduce the second." See Howells to F. A. Duneka, 10 January 1915 (RPB). But he included only one of the four stories he objected to, "Tony," calling it gross and "noisome." And he voiced reservations about Maupassant's "obsessive" treatment of sexual matters, though he was aware, he said, of the Frenchman's "admirable art." See George Arms et al., ed., *Prefaces to Contemporaries, 1882–1920* (Gainesville, Fla.: Scholars' Facsimiles & Reprints, 1957), pp. 164–66.
2. *The Turmoil,* then being serialized in *Harper's Monthly.*

21 JANUARY 1915, NEW YORK, TO FREDERICK A. DUNEKA

Hotel St. Hubert,
January 21, 1915.

Dear Mr. Duneka:

I wish you would let Upton Sinclair use some passages from "A Traveller from Altruria" in an anthology of dangerous thinking which he is making.[1] It will do the book good, and I like to be remembered as a dangerous thinker.

It is all right about the lunch. Call me up any time early next week; I always have an appetite ready.

Yours sincerely
W. D. Howells.

1. Upton Sinclair (1878–1968), socialist novelist of reform, asked Howells in the spring of 1914 to select passages from his books for use in Sinclair's anthology, *The Cry for Justice: An Anthology of Literature of Social Protest* (1915)—and then asked him to write an introduction. Howells responded that Sinclair must make his own choices, that he could not write an introduction, and that Harper & Brothers would have to approve Sinclair's selections from Howells' writings. See Howells to Sinclair, 23 and 26 January 1914 (InU). The upshot was that Harper & Brothers refused substantial reprinting, "so the very charming early novel *A Traveler from Altruria* is represented by only thirteen lines in *The Cry for Justice*," as Sinclair observed in *My Lifetime in Letters* (Columbia: University of Missouri Press, 1960), p. 146.

30 JANUARY 1915, NEW YORK, TO FREDERICK A. DUNEKA

Hotel St. Hubert,
Jan'y 30, 1915.

Dear Mr. Duneka:

I am grateful for all the suggestions on the margin of my proofs,[1] though I could not adopt them all. I am truly sorry Tarkington's story is to end so soon; I hoped it would go on for years.[2]

As for Brand Whitlock if you will look again you will not find that I said his books might "outlive the invasion of Belgium," but only "many events of it."[3] I really think you *ought* to know his "Thirteenth District" which Roosevelt, before his decline and fall, hailed as our greatest political novel; and his "Turn of the Balance" a far greater book; you are only a Kentuckian, though, but Wells as an Ohioan should at least have pretended to know them.[4] Bobbs-Merrill published and rather widely sold them. You had better ask Whitlock for his next novel.*

Yours sincerely
W. D. Howells.

*I happen to know he began one before the war began.

1. Most likely the proofs of the "Editor's Easy Chair," *Harper's Monthly*, March 1915, which discusses the problem of capital punishment and briefly refers to Brand Whitlock's *The Turn of the Balance* (1907).
2. The serial of *The Turmoil* ended March 1915.
3. Neither phrase appears in Howells' brief comment on Whitlock's *The Turn of the Balance* in the March "Easy Chair." Howells refers to this book about "the immemorial inhumanities...practiced in the prisons" as written "by a man who has lately come prominently before the world, and who was trained for the work of writing it by efficient knowledge of 'the criminal classes.' We mean our minister to Belgium, Mr. Brand Whitlock, and his graphic study of prison life...." Earlier comments by Howells also do not contain the quoted phrases: in a New York *Sun* editorial (30 October 1914) Howells is quoted as saying that Whitlock's "rare and manifold gifts have never been meanly or selfishly employed...I am proud to be his

friend"; and in the "Editor's Easy Chair," *Harper's Monthly*, July 1914, Howells reviewed Whitlock's *Forty Years of It*. Whitlock expressed his appreciation and gratitude in a letter to Howells of 19 December 1914 (MH; *Life in Letters*, II, 341–42).

4. Thomas B. Wells was vice-president of Harper & Brothers and associate editor of *Harper's Monthly*; as a fellow Ohioan, Howells suggests, he should be familiar with the writings of the former mayor of Toledo.

9 FEBRUARY 1915, NEW YORK, TO FREDERICK A. DUNEKA

Hotel St. Hubert,
Feb'y 9, 1915.

Dear Mr. Duneka:

I am giving you four stories, with perhaps another to follow: the short ones rather in the manner of "The Mother Bird," which you liked, and have long-ago forgotten.[1]

Now, I would like to know if you have tried my "Primal Memories" among the Philistines anywhere.[2] I understand that the *Saturday Evening Post* is the place to "get money in a basket" as Ford used to say of the *Morning Journal*,[3] and I would willingly share in any plunder of it. My income, by one visitation of God and another has been cut down about $7000 or $8000 this year.

Another thing: the kind Major Leigh, when he wrote me 18 months ago declining to let my farces go to Sergel the universal farce publisher of Chicago,[4] prophesied that you would soon be doing something with my plays which would richly console me for the loss of the untold gold offered me by the Chicagoan. Naturally, with all your larger cares, you have done nothing, not even reprinted the last four comedies from the magazine.[5] Now, I have a notion that if Houghtman-Mifflin and you would let me transfer all my plays to Sergel it would be profit to me and honor to you. I do not in the least know that Sergel would take them now on any terms but what do you say?[6] I have not approached H-M. or him, of course. Why I approach you is because this branch of my many writings is different from the rest, or seems so, and if corded up with all the other drama in Sergel's hands, might blossom anew. I shall not be surprised or pained if you think otherwise.

Yours sincerely
W. D. Howells.

1. Probably "The Return to Favor," "Somebody's Mother," "An Experience," and "The Boarders," *Harper's Monthly*, July, September, November 1915, and March 1916, respectively. They were collected in *The Daughter of the Storage* (1916). "The Mother-Bird" had appeared in *Harper's Monthly*, December 1909.

2. Howells was trying out for the second time his "Primal Memories" (or "Hours of Childhood," as he had called them in his letter to Duneka of 13 May 1914), though he had admitted to Duneka in notes of 4 and 6 June 1914 (MWA) that his "infant memoirs" were "unmagazinable."

3. William Randolph Hearst paid reporters of the New York *Journal* high wages, and with the *Journal* invented yellow journalism. "Ford" is most likely James L. Ford, who wrote satirically about the New York press. See Howells to Duneka, 16 May 1911, n. 1.

4. Charles H. Sergel of the Dramatic Publishing Company in Chicago had offered Howells a twenty percent royalty on five uncollected one-act plays and a $500 advance on royalties in a letter of 5 September 1913 (MH).

5. Howells' last four plays published in *Harper's Monthly* were "Self-Sacrifice: A Farce-Tragedy" (April 1911), "The Impossible: A Mystery Play" (December 1910), "The Night Before Christmas: A Morality" (January 1910), and "A True Hero: Melodrama" (November 1909). A fifth play, "Saved: An Emotional Drama," *Harper's Weekly*, 26 December 1908, had also not been reprinted at the time of this letter.

6. Duneka replied on 10 February 1915 (MH) that he had unsuccessfully tried the *Ladies Home Journal* with the autobiographical material, and that he hoped Howells would be willing to delay a collected volume of plays in a war year bad for publishing. Harper & Brothers never did reprint the plays.

6 MARCH 1915, ST. AUGUSTINE, FLORIDA, TO FREDERICK A. DUNEKA

Hotel Valencia[1]
March 6, 1915.

Dear Mr. Duneka:

I have worked the mud out of my mystery now, I think;[2] and I wonder you did not remember Browning when you blamed it.[3] There are also people who say they do not understand the book of Revelations, and you could justify me to your readers by citing them. If I were you I should use the thing as it now stands. It seems to me a merry jest throughout, and there is a whisk of the forked tale at the end which ought to please people with the belief that I am denying my principles.

Yours sincerely
W. D. Howells.

This is truly a dear old town. I "some think" of buying it, with the peach blossoms and mocking birds all round the little flat we have taken next the nicest sort of hotel.

1. After many delays because of Mildred's dental treatments in Boston, Howells and his daughter left for Florida on 1 March, intending to spend about a month in St. Augustine and to return via New Orleans, from where they would take a river boat up the Mississippi. The traditional winter vacation in Bermuda was ruled out because of the danger of German attacks on American vessels.

2. "The Rotational Tenants: A Hallowe'en Mystery," in *Harper's Monthly*, October 1916. The setting for Howells' fable is the empty cottages of a wealthy beach resort community on All Hallows Eve, in the "blackness of darkness"; and the fable debates the idea of waste as a universal economic principle. At the end the interlocutor asks the Rotational Tenant if he is a capitalist and receives only a shrug in response.

3. Howells is here referring to the obscurity of some of Robert Browning's poetry, a point he brought up again in a later letter to Duneka, 21 March 1915 (RPB): "what are you going to say to the equally obscure author of *Sordello*...?"

21 MARCH 1915, ST. AUGUSTINE, FLORIDA, TO THOMAS S. PERRY

The Valencia*
St. Augustine, Fla. March 21, 1915.

Dear Perry:

We have been here for nearly three weeks in great comfort of bed and board and luxury of weather. The poor Northerners who came for summer are disappointed, but for spring nothing better could be asked. St. A. is really charming, with bits of the past in abundance. If anything the place is overpalmettoed. The "Royal Venetian Band" (all Neapolitans) plays in the Plaza, where there is mild obelisk celebrating in Spanish one of the many "constituciones" given to the Spaniards by their grateful sovereigns, and languid Yankees bask in the sun, or go about trying to find people from their "home towns." Across the way, in charge of a handsome property, is an old Caucasian featured (from his white father) darkey who was once a trick-rider in Barnum's circus, and is, after you, the greatest reader in the world. He has told me personally that, after Shakespeare, I am the greatest author in the world. I find myself much known to his race through my praises of their poet Paul Dunbar.[1] One poor old driver wished to drive me gratis to their church tonight ("a Suvviss of Song") as some slight token of affection for what I had "done for his people."

I am afraid we must give up New Orleans and the Mississippi. Poor Pilla brought the grippe with her, and suffered a week in bed. She is now well; but we dread the chances of travel. We shall try to make Charleston do—two or three weeks hence.

With love to your family

Yours ever
W. D. Howells.

*We have really a little flat next door.

1. See Howells to Douglas, 4 February 1897, n. 1.

15 APRIL 1915, ASBURY PARK, NEW JERSEY, TO SARAH M. PIATT

> Coleman House,
> Asbury Park, N. J., April 15, 1915.

Dear Mrs. Piatt:[1]

Your letter of the 8th has followed me round from Charleston and found me here where I have joined my son's family while Pilla has gone on to Boston to get ready for our summer at York Harbor. When we are young our children belong to us; when we are old we belong to them; both possessions are sweet.

You must not think I have done more than know of the existence of that Authors' Club fund and suggest the diversion of a portion to you.[2] The good and gentle persons in charge have done the rest from their sense that in an unrivalled degree part of it belongs to you. I am glad you are writing or going to write to them, though they feel no claim to your gratitude.

I wish I might see you both, but in the meanwhile take my love, and my heart's wishes for as much comfort as death and age leaves us old people. For me I am mostly very happy in my work still, though for the moment I am often weary of it. But not so weary as of my old body. A little walk tires me, and I have loved so to walk! But I am well, with my 78 years, and this morning Billy promised me 28 more of them—I don't know why. My children are surpassingly good to me. But their mother has now been gone almost five years, and I am often very solitary. Almost every night I dream of her, and sometimes glad dreams. She used to wish we might all go together; I did not understand and laughed. —You have been sorely tried, both of you, but you have each other yet.

> Yours sincerely,
> W. D. Howells.

1. Sarah Morgan Piatt (1836–1919), poet and wife of J. J. Piatt, Howells' collaborator in *Poems of Two Friends* (1860).

2. Mildred Howells' note to this letter in *Life in Letters*, II, 346, reads: "Mrs. John J. Piatt...and her husband having fallen upon evil days, Howells was trying to have the Authors' Club Fund help them. In a letter of March 27th [now lost], Howells had written Mrs. Piatt, 'I suspect the good Goss [Gosse?] is nearer right than you about your affairs, and I am going to try for that additional fund from the Author's Club when I get back to New York: nobody has so gloriously earned it as Piatt and you.'"

23 May 1915, York Harbor, to Aurelia H. Howells

York Harbor, May 23, 1915.

Dear Aurelia:

I hardly know where this letter will find you, but I will send it to the Hotel Royal as you last directed. Of course, with Italy already at war, and with Switzerland shut up or overrun by the hostilities, I am anxious to hear from you and to supply your need of money as soon as I know it. So I will give you my cable address, which is also John's:

Stokwells, New York.

Sign your name *Aurelia*, and John will get it. I wish I had *your* cable address, for it costs me $4 or $5 to reach you at your hotel. Can't you arrange with your banker or bank to let me cable you in their care?

We have been here now nearly a fortnight, and have been watching the leaves and flowers come out. It has been very cool, and we have had the furnace going, but now at last I hope we can let it go out.

I am getting forward my autobiographical papers for publication in the fall,[1] and I want to fill in the Jefferson background. Do you, or does Annie, remember anything of that dreadful summer when I suffered from the fear of hydrophobia?[2] Did father ever mention it in his later life to you? Just what summer was it? I think when I was about seventeen. Everybody whom I could ask is dead, except Eliza, and I could not trust her wild fancy. I think the episode is necessary to a full realization of my life.

I have had all my old letters-home—to father and mother and you—typewritten. There are 8 or 9 thousand of them,[3] and it has cost nearly $100 to do them. I shall not try to write my life farther, but they will be useful to Pilla if she does it.

We have had a great awakening against Germany. As yet she has not answered Wilson's strong letter drawn out by the *Lusitania* atrocity,[4] but we are waiting without anxiety. We have a strong navy, and could keep her off long enough to gather a force for our defence by land. The episode has had the effect of making the German-Americans quiet down or else declare their loyalty. They are worse than the home-Germans, for those cannot help being what they are. But here there is no despotism to make Germans slaves or friends of their national slavery.

John expects to bring his family to K. P. early in June, and then I shall have the dear little boys near by. We are so glad of Abby's good recovery. We are fond of her; she is a good woman, and John and she are very happy.—At last my big flat is rented, but still my income is much reduced, though it is by no means poverty. With our love to all,

> Your aff'te brother
> **Will.**

1. In March Howells had decided to expand "In an Old-Time State Capital," so that it could be published in book form, and he had suggested "Some Years of my Youth in An Old State-Capital" as a title, after Duneka had pointed out that "The public is not interested in an 'Old State Capital', but it is interested in anything associated with Mr. Howells." See Howells to Duneka, 17 and 21 March 1915 (RPB) and Duneka to Howells, 19 and 23 March 1915 (MH).

2. According to Edwin H. Cady, this was in the spring and summer of 1856. See Cady, *Howells,* I, 55.

3. Howells greatly overestimates the number of his letters to his family: about 1,000 survive, and there is no evidence that so large a number of letters was destroyed.

4. Woodrow Wilson's "strong letter" protesting the sinking of the *Lusitania* on 7 May, with the loss of over one hundred American lives, was sent to the imperial German government on 13 May. The president, through W. J. Bryan, his secretary of state, demanded "immediate steps to prevent the recurrence of anything so obviously subversive of the principles of warfare" which the German government, he said, had so wisely maintained in the past. The tone of the note was "firm forbearance," but it also embodied a "real change in his feeling toward the belligerents," according to Ray Stannard Baker, *Woodrow Wilson: Life and Letters* (Garden City, N. Y.: Doubleday, Page & Co., 1927–1939), vol. 5, chap. 7. Howells' approval of Wilson's note was in accord with popular sentiment and was surely influenced by ex-President Taft's immediate public support of Wilson's action.

30 MAY 1915, YORK HARBOR, TO SYLVESTER BAXTER

> York Harbor, Maine, May 30, 1915.

My dear **Baxter:**

Thank you for that list of poets,[1] and for the poem enclosed.[2] I join in your prayer with the hope that the German despotism may perish of its own wickedness,

> Yours affectionately
> W. D. Howells.

and that the kind German common people may forever outlive it.

1. Baxter had, it seems probable, sent at Howells' request the names of new American poets. The consequence may then well have been Howells' striking review article in the "Editor's Easy Chair," *Harper's Monthly,* September 1915, of first and early books of poetry of Amy Lowell, E. L. Masters, Robert Frost, Dana Burnet,

Conrad Aiken, James Oppenheim, Vachel Lindsay, with mention of Anna H. Branch, Arthur D. Ficke, E. A. Robinson, and John Gould Fletcher. Baxter was an early and strong backer of Robert Frost.

2. The poem has not been identified.

2 JUNE 1915, YORK HARBOR, TO THOMAS S. PERRY

York Harbor, June 2, 1915.

Dear Perry:

Both your bread-and-butter letters at hand and contents noted.[1] The plan of the world city suits me exactly, but choose me a lot at the farthest remove from your unnatural family where I may cherish you apart from them on scrod and lobster.

Your visit was for me a mad success, and to-day came B. Tarkington's "Flirt."[2] I'm rather afraid to read it.

I shall be glad of the ink. I *always* use Staffords when I can get it; Carter's was fobbed off on me by the grocer.

John writes that Billy has transferred his interest from submarines to Christ, and required a picture of the Ascension—"like an elevator." Isn't that medievally literal?

With love from both to you all,

W. D.

1. Perry's letters have not been located, but on 24 May 1915 (MeWC) Howells had urged Perry to visit him "this week."

2. *The Flirt*, first published by Doubleday, Page in March 1913, was now being reissued by Grosset and Dunlap. Tarkington, who was summering at nearby Kennebunkport, had been a luncheon guest at York Harbor a few days earlier, apparently at the same time that Perry was visiting Howells. See Howells to F. A. Duneka, 3 June 1915 (RPB) and Virginia Harlow, *Thomas Sergeant Perry: A Biography* (Durham, N.C.: Duke University Press, 1950), p. 204.

29 JUNE 1915, YORK HARBOR, TO HENRY JAMES

York Harbor, Maine, June 29, 1915.

Dear James:

If I wait to write you a fit letter, I shall write none; so here goes a faint response to the kind mentions you make of me in your Mr. and Mrs. J. T. Fields.[1] I read it aloud to Pilla for our common pleasure; she knew *her* if not him and last summer we passed a night at her house in Manchester. Your paper relumed so many old faded fires, and cast, most precious of all, a tender light on your own youth, which used to abash me by its worldly maturity. I remember F.'s bringing me a story of yours with the question of whether he should take it, and my saying, "Yes, and as many more by the same hand as you can get."[2] That is what young ass't ed.s should be saying now; but are they? A change has passed upon things, we can't deny it; I could not "serialize" a story of mine now in any American magazine, thousands of them as they are.

We are much at war for you over here; but we do not seem to help much; we are almost as bad as Russians who don't fight as well as they write. All York Harbor is for the Allies beginning with Mrs. Bell, who lives two doors away from me.[3] She still is the brightest of octogenarians.— Perry was down to see me before dooming himself to that dismal Hancock of his.[4] He is your most pathetically constant adorer, and on the whole I should say your worship was spreading among us. I am comparatively a dead cult with my statues cast down and the grass growing over them in the pale moonlight.

There is now a great wash of young poetry on these shores, and some of it not so bad.[5]—Pilla and I spend our days gardening by day and reading at night. We have a deliciously large, cool house—no such oven as we baked you in at Kittery Point ten years ago.—I am doing my most miserable memoirs,[6] which really make me sick; but I promised to do them. I end them with going off to Venice. It is something awful and I wonder the more at the grace and ease with which you carry off your past in those two blithe books of yours.[7]

Yours affectionately,
W. D. Howells.

1. James's reminiscence in the *Atlantic*, July 1915, recalled the ambiance, in the Fields house, of tradition, literature, European visitors, and publishing as well as Annie Fields's active friendship, after her husband's death, with writers like Sarah Orne Jewett. James speaks of Howells, his "friend and super-excellent confrere," as sowing the seed for the new novel in the *Atlantic*. He also recalls being told by an "amused W. D. H." that Fields found James's "strain of pessimism" in his stories "odd . . . even ridiculous . . . on the part of an author with his mother's milk scarce yet dry on his lips." See Leon Edel, ed., *The American Essays of Henry James* (New York: Vintage Books, 1956), pp. 270, 373.

2. See Howells to Fields, 4 January 1867.

3. Helen Choate Bell. On 2 June 1915 (MH), Howells had commented in more detail on his views regarding German-American relations at this time: "I think it quite possible, though not very probable that we shall send the German ambassador away. That will bring us near war, for we cannot tell a nation that it is inhuman and savage without mortal offence, no matter how true it is. Still it would be so far from actual war, that we might have time to get a little ready to fight. At present our sole equality with Germany is in our distance; if she could get at us she could easily smash us. Everyone knows that and wishes to go slow. Perhaps we shall wait to satisfy her that the *Lusitania* carried no munitions of war before

we break with her, but she really knows that already. I suppose Wilson is doing as well as any one could; we are no readier to fight than China would be, except that we are of a more warlike temper."

4. Thomas S. Perry had a summer house in Hancock, New Hampshire.

5. See Howells to Baxter, 30 May 1915, n. 1.

6. *Years of My Youth.*

7. *A Small Boy and Others* (1913) and *Notes of a Son and Brother* (1914).

1 JULY 1915, YORK HARBOR, TO BRANDER MATTHEWS

York Harbor, Me., July 1st, 1915.

My very dear Matthews:

I was very glad to see your handwriting again, and I wish I could say from my own knowledge that *Saul* was Alfieri's greatest tragedy. Everyone else says so; but I have not read it; Alfieri is not easy reading. I think the *Clytemnestra* is tremendous, but the theme is hackneyed, and the *Filippo*, or *Don Carlos* is awful. The Clytemnestra in my Modern It. Poets is mine-issimo, and Alfieri's too, almost word for word. I'm very proud of it as a bit of work, but it is yours for your book and welcome,[1] if one act of the five will be of any use to you. I wish I had done the whole play, but life is short and gets shorter the longer I live. That is a reason for my sharing, as I do, the regret you express at our not meeting oftener.—I have never seen the English version of Alfieri; but it ought to be good, and probably isn't. *La Locandiera* of Goldoni is an inevitable choice; but I like some of the dialect pieces better: they are all racier, of course—Sior Todaro Brontolon, Le Baruffe Chiozzote, etc.

I wish I could be of any real use, but I am getting uselesser every way. I am old, old! I get tired easily, mind as well as body; I am losing my incentive; as some one says in that saddest novel of Tourguénief's, "The zest is gone."*[2]

> Yours affectionately
> W. D. Howells.

*It isn't either! But I like the heart break of the words.

1. Matthews was selecting plays for his anthology *The Chief European Dramatists* (1916). He included Goldoni's *The Mistress of the Inn*, translated by M. Pierson, but omitted Alfieri, about whom Howells had written in his series of "Choice Autobiographies" in 1877; the Alfieri essay was reprinted in *Modern Italian Poets* (1887).

2. Of the many novels and tales of Ivan Turgenev that Howells knew, *Liza* is surely "that saddest novel" for him. Howells has Colville say to Imogene, in *Indian Summer* (1886): "The samovar sends up its agreeable odor all through his books. Read *Lisa* if you want your heart really broken" (chapter 5). Also, in *April Hopes*

(1888) a group of women talks about *Smoke* and *Liza*, the *Nichée des Gentilshommes* as Mrs. Pasmer calls it, and this lady who "reads her Turgenev in French" says, "I must get *Lisa*, I like a good heart-break, don't you?" See Van Wyck Brooks, *Howells: His Life and World* (New York: Dutton, 1959), p. 106. But it is in Leo Tolstoy's *Anna Karenina* that Anna says to herself, in English, "The zest is gone," as she is driven to the train station where she will throw herself under the train wheels. Howells' misatribution is puzzling. He admired Turgenev and Toystoy above nearly all other novelists; but Liza's "transcendent, hopeless pathos" (*Atlantic*, February 1873) differs measurably from Anna Karenina's violent despair. In any event, the sentence was engraved in Howells' memory: he had used it to tell Hamlin Garland how desolate he felt at the death of his wife. See Howells to Garland, 16 July 1910 (CLSU).

21 JULY 1915, YORK HARBOR, TO AURELIA H. HOWELLS

York Harbor, Me., July 21, 1915.

Dear Aurelia:

I thought you would be interested to see the envelope of your last letter, which shows what a dangerous person you are held to be. Whether it was the Swiss, German, French, English or American Censor who opened the letter I have no idea; perhaps they all did it.—There is no special news here, except that it seems the President has decided to leave it to Germany whether she will drown our people or not. It is rather a droll outcome of the whole matter, and perhaps I don't quite understand it. I will keep sending you papers and you can judge for yourself.

Pilla has been undergoing a strange affliction from some unknown bite or sting on a finger. It festered and from the blood poisoning her hand and wrist swelled; the wound had to be repeatedly opened; but it is now almost healed. She was walking through the tall grass when it happened, and we don't know at all what hurt her; the doctor thinks possibly a spider, perhaps because he can't think of anything else.

I wonder if you and Annie remember hearing father ever talk of my not having any schooling, or any effort being made for me in that way. I am trying to treat of the matter in my memoirs.[1] I suspect we were both proud of my doing for myself; but I remember it once came to my wanting to go to Austenburg Institute and it was decided (mainly by dear old Joe, who grieved over it to me late in life) that they could not spare me from the office or the money for the academy's fees. I dare say I should not have gone, or if I did would have been too homesick to stay. It is odd that without having any such poor chance, I should have been offered professorships in our four greatest Universities—Harvard, Yale, and Johns Hopkins,—besides such colleges as Union (at Schenectady) and Washington at St. Louis.[2] But these all came long after I could turned from literature to accept them.

We are having a wonderfully wet summer, with rain almost every day. It is great growing weather, and our place is beautiful.

Another thing: Did either of you know of poor **Harvey Greene's** being forced out of the army in dishonor by his superior officer who lied against him? I used to hear of it from Joe, who said that Harvey always meant to kill the wretch if they met. But of course this didn't happen; the man died.[3]

With love to all,

> Your aff'te brother,
> **Will.**

1. Howells was writing what became *Years of My Youth* (HE, pp. 97–98). William and Joseph, who was four years older, quarreled often and bitterly, says Howells, but "utter forgiveness" passed between them "long before our youth was passed" (pp. 84–85).

2. For these offers and rejections, see *Years of My Youth*, HE, pp. 96–97, where Howells correctly refers to offers from "three of our greatest universities," rather than four. The error here probably arose from the fact that Johns Hopkins had made offers of an appointment at two different times.

3. For Harvey Green, see Howells to J. A. Howells, 10 April 1857, n. 5, and *Years of My Youth*, HE, pp. 105–6. In a later letter to Aurelia, 4 February 1916 (MH), Howells wrote that "Harvey was a fine fellow, intense and brave; but his life seems to have been a defeat; and poor Jane's."

24 JULY 1915, YORK HARBOR, TO THOMAS S. PERRY

> York Harbor, July 24, 1915.

Dear Perry:

It is so long since I saw you or heard from you that I feel as if I were now accosting you in some blessed planet rather than on your hill in Hancock. How is it with you, and all you? Are you ready to join with James in renouncing Wilson and all his works and swearing fealty to King Jorge? Or don't you believe he's done it, or means to?[1] Not that I should much blame him any way, though nothing could persuade me to bow the knee to e'er a crowned head of them all. I *shouldn't* mind (now I'm past the military age) swapping citizenships with some Frenchman.

I'm sending back with many thanks the De Musset plays which H. J. lent me long ago in our first Sacramento Street days.[2] I don't know that the Caprices of Mary Ann much took me, but you know what a poor beast I am. When did we hold that famous symposium of ours about Artzibashef?[3] I want it for the instructor of an elderly girl here, who says he's beginning to be done in English.

It is Mrs. Bell who mostly keeps us alive.[4]—Poor Pilla has had blood poisoning from some unknown sting on her finger, but she's all-righting now, and joins me in affection to you all.

Yours ever
W. D. Howells.

1. Henry James became a British citizen as an act of loyalty to the country in which he had lived for nearly forty years, and because his status as an alien in the coastal town of Rye made for too many difficulties. See Leon Edel, *Henry James, The Master, 1901–1916* (Philadelphia: J. B. Lippincott, 1972), pp. 528–32. Two weeks later, on 7 August 1915 (NNC; *Life in Letters*, II, 351–52), Howells wrote Brander Matthews: "I am sorry to lose James as an American as well as an Academician; but he had a full right to do what he has done."

2. Alfred de Musset's *Les Caprices de Marianne* appeared in a revised and enlarged two-volume edition of *Comédies et Proverbes* in Paris in 1866. This is probably the edition that James lent Howells in their early acquaintance in Cambridge.

3. "Recent Russian Fiction: A Conversation" between Howells and Perry on Artsybashev, Gogol, Kuprin and others appeared in the *North American Review*, July 1912.

4. Helen Choate Bell.

26 OCTOBER 1915, NEW YORK, TO PAUL KESTER

130 West 57th street,
New York, Oct. 26, 1915.

My dear Paul:

John's sister-in-law, Miss Elizabeth White, has made the greatest discovery of a hero and a plot for a Picture-Play in the career of Coronado, the Spanish conqueror of New Mexico in the 16th century. I ventured to speak of you as gifted in stage-craft, and every way fitted to help her work up such a scheme for the Movies, and I think she will enclose a sketch of the proposed drama for your consideration.

I believe you have met Miss White, and I am sure you will take an intelligent and sympathetic interest in her idea.

Pilla and I were so disappointed in our failure to see either you or your play last spring.[1] We greatly wished to see both; but the chances were against us. She is still in Boston, but I am here with John's family (who join me in love) till sometime late in November.

Your aff'te cousin
W. D. Howells.

1. Kester's play, "The Desert Island," opened at the Baltimore Theatre on 6 April 1916.

31 OCTOBER 1915, NEW YORK, TO MILDRED HOWELLS

130 W. 57,
Oct 31, 1915.

Dear Pilla:

Another incomparable day, with a drive this afternoon through the Park in a trottykins. The motors swarmed to choking on the west side, but the east was decently clear. They all raced at speed-top. Why, why? We will drive *our* Ford always at a walk. The Fords abound here, but declass their owners.

I think I will do a story (in addition to my sketch of St. Augustine) about The Home Towners.[1] I find them pathetically interesting in the retrospect.

Abby has had a let-up in her headache.

New York is dreadful and as yet without the charm I used to feel in it.—I've not been to the Century yet, and will not go till I have the last revise of proof off my hands.[2]

A long hour in bed with Billy to-day when we made a poem about a wood chuck, he furnishing the alternate rhymes and lines.

Jacky is just a sweet pig.

Aff'tely
Papa.

1. "The Home-Towners" was to concern Americans from all over the United States retired in St. Augustine, but it was never published.

2. Although *Years of My Youth* was not published until the following autumn, Howells was probably already revising the proofs at this time. That there were proofs as early as July 1915 is indicated by a letter he wrote on 31 July 1915 to Horace White, requesting suggestions for revisions: "We are contemporaries, we grew up in a new country under conditions much the same, but more favorable I think for you than for me. It has seemed to me that you, better than any other man living, can judge the record of my childhood from my own point of view, and yet bring a mind of different quality and higher training to the criticism of what I have written. Will you do me the great favor to read this proof, and note whatever you find unwise, ungenuine and out of taste in it, and what you think is unadvisable to print?" White acted very promptly, so that on 5 August 1915 Howells was able to thank him for suggested revisions and send him additional proof, which White again returned immediately. Finally, on 8 August 1915, Howells wrote White a third letter, thanking him "again for your kind words about my work, and for your strictures. I will cut out that paragraph about my editing the girl author, for I see that I cannot make

others . . . understand the difference between 'fat' and 'lean' in printer's parlance.—I have reduced my ancestors a little, but I cannot cut them in half." These letters, all in the possession of Polly Howells Werthman, Kittery Point, Maine, have come to light since the writing of the introduction to *Years of My Youth*, HE, pp. xi–xxiii, in 1975, which gives more details about the genesis of the autobiography.

2 NOVEMBER 1915, NEW YORK, TO MILDRED HOWELLS

130 West 57,
Nov. 2, 1915.

Dear Pilla:

I have waited till you were firmly on your back before telling you of a change in my affairs which I think is for the better. As soon as I came down I had a heart to heart talk with Duneka in which (most confidentially) he intimated that he might be out of Harper & Brothers by the end of the year and me with him, that being the tendency of the new Morgan man seeking control.[1] John and I talked the case carefully over, and I decided to do what I have so often, as you know, thought of doing: give up everything but the Easy Chair and be free to market my other stuff. I asked Duneka up to lunch next day, and he came with exactly the same proposition in mind. He was in a much less pessimistic mood, and did not put the change as conditional to my remaining with the Harpers, but said that this new basis would hold in any event. He offered me $5000 for the Chair alone, which was more than I might have stood out for, and I told him what I had been thinking, and accepted. So, without doing anything *but* the Chair I shall have a gross income of—

Easy Chair	$ 5000.
City Bonds	350.
Empire Trust	210.
Royalties on old books	1500
Rents of houses	5000
Rent of big flat	3550
Interest Cambridge house	250
N.E. Trust Co.	180
N.Y. Savings Bank	60
Interest Second Mortgage (Hall)	480
	$16,580.

My net income would be about $14,000. On this we could live handsomely, and if I chose I could run it up to $20,000 by writing outside. Harpers would like the first chance at any such material, and the North

American would probably take anything I offered. Duneka conceded all rights to *The Leatherwood God* in view of the fact that it was imagined and actually begun before my Harvey contract.

I feel very happy in the arrangement, and I hope you will. You see the notion of Harpers is cut salaries, and mine has been large.

You might keep this letter for the figures; I may have forgotten some things. I am going to the storage tomorrow to get bank books, etc.

Aff'tely,
Papa.

1. Colonel George Harvey, having resigned as president and director of Harper & Brothers in May 1915 because of financial mismanagement, was succeeded by C. T. Brainard, who represented the economizing policies of J. P. Morgan & Co., the financial institute most closely associated with the publishing firm. Brainard had recently been appointed the firm's treasurer; he was a man of "uncouth manners and bluntness" and thus "offensive to Duneka, who was the epitome of graciousness...." See Eugene Exman, *The House of Harper* (New York: Harper & Row, 1967), pp. 209–10. For Howells the new arrangement took effect on 1 January 1916. See Howells to Mildred Howells, 10 November 1915 (MH).

10 NOVEMBER 1915, NEW YORK, TO HAMILTON W. MABIE

130 West 57th street,
· Nov. 10, 1915.

My dear Mabie:

Yes indeed, I duly received your Outlook with that kindest notice of my Stratford book.[1] You must know how I value such words from such a Shakespearean as you. They are such words as hardly another man living could speak with the same authority, and I thank you most truly for them.

I like them so much that I would be willing to have you read them in default of any others when you receive my medal for me at the Institute meeting in Boston;[2] I know you are not going to refuse me this office which I have asked in preference of you to any other friend.

Yours sincerely
W. D. Howells.

1. Mabie reviewed *The Seen and Unseen at Stratford-on-Avon* in *Outlook*, 13 September 1914.

2. Mabie represented Howells at the ceremony of the National Institute of Arts and Letters awarding him the gold medal for fiction on 19 November 1915. Howells had sent Mabie his acceptance speech and asked him to deliver it. The medal was delivered to Howells later that month by Ripley Hitchcock, the secretary of the Institute.

7 DECEMBER 1915, NEW YORK, TO FREDERICK A. DUNEKA

> The Hawthorne,
> 70. W. 49
> Dec. 7, 1915.

Dear Mr. Duneka:

While I very much wish and hope that you will see your way to letting the Century people have the book-rights of The Leatherwood God,[1] I quite as much wish and hope that you will not let your decision be affected by that contingency at which we darkly and guiltily (like two conspirators) hinted at our talk yesterday. That is, I expect and desire you to treat the matter as if Franklin Square were to be hereafter what it has been before, with no vile possibility lurking under the eastern horizon; and I believe with my whole corrupt heart that my venture under a new imprint will be to our common advantage. I can arrange for putting the book into that Uniform edition which has gone so long in khaki.[2] The new imprint will remind readers yet unborn that there are a multitude of other books under the old which they have never heard of; we might even get the Centurions to print in the title, "By W. D. H., Author of A Hazard of New Fortunes, The Kentons, The Landlord of Lion's Head," etc., all to the free advertisement of your publications.[3]

> **Yours** sincerely
> **W. D.** Howells.

1. *The Leatherwood God* presented a test case of Howells' new arrangement with Harper & Brothers, which he had explained in his letter to Mildred, 2 November 1915. The Century Company proposed to pay $5,000 for serial use, providing they could publish the novel in book form thereafter, with $1,000 advance against a flat twenty percent royalty. See Douglas Z. Doty to Howells, 6 December 1915 (MH). Harper & Brothers wanted to try the serial elsewhere but keep the novel (see Duneka to Howells, 8 December 1915; MH; but the Century people were insistent on book rights, and Howells signed a contract with them. In a draft of a letter to Duneka, dated 9 December 1915 (MH), Howells canceled a passage that sheds an interesting light on the relationship between author and publisher: "Unless you decided to serialize the story in Harper's on the terms they [the Century] offer me, I do not see what could be done. Even then you could not bring the zeal and liking for it which the Century people feel, and I should know that you had forced yourself to [a] step which must affect the kindness between us. You have honestly believed during our relation of fifteen years that I was not serializable, and I do not say that you have been wrong, though I have repeatedly tried to overcome your reluctance."

2. The uniform edition never materialized after the failure of Harper & Brothers to continue the Library Edition of 1911 past six volumes embodying eight titles.

See Howells to Duneka, 3 February 1914, n. 3. The original Library Edition was bound in deep green, but was reissued in a cheaper khaki binding and substantially trimmed margins.

3. The title page of the novel does not list earlier works under the Harper imprint.

15 DECEMBER 1915, NEW YORK, TO HENRY JAMES, JR.

> The Hawthorne
> 70 W. 49 st.
> Dec. 15, 1915.

Dear Mr. James:[1]

I had not heard of the sorrowful news you tell me.[2] I cannot say anything. But I wish he could have lived to know the Allies were winning, however they seemed to be losing. If he is still living when your next letter reaches your mother let her give him my dearest love. He is the last that is left of my earthly world.

> Yours sincerely
> W. D. Howells.

1. See Howells to H. James, Jr., 15 August 1913, n. 1.
2. Howells' friend of half a century had suffered a stroke on 2 December. See Leon Edel, *Henry James, The Master, 1901–1916* (Philadelphia: J. B. Lippincott, 1972), p. 560.

26 JANUARY 1916, ST. AUGUSTINE, FLORIDA, TO KATE D. WIGGIN

> 246 St. George Street,
> St. Augustine, Fla., Jan'y 26, 1916.

Dear Mrs. Riggs:[1]

I have given above what seems to be my present earthly address in the most heavenly air.[2] How any body can bear to stay in New York even for the sake of the Colony Club, passes my understanding. Send poor old Silas along and I will gladly write in him for you.

Why should you protest your "undiminished affection" for me? Have I written any novel half as popular as yours[3] that you should love me less than ever?

The Poinsettias are in bloom, and the peaches are "all blowed out" as they saying at Kittery Point. The mocking-birds are singing all the day.

Yours with faded regard,
W. D. Howells.

1. Kate Douglas Wiggin (Mrs. G. C. Riggs) was an expert in kindergarten education and author of popular children's books, who when she was a young woman in Santa Barbara, California, liked to play the "verbose, light-hearted (and lighter-headed!) heroines" of Howells' farces. Quoted from Wiggin's *My Garden of Memories* (1923) in Cady, *Howells*, II, 230–31.
   2. Howells and Mildred had left New York on 4 January.
   3. *Rebecca of Sunnybrook Farm* (1903) sold more than 750,000 copies.

26 JANUARY 1916, ST. AUGUSTINE, FLORIDA, TO HENRY JAMES

246 St. George Street,
St. Augustine, Florida, Jan'y 26, 1916.

My dear James:
   I hope this may find you mending from your break, which has been such a sorrow to all of us who love you.[1] To me the news of it was so disabling that I did not know how to make you the offer of my sympathy, but I knew you would know you had it. Though I have written so seldom to you, you may be sure that no event or circumstance of your life has been unnoted by me, and especially none in this *dies irae*, when you have been moved and stirred so deeply. I am much older than you, and I shall soon be in my eightieth year; but I have somehow always looked to you as my senior in so many important things. You have greatly and nobly lived for brave as well as beautiful things, and your name and fame are dear to all who honor such things.
   Pilla is with me here where I have fled from the cold and colds of the North, and she joins me in the love which I need not protest to you. If Mrs. William James is with you as I hope, share it with her.[2]

Yours ever
W. D. Howells.

1. See Howells to H. James, Jr., 15 December 1915, n. 2.
   2. Alice James stayed with her brother-in-law until he died on 28 February 1916. See Leon Edel, *Henry James, The Master, 1901–1916* (Philadelphia: J. B. Lippincott, 1972), p. 560.

11 FEBRUARY 1916, ST. AUGUSTINE, FLORIDA, TO SINCLAIR LEWIS

St. Augustine, Feb'y 11, 1916.

Dear Mr. Lewis:

I did not like your boy in the beginning; I thought him overdone; and so dropped the book for a while.[1] Today I took it up and read about the flying, from the mob scene in California to the end of the flying at New Haven. It was all *good, better, best.* The go was full of throbs, and the people real and palpable. I am awfully glad of it. Now I shall keep on to the end—I hope.

We expect to go to Palm Beach by boat on Monday; I hear you are going later. We expect to be at the Hotel Saltair, West Palm Beach.

With our best joint regards to Mrs Lewis and yourself,

Yours cordially
W. D. Howells.

1. The "boy" is Carl Ericson, "the Hawk," in *The Trail of the Hawk* (1915). Lewis (1885–1951) had given Howells a copy of the novel during a mid-winter meeting in St. Augustine. Less than fifteen years later, in his December 1930 acceptance speech for having been awarded the Nobel Prize in literature, Lewis accused Howells of atrophied gentility and having exerted a deadening influence on American letters. See Mark Schorer, *Sinclair Lewis: An American Life* (New York: McGraw-Hill, 1961), pp. 231, 552. Yet in *Dodsworth* (1929) he had made Sam Dodsworth exclaim: "Say do you realize that at the time Dickens described the Middlewest—my own part of the country—as entirely composed of human wet rags, a fellow named Abe Lincoln and another named Grant were living there; and not more than maybe ten years later, a boy called William Dean Howells (I heard him lecture once at Yale, and I notice that they still read his book about Venice *in* Venice) had been born? Dickens couldn't find or see people like that. Perhaps some European observers today are missing a few Lincolns and Howellses!" (p. 253).

16 FEBRUARY 1916, ST. AUGUSTINE, FLORIDA, TO THOMAS S. PERRY

246 St. George St.,
St. Augustine, Feby 16, 1916.

My dear Perry:

I am sending you, with much love, half dozen bottles of Scuppernong wine which I think will remind you of your native Tarragona and your ancestral port. I suppose you know the vine which grows wild along with the rattlesnakes in the woods here, and bears its fruit in blobs of three or four, as big as damson plums. The wine is made by a German woman three or four miles from town here, and she has promised this day to express the case to you.—We have been having a beautiful summer which the almanac would call winter, but with only five days of frostless cold out of our two months so far.[1] Much of the time we have fervently desired the shadow, as we walked to our lunch at the Italian trattoria across the plaza up St. George street. We are keeping house in a camping-out way, and seeing a good many amiable people, but not too many. I work all morning, and after lunch I nap, and then drive or go to the movies. These are better than we saw at York Beach, last summer, and better still in the making where we sometimes see them amidst our conscious picturesqueness.

Among our acquaintance we count four retired generals who like the climate, and no end of friendly folks besides. The English-born rector lives across the way, and we exchange pro-ally opinions; but I do not go to his service.

I wonder if I have told you that a serial of mine—The Leatherwood God—will begin in the Century for April. I believe I have already made you read it, but you had better read it again.

What better books can you have been reading in your several languages?—Do you hear directly anything about poor James? I was so stricken down with him that I could not write until a few weeks ago.[2]

With our love to you all,

Yours ever
W. D. Howells.

1. Actually Howells had arrived in St. Augustine only a little more than a month earlier.

2. See Howells to James, 26 January 1916. After Howells had received word of James's imminent death, he wrote Perry on 1 March 1916 (MeWC): "Here is a touching letter from Mrs. Wm. James, about him who seemed so imperishably vital. It is an immense loss."

7 MARCH 1916, ST. AUGUSTINE, FLORIDA, TO FREDERICK A. DUNEKA

246 St. George Street,
St. Augustine, March 7, 1916.

Dear Mr. Duneka:

No one knew James as I did from the first, and if you will announce from me, to appear in an early number of Harper's, a paper about him, biographical, personal, critical, I will write for you such a paper as I wrote about Longfellow, about Lowell, about Holmes, and better.[1]

This is an offer under our agreement, and I should like your decision, for if you do not want the paper I am likely to do it for some one else.

Yours sincerely
W. D. Howells.

P. S. There is a kind of "bounce" in this which I do not like; but you will understand that it is not *real* bounce. I think I had better not promise the paper for any certain time, and if you like the notion of it you had better say it "will appear in a forthcoming number." I should like to have it heralded because people will naturally expect something of the kind from me, and perhaps wonder why they do not get it.

1. Only a few days earlier Duneka had asked Howells to pull together his criticism of *Daisy Miller* and to write an additional paragraph on the death of James. Howells sent the critical piece, but added: "I have tried for the additional paragraph which you suggested; but I shall not care if you omit it. I really could not write more of James's death yet." See Howells to Duneka, 5 March 1916 (RPB). But he changed his mind as he came to consider his unique relation to James and thought about similar pieces he had written on the literary careers of Longfellow (*Harper's Monthly*, August 1896), Holmes (*Harper's Monthly*, December 1896), and Lowell (*Scribner's*, September 1900). The criticism of *Daisy Miller* appeared in 1916 as preface to a text printed from the plates of an illustrated Harper & Brothers edition of 1906. Subsequently, Boni & Liveright published Howells' introduction and the novella in 1918, in the Modern Library. See George Arms et al., ed., *Prefaces to Contemporaries, 1882–1920* (Gainesville, Fla.: Scholars' Facsimiles & Reprints, 1957), p. xviii.

17 MARCH 1916, ST. AUGUSTINE, FLORIDA, TO FREDERICK A. DUNEKA

St. Augustine, March 17, 1916.

Oh! oh! oh!
Oh! oh! oh!
How *could* you ask it? No, certainly not in a month, unless I have a fool's own luck. But I will begin it on Monday, after thinking it all over, and will do the best I can.

Wont it warn the interlopers off if you say "in an early number," instead of rigidly "in June"? Who will dare if it is known I am doing it?[1]

I had just got warm in my St. Augustine, and John's pictures are so inspiring![2] Well, heaven is over all. I will try! The Easy Chair is in my way before April 10th, and I must turn aside and break my shins on it, and then limp on.

Yours ever
W. D. Howells

1. For Howells' memorial article on Henry James, see Howells to Duneka, 7 March 1916.

2. John Howells was making sketches, "splendid and full of . . . strange force," as Howells wrote Aurelia on 19 March 1916 (MH), for his father's two-part essay, "A Confession of St. Augustine," *Harper's Monthly*, April–May 1917. Seven of his sketches illustrate part 1.

18 MARCH 1916, ST. AUGUSTINE, FLORIDA, TO FREDERICK A. DUNEKA

St. Augustine, March 18, 1916.

Dear Duneka:

I ought to say, before we go further with the James paper (I have already begun it, you see!) that the price, to Messrs. J. P. M. & Co., will be $2500. You know I could get that from another magazine, though of course to the Colonel, who commanded my affections as well as labors, it would have been less.[1] The price is irrespective of time and place.

Yours sincerely
W. D. Howells.

1. For the role of J. P. Morgan & Co. and the resignation of Colonel George Harvey, see Howells to Mildred Howells, 2 November 1915, n. 1. Harvey, together with Howells and Finley Peter Dunne, was a member of Mark Twain's exclusive "Damned Human Race Luncheon Club." See *Twain-Howells*, p. 828.

23 MARCH 1916, ST. AUGUSTINE, FLORIDA, TO FREDERICK A. DUNEKA

St. Augustine, March 23, 1915.[1]

Dear Mr. Duneka:

I am truly, almost humbly, grateful to you for refusing to give the price I asked for the James paper,[2] because now I need not lash myself on to doing it within a certain time. My demand was the measure of the strain I must undergo in that case as well as of the thing's intrinsic value; the market value would be always your affair. I doubt now whether I shall ever write the paper; certainly if I do it will not be immediately. The relief is more than I could express without theatre, and it is for this that I thank you. I shall gladly return to mousing about this strange, beautiful, factitious, fatuous place, and remand my memories of James to the past where I should have suffered so much in calling them up.[3]

Sincerely, almost affectionately, yours
W. D. Howells.

1. The content and context of this letter clearly establish Howells' dating as erroneous.

2. Replying to Howells' letter of 18 March, Duneka had responded on 20 March 1916 (MH) that Harper & Brothers could not pay $2,500, even though the article might be worth it, and that no other magazine would "dare venture such a figure." He proposed instead to pay "$500. or $600. a number," perhaps for three installments. Later in the year Howells refused to write a memorial notice of James for the Authors Club, saying: "If I should write anything about him I should wish it to be something fully representative of my mind about him, and I find that touching any subject impairs its freshness for me, and so far disables me." It seems worth noting, however, that in the spring of 1910 Duneka had paid Howells $1,500, in addition to his annual salary from Harper & Brothers, for the three-part essay, "My Memories of Mark Twain."

3. Five years later, at the very end of his life, Howells was working on two manuscripts, one an "Editor's Easy Chair" review of Percy Lubbock's two-volume edition of James's letters, the other an essay, "The American James." See *Life in Letters*, II, 394–99.

25 MARCH 1916, ST. AUGUSTINE, FLORIDA, TO HAMLIN GARLAND

St. Augustine, March 25, 1916.

My dear Garland:

I somehow thought you would be first to speak a good word for my story,[1] and there is no one whose good word could be welcomer. I thank you for it, and I hope the thing will not disappoint you as it goes on. Nancy is the chief figure of the drama, and you are right in expecting my best of old Braile; he is a sort of grim chorus, but he has his part in the action.

We expect to go North in a fortnight, and be in New York about April 20, for a week. Your New York experiment interests me; you are right to make it.[2]

I want a good long talk with you.

My daughter joins me in best regards to your wife and you. With love to your little ones,

Yours ever
W. D. Howells.

1. Garland was reading the first installment of *The Leatherwood God*, *Century*, April–November 1916. A few days later Howells received a letter, dated 30 March 1916 (MH), from Douglas Z. Doty of the *Century*, commenting on the success of the novel: "Your appearance in our magazine has made a wide stir and brought us hearty congratulations from many quarters. We are all of us feeling happy at the very auspicious launching of your latest work."

2. Garland's "New York experiment" meant establishing his family in New York City. See Jean Holloway, *Hamlin Garland: A Biography* (Austin: University of Texas Press, 1960), p. 225.

2 MAY 1916, NEW YORK, TO ALBERT MORDELL

120 West 57th St.,
May 2, 1916

Dear Mr. Mordell:[1]

I think you take very magnanimously my difference of opinion which must remain until yours is changed. There was no reason why I should not treat you civilly, and I am glad you felt that I had done so. I wish for your own sake, rather than mine, that you had not agreed with Moore that I had "imitated" Henry James; that senses of a grotesqueness unworthier of you than of him, for he had so long been a [illegible word] expatriate in Paris that he felt obliged to prove his familiarity with continental literature by insulting ours.[2]

Yours sincerely
W. D. Howells.

1. Albert Mordell (b. 1885), by profession a lawyer, wrote on literary topics and later collected a volume of Howells' writings about James's fiction, *Discoveries of a Genius: William Dean Howells and Henry James* (1961). Howells had reviewed Mordell's *Dante and Other Waning Classics* in the "Editor's Easy Chair," *Harper's Monthly*, May 1916. On 19 November 1939, Mordell wrote to George Arms in explanation of the matter referred to in this letter: "I recalled that Howells...had some quarrels of his own with Dante and Milton. I therefore sent him my book...."

2. In "The Early Lucid Henry James," *Book News Monthly*, April 1916, Mordell wrote: "It was George Moore who said that James went abroad and read Turgenev while Howells stayed at home and read James. Howells, in his *Modern Instance*, resembles James.... No one would ever accuse Howells of being obscure as a stylist, yet James's early novels are no more intricate than any of Howells's novels."

6 MAY 1916, NEW YORK, TO EDITOR, NEW YORK EVENING POST

May 6, 1916.

To the Editor of the Evening Post.[1]
Sir:

You had so clearly and aptly characterized the cruel folly of the English Government in putting its Irish prisoners to death that at first it seemed to me nothing was left for your readers but to assent to your wise and just words.[2] Now it seems to me that they ought not to assent tacitly, but that each of them has a duty to speak out in approval of what you have said.

Nothing more lamentable in the course of the war now raging has come to pass than this act of bloody vengeance by the English Government. Vengeance, mere vengeance it is, for it testifies solely to the power of England, to the often wrong of her hard hand against her good heart. It would appear that in the hundred years which have elapsed since the hanging of Emmet, England has really learned nothing in the right treatment of Ireland, where in spite of so many centuries of conquest, those who struggle against England's power cannot be traitors, cannot be rebels, as the men of Ulster lately were in their defiance of the Home Rule measures brought to bear in the British Parliament, upon the Irish situation. This was the golden hour for the sort of justice which we misname mercy, this was the moment, not indeed, wholly to forget the violent madness of the Irish rising, but above everything, not to overmatch it with the madness of English resentment. The shooting of the Irish insurrectionists is too much like the shooting of prisoners of war, too much like taking a leaf from the German classic of Schrecklichkeit; and in giving way to her vengeance, England has roused the moral sense of mankind against her. What a pity, what an infinite pity! She has left us who loved her cause in the war against despotism without another word to say for her until we have first spoken our abhorrence of her inexorable legality in dealing with her Irish prisoners.

William Dean Howells.

1. Rollo Ogden (1856–1937), editor of the New York *Evening Post* (1903–1920), a scholar and a champion of reform, went to the New York *Times* in 1920.

2. "The Irish Executions" appeared as an editorial in the New York *Evening Post* of 4 May. Howells' letter was printed in the *Post* on 8 May, and reprinted without his knowledge or consent in the *Nation* of 18 May. See Mildred Howells' account in *Life in Letters*, II, 356–60. Ogden responded, in a letter to Howells, dated 8 May (MH): "If a man has a name I don't suppose he can do better with it than sign it, at a time like this, to a just and humane sentiment." On Easter Monday morning, twenty Irish volunteers set up a headquarters for the uprising in the general post office in Dublin, and under the leadership of Patrick Pearse and James Connolly proclaimed a Republic. During the following week 103 British soldiers and 450 rebels and civilians were killed. On Saturday, Pearse signed an unconditional surrender. General Sir John Maxwell ordered fourteen rebel leaders shot, including the seven signers of the Proclamation of the Republic. Sympathy for the rebels had not heretofore been strong, but with the executions the reputations of the dead revolutionaries were transformed overnight—a transformation that W. B. Yeats celebrated in his poem "Easter 1916" and the lines, "All changed, changed utterly: / A terrible beauty is born." See Edward Norman, *A History of Modern Ireland* (London: Allen Lane, Penguin Press, 1971), pp. 259–64.

16 JUNE 1916, YORK HARBOR, TO WALDO R. BROWNE

York Harbor, June 16, 1916.

Dear Mr. Browne:

Thank you for letting me see your letter so splendidly just and right regarding England and her lamentable mistake, and so only too kind to me. Your words have touched me deeply; I wish that I deserved them.[1]

I never wrote to the *Nation*, but to the *Evening Post*, and by their office juggle my letter appeared in the *Nation* as if I had addressed myself to that paper. Perhaps you will like to see the letter of thanks which the editor of the *Post* sent me.[2] I should like to have it back, of course.

I do not remember writing anything about the Anarchists except my letter to the *Tribune* deploring their unjust fate,[3] and I can think of nothing at all about Altgeld.[4] I met him only once—at Hull House, and had the joy of telling him how glad of him I was.

Yours sincerely,
W. D. Howells.

1. Browne had written Howells on 19 May 1916 (MH) thanking "an old friend of my father's for the nobly conceived and expressed letter in this week's issue of 'The Nation'." See Howells to the editor of the *Evening Post*, 6 May 1916, n. 2. On 10 June 1916 (MH) Browne wrote again, enclosing his own letter to the *Nation* in regard to England's treatment of the Irish rebels. The *Nation* had refused to publish Browne's letter on the ground that its argument was "not quite invulnerable," even though Browne felt the real reason to be the editor's pro-English attitude.

2. See Howells to the Editor of the *Evening Post*, 6 May 1916, n. 2.

3. Browne had informed Howells in his 10 June letter that he would probably write a biography of the former governor of Illinois, John P. Altgeld, adding: "If you have ever published anything relating directly to Altgeld, or to the Anarchist case, I wonder if you would be kind enough to let me know where I can find it." See Howells' letters to the editor of the New York *Tribune*, 4 and 11 November 1887; and, for the publication of Howells' letter to Browne's father in the Chicago *Tribune*, see Howells to F. F. Browne, 11 November 1887, n. 1 and n. 2.

4. Altgeld pardoned the three surviving anarchists in 1893 and ended his political career by his action. Vachel Lindsay celebrated Altgeld in a poem as "Eagle that Will Not be Forgotten."

4 JULY 1916, YORK HARBOR, TO AURELIA H. HOWELLS

York Harbor, July 4, 1916.

Dear Aurelia:

We have had John and Abby with their boys over to lunch, and they have just started home in our Ford car. (I don't know whether I've told you of our buying it; but it's all we could wish.) We had meant to go back with them for supper, and the evening's fireworks, but it's pouring rain, after 24 hours of it, with and without thunder-storming, and we wisely gave it up. This has so far been a wonderfully wet year, and we don't see the end yet.

I hope the *Atlantic* people sent Vevie the July number with her admirable article;[1] but I will send it too, to make sure. In my last letter I made some suggestions as to future contributions. It will be best to send what she writes to Mr. Sedgwick direct.[2]

I am not writing so much this summer as usual, partly because I don't find my stuff so satisfactory, and partly because I find that writing tires me more than it used, just as walking does.—It is odd how I find father's figure and bearing in mine, and his face looking at me from the glass. The individual life is a repetition of the life that has been. I can understand how people weary of it. The fear of death, of ceasing to be, continues after the love of living has lessened. That is partly the effect of the absences which have replaced the familiar presences.

The wet has made the country very beautiful, but it is tiresome; yet last week which it dried up and warmed up I was impatient, and wanted the rain and the hearth fire again.—The possibility of war with Mexico is dreadful, and is the effect of Wilson's folly. Some excuse can be made for his German policy, but none for his Mexican muddling. There is some comfort in the overwhelming prospect of Hughes's election.[3] The Roosevelt men have come back, and if the Republicans get into power, our troops will be withdrawn from Mexico where they ought never to have been sent. This is wickeder than the old Mexican war of 1846, which father so abhorred, and more stupid and objectless. All our poor volunteers are being rushed to the border, and may be sent across, any day[4]—men who were once dear little boys like Billy and Jacky.—We had a wild time when we sat down at lunch, they blowing the 4th of July horns their aunt had got them, but they quieted down directly and were delightful to the end. I wish I could have them with me all the time; but that is not in nature.

With love from us both to you all,

> Your aff'te brother
> **Will.**

1. Marie Marguerite Fréchette, "Switzerland's Part," *Atlantic*, July 1916. Vevie argued that by remaining neutral the Swiss were fulfilling, in their charitable treatment of internees and others, the ideal of democracy at stake in the war, and that their charity was second only to their patriotism.
2. Ellery Sedgwick, the editor of the *Atlantic*.
3. In the November presidential election Woodrow Wilson won by a narrow margin

over the Republican candidate, Charles Evans Hughes. Howells' contempt for Wilson is succinctly expressed in a later letter to Aurelia, 19 October 1916 (MH): "What made you think I could possibly vote for Wilson? I think he is the falsest and basest politician since Buchanan. . . . Fortunately the fighting favors the Allies whose success is our only hope, unless we can elect an *American* president."

4. Wilson had been confronted with a complex situation in Mexico from the beginning of his administration: ten days before his inauguration the Mexican Revolution had been precipitated by the murder of President Madero. Events took a particularly serious turn when, on 16 March 1916, General John J. Pershing was sent with 10,000 American troops on a punitive mission against Pancho Villa across the Mexican border. See Louis M. Teitelbaum, *Woodrow Wilson and the Mexican Revolution (1913–1916)* (New York: Exposition Press, 1967), p. 323.

6 JULY 1916, YORK HARBOR, TO HENRY E. KREHBIEL

York Harbor, Me., July 6, 1916.

My dear Krehbiel:[1]

I translated *Un Drama Nuevo* by Estebanez for Lawrence Barrett,[2] and his widow, wherever she is, probably has the play; at least I have never heard of her parting with it. The plot is not like *Pagliacci*;[3] for *La Femme de Fabain*[4] I can't speak—I never saw or read that. I have no copy of *Yorick's Love*, which I somewhat disgustedly and disgustingly adapted from the Spanish, but where I did not tamper with that the play is fine. Do you want it for a movy? I think it would be good.—You could get the U. S. Legation to get you a copy of *Un Drama Nuevo* at Madrid, probably.

Yours sincerely
W. D. Howells.

1. Henry E. Krehbiel (1854–1923) was music critic of the New York *Tribune* and espoused the cause of Wagner and the romantic composers in the United States.

2. Howells had translated and adapted *Un Drama Nuevo* of Manuel Tamayo y Baus (Estébanez) in the summer and fall of 1877 for the popular actor Lawrence Barrett. See Howells to Hay, 29 October 1878. In a letter of 17 October 1916 (MH) to a Mr. Baker, Howells recalled Barrett as "an heroic nature, and ridiculous as well as sublime."

3. *I Pagliacci* (1892), an opera by Ruggiero Leoncavallo, belongs to the realistic school of Italian opera in which common people are portrayed in everyday situations.

4. Howells' spelling of the last word of this title is not entirely clear; it could be read as either "Fabarin" or "Fabain." In either case he most likely referred to *La Femme de Tabarin* (1887), a play by Catulle Mendès (1843–1909).

8 AUGUST 1916, YORK HARBOR, TO THOMAS S. PERRY

York Harbor, August 8, 1916.

My dear Perry:

Thank you for all your friendly concern. I seem to be over my plague, but it has left me weaker than I imagined being. I eat, and then after a few pages like this, I sleep—three or four naps a day.[1]

I've been reading Thackeray a good deal. His novels are ridiculously bad: things happen as the most childish readers would like them to, and happen, Whack! so as to put no strain on their anxieties. *Roundabout Papers* good, but talky; *Four Georges* the best of him; *English Humorists* a swash of sentiment. Yet he is a man, and would like to have known how to be more of one.[2]

The English, the average, *cannot* write a novel. Yet God made them, and put good hearts in and good heads on them.

I hope we shall see each other yet before the summer goes.

There! I'm tired.

Yours ever
W. D. Howells.

1. Two weeks earlier, on 25 July 1916 (MeWC), Howells had written Perry that he had been in bed "for a fortnight with bronchitis" and that his "career here since early June seems to have been one long unconscious slump in health."

2. Howells' sense of Thackeray's qualities changed throughout his life, from early adulation to scornful attack in the "Editor's Study" years (1886–1892) to the mixed reaction of this and other late letters. See Howells to Gosse, 16 November 1882, n. 1.

25 AUGUST 1916, YORK HARBOR, TO PAUL KESTER

York Harbor, Me., August 25, 1916.

My dear Paul:

Miss Sabine writes me that you have seen her and her version of S. Lapham.[1]

Frankly, I am afraid she is not arriving. Would you mind saying what *you* think under a seal of the secrecy sacred among Cymru? Would you let her see our dramatization? I have a copy.

I wish she would give up her job.

All managers, as we know, are thieves and murderers, but I know one who is not so steeped as others in human gore, and I would like to show him our play.

I would not wish to crowd Miss S., who seems a good soul, but if she is *not* arriving?

I hope you and your family, (to whom our love) are well. We are *not*, but sunk in sullen wells of cold.

Your affte cousin,
W. D. Howells.

Of course it could be made worth her while.

1. Although Howells and Kester had collaborated on the dramatization of *The Rise of Silas Lapham* in the late 1890s (see Howells to Kester, 10 June 1898), Lillian Sabine was working on an independent adaptation of the novel for the stage. Her efforts were successful, and the play was produced by the Theatre Guild at the Garrick Theatre in New York for forty-seven performances in the fall of 1919. See Walter Meserve, *The Complete Plays of W. D. Howells* (New York: New York University Press, 1960), p. 483. Howells wrote to Sabine on 15 October 1919 (copy at MH), giving her "a renewal of the dramatic rights" to *Silas Lapham* and conceding to her also "the film rights for a period of two years, these rights to revert to me if at the end of that period the piece is not filmized and producing an adequate income."

10 SEPTEMBER 1916, YORK HARBOR, TO THOMAS S. PERRY

York Harbor, Me., Sept. 10, 1916.

Dear Perry:

We had a glorious week buzzing round in our Rocky Ford, which did not take us to Hancock, but glory-crowned our vast shadows on the crest of Poland Spring.[1] The tour ended in the good weather it began in, and tonight I am off to Boston for some teething tomorrow morning.

I wish we could have dropped in on you, for the right talk does not grow on all the shores of Y.H—only on Mrs. Bell's point.[2] I should like to know more of Miss West's (or anybody's) sensible book about H. J.,[3] who is in much danger of being made a crazy cult of, for no fault of his.

To think of your going up Mt. Washington with a field-glass! I can scarcely climb to the height of Norwood Farm's trolley-stop with a toothpick. Oh, I am old, and my legs and wits are very tired.

Pilla joins me in love to you all.

Yours ever
W. D. Howells.

1. Hancock, New Hampshire, Perry's summer retreat, is located about 90 miles west of York Harbor; Poland, Maine, is situated in Androscoggin county, about the same distance to the north.

2. Helen Choate Bell, Howells' York Harbor neighbor.

3. Rebecca West's *Henry James* (1916), which Perry presumably recommended to Howells, is an early study attempting to evaluate the whole body of James's writings in fewer than 20,000 words. West believes that James lost his "native reactions" early and that his detachment from America affected his entire career. She sees him as New England and Puritan and as a proponent of art for art's sake; but in the end she finds that criticism breaks down before his masterpieces, in the "white light of his genius."

8 OCTOBER 1916, KITTERY POINT, TO HAMLIN GARLAND

Kittery Point, Oct. 8, 1916.

Dear Garland:

It's very interesting about your going out with your moving-picture people;[1] I wish I were young enough to do such a thing, and I wish you luck of your venture with all my heart.

We left York Harbor last Monday and I am here with my son's family for October, hoping to finish the scenario of my next novel The Home-Towners.[2] I bring moving-picture folks into it; you know they abound in St. Augustine, where I have put the scene of the story. It will be quite different from all my other things.

No, my dear boy, no lunches or anything else to honor me. I never did like honoring, and now I couldn't bear it even friends like you and Matthews. Besides, I don't know when or how long I shall be in New York.

Yours ever,
W. D. Howells.

1. Garland had proposed to Colonel Brady, scenario director for Vitagraph, in Brooklyn, that he "picturize" Howells' *Leatherwood God*. Garland was for a time filled with the "mirage" of success in films, and signed a contract with Vitagraph to produce *The Captain of the Gray-Horse Troop* and three other of his western books. See Jean Holloway, *Hamlin Garland: A Biography* (Austin: University of Texas Press, 1960), pp. 225–27. As a regular moviegoer, Howells too was fascinated with the art of film making and wrote Garland, on 17 July 1916 (CLSU), "to tell Col. Brady that I shall be glad to have him do my story on the same terms and conditions as he does your stories. I fancy there won't be much money in it, but I am glad of a little."

2. See Howells to Mildred Howells, 31 October 1915, n. 1.

8 OCTOBER 1916, KITTERY POINT, TO LAWRENCE GILMAN

Kittery Point, Oct. 8, 1916.

Dear Mr Gilman:[1]

Thank you for the kind words from yourself and Mr. Huneker. He wrote something I thought sound and true, and I wrote to tell him so.[2] I always need humbling and praise like yours does the work.

Yours sincerely
W. D. Howells.

1. Lawrence Gilman (1878–1939) was the music, dramatic, and literary critic of the *North American Review*. He had been music critic of *Harper's Weekly* and managing editor before its demise in 1913.

2. James Gibbons Huneker (1860–1921) was a musician and dramatic and literary critic of the New York *Sun*. He wrote "The Great American Novel," New York *Times*, 16 July 1916, a piece that delighted Howells, who wrote Huneker of "that monstrous misconception," "that gross impossibility," which "I like to see you bang...about." See J. G. Huneker, *Steeplejack* (New York: Charles Scribner's Sons, 1920), II, 240; and Arnold T. Schwab, *James Gibbons Huneker* (Stanford, Calif.: Stanford University Press, 1963), pp. 221, 349. Earlier, Huneker had urged readers of contemporary fiction to read Howells for "a sense of proportion, continence of expression, the art of exquisitely simple prose, and vital characterization." See *Puck* 76 (2 January 1915), 21.

13 OCTOBER 1916, KITTERY POINT, TO THOMAS S. PERRY

Kittery Point, Oct. 13, 1916.

Dear Perry:

I *could* not read the essay on James,[1] and I am sending it to Mrs. Bell—whom heaven help and bless!—at Boston, for she has left York Harbor by now.

I am here with my dearest boys and their parents, while Pilla is rioting at the Womens City Club in Boston. Just when we shall join forces for the winter I don't know, or where we shall open our campaign. Probably in New Orleans but always possibly in Florida, which I recur to tenderly. Besides I have begun a novel and have put the scene at St. Augustine.[2]

As I draw near my 80th birthday I feel older and older, that is physically wearier. I did not suppose any one could be so dog-tired as I feel at times. This is possibly an effect in part of my midsummer's sickness; the past which I shall never be well of. I see my father's old, bent figure in the glass oftener. Age is a cruel thing, but I have had a good time and I still have—at times, and when I get fairly launched on my novel I dare say I shall be quite young again.

When do you return to Boston? I shall call you up at 312 perhaps before you expect.

Yours ever
W. D. Howells.

1. For Rebecca West's *Henry James*, see Howells to Perry, 10 September 1916, n. 3.
2. The projected novel, "The Home-Towners," was never completed.

28 OCTOBER 1916, KITTERY POINT, TO R. F. WORMWOOD

Kittery Point, Me. Oct. 28, 1916.

Dear Mr. Wormwood:[1]

I am almost ashamed to think how little The Leatherwood God owes to my invention. The facts are of full record in a volume of Robert Clarke Co.'s Ohio Valley Series (Cincinnati) by Judge Tannyhill.[2] Of course I made the people, some, and some I patched together from the true narrative, which for fifty years had tormented me as the history of an extraordinary event, and an insoluble problem.

If you should be thinking of making any public mention of my novel, I am very willing you should trace all parallel between the true and the imagined characters.

The Cochrane affair is new to me, and very interesting. Can you send me any printed account of it?[3]

I expect to be all next week at the Hotel Bellevue, Boston.

Yours sincerely
W. D. Howells.

1. R. F. Wormwood was the editor of the Biddeford *Daily Journal* (Maine), and the circumstances of Howells' correspondence with him are explained in a letter Wormwood wrote to Mildred Howells, 15 January 1923 (MH): "The reference to the 'Cochrane affair' may be explained as follows: [¶] Many years ago there appeared in York county one Jacob Cochrane as leader of a religious movement which was later referred to locally as 'the Cochrane craze.' This Cochrane was, evidently, a man of considerable natural ability, but at this late date it is impossible to determine whether there was more of the religious fanatic or just plain charlatan in his makeup. This much can be said, however: He divided churches, he broke up families and he left upon the communities where he preached and exhorted an impress of his personality which remained long after his death. [¶] When 'The Leatherwood God' appeared

I was struck with certain points of resemblance between its chief character and Jacob Cochrane. The possibility that your father knew the story of the Cochrane craze and that it had provided more or less raw material for his story led to the correspondence."

2. R. H. Taneyhill, *The Leatherwood God: An Account of the Appearance and Pretensions of Joseph C. Dylks, in Eastern Ohio in 1828* (Cincinnati: R. Clarke & Co., 1870), appeared as no. 7 in the "Ohio Valley Historical Series."

3. Wormwood explained to Mildred Howells that the "story was printed in the Biddeford Journal, and from that paper I clipped the tale and preserved it in a scrapbook."

OCTOBER 1916, KITTERY POINT, TO HENRY B. FULLER

Kittery Point, Me.,

My dear **Fuller:**

I am afraid that "late phase" must find its fullness in some other air than this. I am nearly eighty years old and tired, tired. It is a strange experience. I used only to need the chance to work, now the chance dismays me. Certainly I hope the L. God will prosper, but I dread to know whether.[1] My daughter and I are planning another winter in the South: Pinehurst, St. Augustine and perhaps New Orleans. We expect to spend November in New York, where I wish so much we might see you. It has been pleasant to meet dear old Garland; but I believe he is to be with his family in Passadena, moving the Movies.[2]

Your work for the Free Verse[3] interests me, but does not persuade. If it has come to stay, nothing can oust it, and I must content myself with deploring it.

Do have Houghton-Mifflin send me your "book of short things."[4] Sometimes I can do a good book a good turn, but the conditions of my work are grudging.

Yours affectionately
W. D. Howells.

1. *The Leatherwood God* was published in book form on 2 November, three days after Howells left Kittery Point. These dates provide a basis for an approximate dating of this letter.

2. See Howells to Garland, 8 October 1916, n. 1.

3. "A New Field for Free Verse," *Dial* 61 (14 December 1916), 515–16.

4. Fuller described his *Lines Long and Short: Biographical Sketches in Various Rhythms* (1917) as "a set of 20-25 *vers libre* biographies ... each piece about 160–170 lines; many of them condensed short stories, in pseudo-poetic guise." See J. Pilkington, Jr., *Henry Blake Fuller* (New York: Twayne Publishers, 1970), p. 144.

19 November 1916, New York, to Frederick A. Duneka

> *St. Hubert*
> *One Twenty West Fifty Seventh Street*
> Nov. 19, 1916.

Dear Mr. Duneka:

Mr. Wells writes me that he has told you of my wish to be relieved from the promise I gave you last fall when we arranged the new basis for the Easy Chair, and you asked that I should offer everything I did to Harpers first.[1] This was an afterthought of yours, but I willingly assented because I naturally supposed that what I offered would be accepted; in fifty years the invariable acceptance of my work everywhere had perhaps spoiled me for refusal; but the first thing I offered Harpers, some months ago, was unconditionally refused.[2] I have no criticism to make of this adverse judgment; but I feel that my sort of fiction is no longer desired at Franklin Square, and I think I should be free to offer it elsewhere without having to explain that it has failed of liking there. The present condition seems hampering to both sides, for I do not suppose that the Harper editors like to refuse any more than I like to be refused. This is all, and I would not have voluntarily brought the matter to your notice; but Mr. Wells's talk will no doubt have prepared you for this appeal.

I feel very deeply for you in your continued debility,[3] and I wish I could fully express my sense of the consideration you have always shown me; but I can only assure you of my grateful regard.

> Yours sincerely
> W. D. Howells.

1. Thomas B. Wells, the associate editor of *Harper's Monthly*, had written Howells on 17 November 1916 (MH), explaining that he had discussed the matter with Duneka and suggesting that Howells write Duneka "a letter telling him just exactly how you feel on this question."

2. This is possibly a reference to "The Home-Towners," the only major piece of fiction Howells had been contemplating since the fall of 1915. However, in his reply of 20 November 1916 (MH), Duneka indicated that he could not "recall any story of yours having been declined." He pleaded with Howells to reconsider his request, pointing out that no other periodical would give Howells "a more hospitable welcome" than *Harper's Monthly* had extended to him over the years. His invalid state keeping him at Summit, New Jersey, Duneka felt that Howells' "turning elsewhere hurts especially since I must do my work under the handicap of only indirect contact with Franklin Square and its friends." In the two letters that conclude this exchange (Howells to Duneka, 22 November 1916 [RPB], and Duneka to Howells, 22 November 1916 [MH]) Howells maintained his ground, leaving Duneka to "hope that . . . you may feel inclined to let us have something of a fictional nature."

3. Mildred Howells observes that Duneka's illness was "painful and hopeless" and that Howells "made a journey out to Duneka's home in New Jersey to see him before going South." See *Life in Letters*, II, 365.

23 DECEMBER 1916, ST. AUGUSTINE, FLORIDA, TO FREDERICK A. DUNEKA

Hotel Alcazar,
St. Augustine, Fla., December 23, 1916.

Dear Mr. Duneka:

I want to recall myself to you on Christmas Day, when I hope this will reach you, with the wish of my whole heart for your full recovery. I have been thinking of all your generous friendship during the fifteen years when we were together, and of the kind things you did to me, down to the day of our parting.[1] How patient you always were with me, how sympathetic, how considerate of my foibles. I grow older and older on your hands, but you never let me know you know it, and now when I begin to know it from within myself, I must wonder at your forbearance. I should like to remind you of all the instances of your kindness, but I shall never forget them, and I trust you will remember them. We lived through a hazardous experiment; may you live through the years of your power again, and use it to befriend some worthier object. May I assure you of my very earnest affection?

Yours sincerely,
W. D. Howells.

1. See Howells to Duneka, 19 November 1916, n. 3.

31 DECEMBER 1916, ST. AUGUSTINE, FLORIDA, TO ANNE H. FRÉCHETTE

Hotel Alcazar
Saint Augustine Florida . . .
Dec. 31, 1916.

Dear Annie:

I want to thank Achille for his sonnets, which brought back my sense of Switzerland with a grace felt even through my translation of his beautiful French.[1] I am so glad he is well again; his poetry, I take it, is a return of health. My affectionate regards to him.

That was a fine and sincere letter from Sedgwick to Vevie. I don't know just what her paper is, but I suggest her trying it with the North American Review (171 Madison Avenue.) Let her write to Miss Elizabeth Cutting, the assistant editor.[2]—I hope this will find Aurelia well of her lumbago. I have tried many other miseries, but not just that; still I can be as sorry for her as if I knew personally about it. Just now I have a prolonged indigestion, and I who used to eat anything can now eat *hardly* anything. It affects my pneumo-gastric nerve, and my heart jumps and comes down with a thump. But this is an old bother with me.—I got much of my family lore out of father's beautiful and modest memoir.[3] Haven't you read it? Then there were scraps of hearsay which had stuck in my memory. But I feel my book very inadequate; it was hard to do and I did it badly in great part. All my later work has been hard. Have you read The Leatherwood God? The English have received it intelligently, and the American critics though kind, most ignorantly.[4] What strange animals some of them are. What strange animals nearly all of us seem in our shameful situation! The English have no right to blame us, but I burn with shame before the French, that generous people. Our President flounders from bad to worse; he cannot write his ridiculous notes intelligibly.—We are in one of the two great hotels here, which is filling up, and will overflow soon. But the people are not interesting; I envy you the sort you see in Switzerland. The Americans seem not to think, any longer. But I see them here at their idlest and emptiest.—I am trying to do a novel,[5] but on this bare ground it is hard sledding. I think I shall hardly finish it, though the notion of it pleased me at first greatly. I feel my years, which are almost eighty.— I oughtn't to grumble, for at least I have my health when most people are sick and sore from long living.—How dearly I should like to see you and talk with you!—I never hear now from Eliza. Do you?—Sam wrote, for him, a very good letter about my recollections.[6] I don't know how they are getting on. It must be hard for him to dog round to his job where he seems to have to sit among the cinders of the furnace room; but I've made it easy for him to have two or three holidays a week.—The John family are well, and Billy is going to school very joyously. He writes me at times unexpectedly. His longest letter is: "Dear Fafa: I am going to tell you a funny joke. This is it. If you go to the market and you want to buy a summer squash, and they can't give you any, get an egg, and throw it up and it will come down *squash!* Billy." Jacky is a tender little angel with a quick temper.

Love to all.
Will.

1. None of the poems, either in the original or in translation, has been located.
2. Howells had previously advised Marie Marguerite Fréchette to submit her

writing to Ellery Sedgwick, editor of the *Atlantic*. See Howells to Aurelia Howells, 4 July 1916. Apparently Sedgwick had declined her latest submission. No article under Vevie's name appeared in the *North American Review* between January 1917 and June 1918.

3. *Recollections of Life in Ohio, from 1813 to 1840* (1895).

4. For a discussion of the critical reception of the novel, see *The Leatherwood God*, HE, pp. xxiii–xxix.

5. "The Home-Towners."

6. *Years of My Youth.*

21 JANUARY 1917, ST. AUGUSTINE, FLORIDA, TO MARY R. JEWETT

St. Augustine, Florida. Jan'y 21, 1917.

Dear Miss Jewett:[1]

Thank you for remembering me among your sister's friends. All the poems are like her, gentle and fine and true. But I like best the ones addressed to her father.[2] She used so often to speak to me of him, and tell me of their companionship, and all that she owed to it.

My daughter joins me in affectionate regards.

Yours sincerely
W. D. Howells.

1. Mary R. Jewett (1847–1930), older sister of Sarah Orne Jewett, who died in 1909, had sent Howells a copy of her sister's *Verses* (1916). The imprint of the volume specifies "Printed for Her Friends."

2. Howells refers to "To My Father, I" and "To My Father, II," the poems which open the privately printed volume.

10 FEBRUARY 1917, SAVANNAH, GEORGRIA, TO HAMLIN GARLAND

De Soto Hotel
Savannah, Ga. February 10th, *1917*

Dear Garland:

Yes, the Larkin Mead plaque will do for the '80s,[1] but *I* can't give you leave to use the St. Gaudens;[2] only the widow St. Gaudens can do that, and she is at Miami or Palm Beach, Fla. I enclose the well-known aetat. 70 one,[3] and John can give you the most actual thing (and fine) of me with my arms round my two grandsons; he did it, and has it.[4] Mrs. J. Q. A. Ward (Morningside Drive) has a plaque of me done by Ward in Columbus about 1860, worth reproducing for the period.[5]

Luck and love to you.

Yours sincerely
W. D. Howells.

1. Larkin G. Mead, Jr., Howells' brother-in-law, had made a medallion of Howells' profile in 1882 or early 1883. See Howells to Gosse, 3 April 1883. A cast of the bas-relief is now located in the John Hay Collection, Brown University Library. Garland was collecting information about portraits of Howells in connection with either his plans for the eightieth birthday commemoration (see Howells to Garland, 18 March 1917) or the efforts by the National Institute of Arts and Letters to gather such materials for its archives.

2. A cast of Augustus Saint-Gaudens' bas-relief of Howells and Mildred Howells (1898) is located in the National Portrait Gallery and has been reproduced many times. See Margaret Chrisman, *Fifty American Faces* (Washington: National Portrait Gallery, 1978).

3. The "well-known" photograph appeared in the New York *Times*, Pictorial Section, 24 February 1907. It is used as the frontispiece in volume 5 of this edition.

4. See the frontispiece to this volume.

5. An 1898 cast of the bas-relief by J. Q. A. Ward (ca. 1862) is also located in the National Portrait Gallery.

19 FEBRUARY 1917, SAVANNAH, GEORGIA, TO THOMAS S. PERRY

De Soto Hotel
Savannah, Ga. February 19th, *1917*

Dear Perry:

It's good of you to tell me of those English notices,[1] and I improve the occasion to tell you that we shall be working northward soon. St Augustine in Dec. and Jan. was hot and flabby, but here in Feb'y we have had it good and cold at times and at others beautifully fresh and warm like today. It is a place where I would willingly live, an English looking place, like say Leamington, but much nobler in its layout. The spirit of Oglethorpe[2] lingers in the civic life and we have met people we would like to meet again—both men and women. Half the pop. has called and had us to dinner (2. pm. and supper 7. pm.) It is very Confederate in the monuments, but actually thoroughly reconstructed.

We expect to go this week to Tryon, N.C. viâ Columbia, S. C. Tryon is in the mts., and is very bland with a sunward exposure.

We have read a lot of books and are now (after fifty years for me,) deep in Middlemarch. G. E. *was* a great creature. Also Barry Lyndon, by far Thackerays best as I know from twenty other readings of all the others.[3]

I hope to see you by May. I wish I could talk of Berlin with you.

Pilla joins me in regards to your house-poets and all your house.

Yours ever
W. D. Howells.

1. The "English notices" may refer to reviews of either *The Leatherwood God* (see Howells to Anne Fréchette, 31 December 1916, n. 4) or *Years of My Youth*, which had also been published the preceding year. See *Years of My Youth*, HE, p. xxvii.

2. James E. Oglethorpe (1696–1785) was the English general who secured a charter to establish Georgia and founded Savannah in 1733.

3. Later that year, on 10 September 1917 (MeWC), Howells wrote to Perry: "We are reading Thackeray with vast delight. Even 'Philip' which I always supposed was so poor. He *was* a great fellow, T. was, in spite of me."

28 FEBRUARY 1917, TRYON, NORTH CAROLINA, TO THOMAS S. PERRY

Tryon, N. C., Feb'y 28, 1917.

My dear **Perry:**

Your praise of me at the Sun dance[1] was such as to give me the delicate pleasure of perfectly adjusted blame. Indeed you were too good to me, and I am beholden to you much. When I think what you might have said—but I will not be fulsome.—I recall especially H. James bringing us together,[2] and also a meeting in (?) Holworthy.[3] Fay, who was Hercules and Reverend,[4] once said to me, "Perry has a genius friendship," and he was right. I liked your recalling our benefactor of the subscription book.[5] "You can call this copy worth $40,000." So we did, but it did not come.—John thought you far the best of the Sympoters.

We are here in the mud of the N. C. Mts., and when we were in Savannah we were in a better place—one altogether lovely in fact. I think we are not long for these tops—but who knows?

With our love to you all

Yours ever
W. D. Howells.

1. The "Sun dance" was a full page spread, "His Friends Greet William Dean Howells at Eighty," with photographs, in the New York *Sun*, 25 February 1917. Booth Tarkington, Douglas Z. Doty, Hamlin Garland, Charles Hanson Towne, and T. S. Perry all commented on Howells in the article.

2. Perry reported in the *Sun* tribute that he had tried to visit Howells in Venice "fifty years ago this spring," but had missed the writer of the Venetian letters in the Boston *Advertiser*, who had returned by this time to the United States. Perry added: "On my return to this country a year or more later, I was taken to call on Mr. Howells by Henry James, and this time he was at home." The next summer, in 1869, Perry met Howells in Quebec, and because of his scorn for the Canadian scene inspired Howells' portrait of the supercilious Miles Arbuton of *A Chance Acquaintance* (1873). "I bear no malice," Perry concluded his anecdote: "If one can't be immortalized in one way one must try another."

3. Perry and Howells presumably met in Holworthy Hall at Harvard University in 1870 when Howells gave his series of lectures on "New Italian Literature"; Perry held at that time a teaching appointment in French and German at Harvard.

4. See Howells to Fosdick, 21 April 1901, n. 2.

5. Perry in his speech had recalled their working together on the *Library of Universal Adventure by Sea and Land. Including Original Narratives and Authentic Stories of Personal Prowess and Peril in all the Waters and Regions of the Globe* .... The compilers selected such tales of horror that they would not let their own children see the book. Their "benefactor," "full of hope and energy" must have been a Harper subscription agent who promised "Pactolian streams" of gold. See Virginia Harlow, *Thomas Sergeant Perry: A Biography* (Durham, N.C.: Duke University Press, 1950), pp. 137–38.

18 MARCH 1917, AUGUSTA, GEORGIA, TO HAMLIN GARLAND

Augusta, Georgia, March 18, 1917.

My dear Garland:

I do not know whether to be more daunted or delighted by the program of the meeting which you have sent me.[1] If I could somehow be put outside of the whole affair, I think I could be not wholly unhappy in hearing the verses and the songs and the little play which you promise. As it is, and at the worst, I can count upon unmixed pleasure in the chairman's remarks, for I shall not have to make them, and I know they will be of the kindness which is the warp and woof of our long friendship.

In the presence of so much potential immortality may I single out the fixed fame of our divine McDowell as renown which I hope not quite forgottenly to share with him in the verse which his music has given wings?[2] As for the rest who have joined in your design to flatter me out of the sense of my eighty years, but whom I must not distinguish by name, they may be sure that the gratitude which remains unspoken in my heart will be life-long, if not so long as the arts in which we are all, young and old, brethren.

Ten or twenty years from now I hope to join you and them in commemorating the birthday of some other octogenarian. Now I must remain in all affection, my dear Garland,

Yours and theirs,
W. D. Howells.

1. Garland, as chairman of the Joint Committee of the Literary Arts, was arranging a dinner honoring Howells' eightieth birthday, to be held on 21 March, in Howells' absence, at the National Arts Club in New York. The program, which is bound into a volume of tributes (MH), lists the following events: readings from Howells' prose and verse; three songs by Edward MacDowell based on Howells' verses; a presentation of Howells' farce *The Register*; and readings of letters of congratulations. The volume of personal tributes, to which Howells jokingly referred as "the

bound volume of obituary testimonials" (Howells to Garland, 7 April 1917; CLSU), finally reached Howells in September, at which time he sent Garland an official letter of acknowledgment to be printed and distributed "to each of those who took part, by word, act or letter, in the commemoration." See two letters from Howells to Garland, 7 September 1917 (CLSU), one a personal note, the other the official letter.

2. Edward A. MacDowell had set three of Howells' poems to music: "Folksong," "The Sea," and "Through the Meadow." See Gibson-Arms, *Bibliography*, p. 43.

12 APRIL 1917, ATLANTIC CITY, NEW JERSEY, TO PAUL KESTER

The St. Charles
Atlantic City, N. J. . . . . April 12, 1917.

My dear Paul:

Night before last, well toward morning, I finished your very great book.[1] If there is justice in fate it will count with the three or four American novels which merit remembrance. In its characterization of types and conditions it is powerful, and a whole state of things survives and abides in its page. I wish I could tell you all I feel about it; but I can speak only of your magnificent hero, the brute-egotist and fool-martyr, Brent. He is magnificent. Your Southerners white and black are all true, and I wonder how they will work out their hopeless problem. Your terrible book leaves that as it must & where it finds it.

The thing ought to make a great effect with the public, and I could wish the great War over that it might have a fair chance.

Of course I should like to write about it, but I don't know where exactly—the Easy Chairs creaks along so heavily and slowly.

You have done a vast thing; I wish I had you here to give the particulars of praise which I can't write.

Greet your mother from me on having such a son.

Your aff'te cousin
W. D. Howells.

1. Kester had sent Howells *His Own Country* (1917), a novel in which the mulatto hero returns from Canada to his birthplace in the South. Howells wrote about the novel in the "Editor's Easy Chair," *Harper's Monthly*, August 1917, calling the novel "a unique contribution to our fiction." Apparently Kester intended to use Howells' letter in advertising the novel, but Howells vetoed this plan in a letter of 20 April 1917 (NN): "the publication of my letter or the commerical use of it would be a very unfair form of advertising. I would rather do this for you than for any one else, but I have the inflexibility of the virtuous against it, for it spoils all confidence between friends and takes an unfair advantage of enemies."

13 JUNE 1917, YORK HARBOR, TO AURELIA H. HOWELLS

York Harbor, June 13, 1917.

Dear Aurelia:

I decided to send your money by cable again, and by this time, or days before, you will have got $200 without deduction,* unless your Montreux banker charges you a commission, for I've paid the cabling. I didn't like to take the chances of the mail. Of course I shall hear from you at once, unless Switzerland keeps selling the Germans cattle, and the Allies bottle her up, as they must: it doesn't matter that the cattle are her own. It is all dreadful, but we don't realize our own part in it yet, though the conscription has taken its first step,[1] and we are all, who can, buying U. S. bonds. In different ways most of our friends have sent fathers or sons over to take what part they can in the war which seems so incredible. The Allies' envoys stirred us up all they could,[2] but we shall not believe in it till we get our own mortality lists, and our wounded begin returning. We are serious, but we cannot believe it all.— Everybody is trying to do something but our own family is out of the fighting because of age and disability. The poor little boys long to be boy scouts, but I'm glad they're so far off from soldiering yet. The Americans who realize the situation are very serious, and accept it as a dire necessity, unless the Germans, who seem the worst people in history, are to rule the world. We have had the latest and coldest spring I ever knew—almost a month behind time. I hear nothing direct from Sam, but I believe he is getting on all right.[3]—It is joyful to have John's family at Kittery Point. While Pilla was dentisting in Boston, I spent three glad days with them. Abby and John are both better, and the boys are full of health and happiness at being in the country. They are such dear boys. With love to all,

Your aff'te brother
Will.

(*though my memo. from my banker makes it yield only 994 francs)

1. The United States had broken off relations with Germany in February 1917 and on April 6 entered the war; in June the first American troops landed in France. President Wilson signed the Selective Service Act on 18 May, providing for the registration of about 10 million men between 21 and 30 years of age. Howells, who had been very critical of Wilson's policy of neutrality (see Howells to Aurelia Howells, 4 July 1916, n. 3), now supported the president. On 7 April 1917 (MH) he wrote to Aurelia: "Yes, we are at war with that wicked Germany, and Wilson has justified himself with all whom his delays have made unjust to him. We are excited in a

way, and buy all the newspapers, but we are not conscious of hostilities; possibly they may never come to us, and we hope that with us it will always be a sea-fight." Six months later, on 4 December 1917, Howells wrote Wilson a complimentary letter, now lost, to which Wilson replied on 6 December 1917 (MH): "I am warmly obliged to you for your gracious letter of December fourth. It gives me very deep pleasure that you should so entirely approve my address to the Congress, and your words carry with them a delightful reassurance."

2. The French and English delegations under Marshall Joseph Jacques Césaire Joffre and Foreign Secretary Arthur James Balfour, respectively, had made a highly publicized visit to the United States in late April for the purpose of ascertaining the American commitment to the war effort. See David F. Houston, *Eight Years with Wilson's Cabinet, 1913 to 1920* (Garden City, N.Y.: Doubleday, Page & Co., 1926), vol. 1, chap. 17.

3. Although Sam was still continuing in his position in the Government Printing Office in Washington, Howells felt that his brother was increasingly unable to do his work and thus should retire. Such a step would mean that Howells would have to substantially enlarge his regular contributions to Sam's income, but he was willing to do so and, on several occasions, wrote to Paul Kester to help Sam find cheaper retirement housing in Alexandria, Virginia. See Howells to Kester, 19 April 1917 (NN).

29 JUNE 1917, YORK HARBOR, TO THOMAS B. WELLS

York Harbor, June 29, 1917.

My dear Wells:

I would rather trust your judgement than the New Republic's, and I gladly consent to the deal with Bones & Bloodroot. Three cents is no great sum, but if your fancy multiplies it often enough it really comes to something handsome.[1]

Yes, Clemens was a good judge of books except when it came to Jane Austen; there he fell down. Payne is now so fond of his letters that he wants me to recollect a lot that don't exist, in hopes of palming them off on you.[2]

Sincerely yours,
W. D. Howells.

1. In a letter of 26 June 1917 (NNC), Wells had called Howells' attention to the "nice little" reprint series that was advertised by the "delightfully anatomical" Boni & Liveright in the *New Republic*. He passed on to Howells the young publishers' request to put *A Hazard of New Fortunes* and *The Son of Royal Langbrith* in the series at six cents royalty per copy, which was to be divided equally between Howells and Harper & Brothers. *A Hazard* appeared in the "Modern Library" in November 1917.

2. Wells had also praised Mark Twain's sound literary judgment in the recently published *Mark Twain's Letters*, edited by A. B. Paine. A sampling of the letters from Clemens to Howells and others had appeared in *Harper's Monthly*, May 1917.

29 JUNE 1917, YORK HARBOR, TO HAMLIN GARLAND

York Harbor, June 29, 1917.

My dear Garland:

Things are going very well with me, thank you. Never since I came to eighty have I been so well. I work as of old, or of young, and if the stuff is not so good as before, still it is stuff, and I don't complain. I shall be glad to see your novel, and I rejoice to hear that Fuller has gone back to his natural job.[1]

After all, I didn't write to those bosses of the societies which celebrated me in March, for I thought it would seem invidious to single some out for my gratitude and spare others. When shall I see the collected tributes?[2] I think that will be the time to offer my thanks to all for all, which I feel to have been a great thing.

It is a pity you cannot go back to New Salem, but New England is no bad place. What about Peterboro which you preached up last year? Asbury Park is a beautiful place, but rather sharky and undertowy, I'm afraid, come to think of it.

I have done three Easy Chairs hand-running, so as to have a good space of time for three papers about people of my Venetian period, which I've contracted.[3] My last Easy Chair is largely about Sir Oliver Lodge's book, *Raymond*. Have you read it? Not very important, but very touching, and not uninteresting.[4]

My love to you all.

Yours affectionately,
W. D. Howells.

1. Henry Blake Fuller was writing again after a long absence from literature.
2. See Howells to Garland, 10 February 1917, n. 1.
3. The three Venetian papers, all in *Harper's Monthly*, were "Overland to Venice" (November 1918), "An Old Venetian Friend" (April 1919), and "A Young Venetian Friend" (May 1919). They have been collected in *Years of My Youth*, HE, pp. 207–52.
4. Howells is referring to *Raymond or Life and Death* (1916), which he reviewed in "Editor's Easy Chair," *Harper's Monthly*, November 1917. He calls it "a most tedious and unconvincing book," full of "mediumosity" on the old question "If a man die shall he live again?"

10 JULY 1917, YORK HARBOR, TO SARAH M. PIATT

York Harbor, Maine July 10, 1917

Dear Mrs. Piatt:

We who are left behind are lonelier if our years are many, but I think we are comforted sooner than if our years were few. There is a sense of reunion in them, an imagination, stronger than the hopes of youth. In my age I dream more than I read and hardly a night, never a week, passes, but I dream of my lost wife. It doesn't matter whether the dreams are kind or unkind, they bring her back. She suffered greatly in the beginning of her long sickness, but the blessed morphene saved her from that, and the sickness became a dream.

I know how it is with you now while your sorrow is still so new;[1] but after long unbelief I am getting back some hope again, and I am at last getting back peace, which seemed gone forever. Last night my daughter and I read far into Plato's *Phaedo*; and she said of the endeavor to realize the life hereafter, "It will be so simple I shall say, Why didn't I think of that before? I might have known it."

I wish I could have written better about Piatt,[2] and established him with others as he remains in his sweet manly poethood with me. There are things of your own, dear friend, which I prize no less than his—especially among your pieces about children: one bidding them goodnight forever,[3] since they will never be the same after any slightest [illegible word]. My little grandsons are the joy of my life, and I see them changing, but I keep them unchanged in my heart.

This is mere meandering; but I never could write letters.

Yours affectionately,
W. D. Howells.

1. John J. Piatt, husband of Sarah M. Piatt, died in the spring of 1917.
2. Howells devoted the "Editor's Easy Chair," *Harper's Monthly*, July 1917, mostly to Piatt's life and poetry, characterizing him as "first of the Western poets to feel the beauty of that newer world and to translate it in . . . art which can never be old."
3. "Last Words: Over a Little Bed at Night," in *A Woman's Poems* (1871).

22 JULY 1917, YORK HARBOR, TO HAMLIN GARLAND

York Harbor, July 22, 1917.

My dear Garland:
So far as I know your book is without its like in literature.[1] It is perfectly true to life, and beautiful with right feeling, from first to last. I wish every American, every human being might read it. Never before has any man told our mortal story so manfully so kindly. I would

like it to go on forever. But I miss two galley slips, 160–161, and where are they? It often needs proof reading.

Are you coming to see me? Say when.

Yours affectionately
W. D. Howells.

P. S. Why do you say I have, or had, a large head?[2] The average hat of the dining room hat-rack comes down over my ears.

1. *A Son of the Middle Border*. Howells reviewed Garland's account of his child-hood and youth in the New York *Times*, 26 August 1917.
2. Garland's recollection of his first meeting with Howells includes these lines: "Suddenly the curtains parted and a short man with a large head stood framed in the opening. His face was impressive but his glance was one of the most piercing I had ever encountered." See *A Son of the Middle Border* (New York: Macmillan, 1917), p. 386.

19 AUGUST 1917, YORK HARBOR, TO WILLIAM GRIFFITH

York Harbor Aug. 19, 1917.

Dear Mr. Griffith:

Of course I have been very greatly interested in Mr. Harvey's book;[1] a man does not have a whole volume written about him, whether of praise or blame, or both, as this is, without great inward stir. But what word can I send him who shrank from sending his words to me? Reading the book was like looking at myself a long time in a mirror where I saw some one of my name and work powerfully reflected, and being possessed with the doubt whether it was really I.

I should like you to tell Mr. Harvey above all things that I am grateful for his words about Marcia Hubbard, and then for his just sense of the Lapham girls;[2] I wish he had included their mother with them; you see what a greedy chooser even a tacit beggar can be; and I can think of a hundred points where he gave me such unstinted glory without similarly satisfying me. It is perhaps the kind of thing that I might well have coveted on coming back from the dead half a hundred years hence to get.

There is no use talking; but I realize that he has boldly done the bravest kind of thing; I hope he may never think himself wrong in his praise of me. When it comes to his blame I cannot be so sure he is right, naturally. The sissyism doesn't seem very ben trovato in either the new saws or ancient instances. But I wish to thank him for being so luminous on some cloudy aspects of Poe.[3] His exegeses might very well bring that tipsy spirit reeling back to hiccup his thanks from the fields of asphodel. It is a very convincing thing and it does not matter that I do not like it.

I thank you for sending me the book.

Yours sincerely,
W. D. Howells.

1. Alexander Harvey (1868–1949), *William Dean Howells: A Study of the Achievement of a Literary Artist* (New York: B. W. Huebsch, 1917) was the first book-length work on Howells. It was sent him by William Griffith, a colleague of Harvey on the staff of *Current Opinion*. Griffith explained in a letter of 23 October 1928 (MH) to Mildred Howells: "As I recall, he [Harvey] was hesitant about sending the book to your father, but gave me permission to do so."

2. Harvey (who opens his "study" by attacking the English and American Philistines) found Marcia Hubbard in *A Modern Instance* vivid and passionate; and he called the episode in *The Rise of Silas Lapham* in which Irene gives her trinkets to her sister Penelope the "most thrilling scene in fiction." Harvey tends to emphasize the physicality and charm of the Lapham girls.

3. Harvey speaks of Howells as a "lord of language" and "a great literary artist" in the first part of his critique. But in the final two chapters he condemns Howells as the leader of the "sissy school of literature" and praises Poe for his mastery of the voluptuous and erotic in extended analyses of the major poems, especially "Ulalume."

23 AUGUST 1917, YORK HARBOR, TO THOMAS S. PERRY

York Harbor, Aug. 23, 1917.

My dear Perry:

Alexander Harvey is certainly not George Harvey, but otherwise I know nothing about him except that his publisher says he is young and too modest to send me his book,[1] which the pub. then sends. After a first look into it I thought I could not bear to read it, yet did so finally, in spite of my small stomach for things about me. First he skies me, inordinately, and then drivels over me with talk about "sissyism." All of us, it seems, who are not drunken blackguards are sissies, and I the worst for having kept our authorship sober, as editor and critic. Of course you have seen what the book is, and there is no use telling you. I cannot help being glad that he values some characters of mine: but I am no such prodigy as two thirds of his book makes me out; I warn you of that. Still, my curiosity haunts about him. Perhaps he will answer my letter to his pub.

I am very old, thank you, and my dry work and the wet weather try me. I have had a great stir in reading Garland's autobiography; really a great thing, amongst the greatest of its kind.[2]

Society in York is having its Dog Days, and I am sick of it—Mrs. Bell remains divine. What a wonder she is! She has just lent me Eckermann,[3] which I had not read. But I would rather be in Y. H. than in Weimar.

Yours ever
W. D. Howells.

He hates the English, Russians, Spanish because he knows no better, or does not know *them*.

1. See Howells to Griffith, 19 August 1917.
2. *A Son of the Middle Border*. See Howells to Garland, 22 July 1917.
3. Helen Choate Bell had given Howells J. P. Eckermann's *Conversations with Goethe* (1836), probably in the standard English translation by John Oxenford, first published in 1850 but frequently reprinted.

31 AUGUST 1917, YORK HARBOR, TO THOMAS S. PERRY

York Harbor, August 31, 1917.

Dear Perry:

Yes, I have been in Weimar, and in spite of happening on Sedan Day there I greatly loved the place.[1] It seemed a sort of Old Cambridge and Old Athens blended, and Goethe's love of Italy had got into the profiles of the children. At our hotel I fell into the keeping, as for our railway carriage, of a man who impressed me as absolutely good and kind. He was a pastor and a German; how could he be so disinterestedly affectionate and lovable? I have often wished since that I could have kept him with me for life. Read a rambling, scambling book of mine called Their Silver Wedding Journey and know all about Weimar.[2] Eckermann is holding out delightfully.[3] There was a lot of meat in old Gutty which wasn't the flesh and the devil, quite. I wish I had known him. He would have been a great addition to York Harbor society.

This is the last of summer. The other day the poetic Jacky pointed out the goldenrod and said, "That's winter."

Yours ever
W. D. Howells.

That was a fine letter of M. Storey's in the B. Herald about the Nigs.[4]

1. Howells had visited Weimar on 1 September 1897, the twenty-seventh anniversary of the Battle of Sedan, in which Prussian troops overwhelmed the French and captured Napoleon III. He wrote his sister Aurelia on 5 September 1897 (MH; *Life in Letters*, II, 79–80): "It is a most charming old town—the only one in Germany I've seen where I would be willing to live." Howells' comments about Weimar are connected with his concluding remark in his letter to Perry of 23 August 1917.

2. For the chapters on Weimar, see *Their Silver Wedding Journey* (1899), II, 235–84.

3. See Howells to Perry, 23 August 1917, n. 3.

4. Moorfield Storey (1845–1929), anti-imperialist at the turn of the century, was president of the NAACP (1910–1929) and a defender of the rights of American Indians. Storey had visited Howells in Augusta, Georgia, in late March. See Howells to Perry, 26 March 1917 (MeWC). His "fine letter," headed "Our Negro Problems" (Boston *Herald*, 30 August 1917), answered the argument of F. W. Jones, a Southerner, that any attempt to readjust relations of black and white would be a "step backward" to the "horror" of reconstruction. Storey insisted that "Negro aggression" was as nothing in the face of Ku Klux Klan activities and of lynchings North and South that "stain the name of the United States"; and that all that Negroes wanted was equal rights before the law—that is, justice. Despite German efforts to incite them, Negro troops were loyal, Storey insisted.

13 SEPTEMBER 1917, YORK HARBOR, TO ALEXANDER HARVEY

York Harbor, Sept. 13, 1917.

Dear Mr. Harvey:[1]

I am afraid my next novel is the one just behind me, for I do not believe that there is any before me. Even if there were I cannot think that the fable of an octogenarian could deal profitably with love. I respect that passion in young people if it inspires them to marriage, but otherwise it can only at best have my pity. It is then the source of more unhappiness than anything else in the world, and I wish people to be happy, just as I wish them to be good.

You see, I am an old fogey (as we used to say) but I think I understand your feeling about life for I have not quite forgotten its like in my own case; and you may be sure that I value your caring for my work and the reason of it. I wish I could see so little to blame in it in one aspect, and so little to praise in another; I am sure I am right in desiring always to be decent. I know we are naked under our clothes but I know we have always our clothes on unless we are savages. Do believe that I feel your generosity toward the people I have tried to portray recognizably. But I think my luck with their likenesses is the effect of trying for them rather than forecasting them. Perhaps we shall some time meet and then find that we agree about more things than we now think.[2]

Yours sincerely,
W. D. Howells.

1. See Howells to Griffith, 19 August 1917, n. 1.

2. To his astonishment, on meeting Harvey, Howells found him "not the callow ass's colt we figured him, but a staid old horse of fifty with a son in the army. He stood differing from [it] like a hero and martyr, so that I had not the heart to master him much." See Howells to T. S. Perry, 7 December 1917 (MeWC).

20 SEPTEMBER 1917, YORK HARBOR, TO FREDERICK A. DUNEKA

York Harbor, Sept. 20, 1917.

Dear Mr. Duneka:

This script will remind you of one of your old detestations, but I have become so fond of it that I can't quite give it up.[1]

I hope you have had a good summer. Wells writes me that you are still interested in our common shop and are doing a lot of work for it.[2] My own work comes harder than it used, just as my walking does. If I get over a mile of ground and grass, I feel that I am young again, but I don't blow about it so much as I blow. You know that when I gave up every thing but the Chair, I didn't mean to do anything else, but one thing and another tempts me. The world is still interesting, and there are books that I want to write of so much that I have broken into the Sunday Times Review, and done a page about dear old Garland's autobiography—a mighty good book. You ought to read it, and Poole's new book, and Paul Kester's; Abraham Cahan has done a pretty great autobiographical novel, but it is too sensual in its facts, though he is a good man.[3] Why do they want to get so much dirt in? Have you seen a strange book wholly about me by a certain Alexander Harvey?[4] After two thirds I wouldn't have spoken to you; after the last third you wouldn't have spoken to me. Just now I'm reading Froissart; mighty good stuff; and I have read up the Polyponessian war, and Edward 3d, and other histories; I'm reading The Newcomes to my daughter, and I have read her "Philip;" not so bad as I expected.[5]—We have had a long rainy, foggy summer, and now dust and drouth. To day we have dug our potatoes—three bushels, magnificent. Last month I fell over in my corn-patch, and almost broke a rib, but not quite, though I am still sore from the bruise.

I think often of our years together—touch and go-ment's mostly—and always tenderly of your wise kindness.

My daughter joins me in best regards to Mrs. Duneka and you.

Yours affectionately,
W. D. Howells.

1. By 1890 Howells had proposed to the Hammond typewriter manufacturers a script type face, which they put on the market and called the W. D. Howells Special. It is used here. See *Twain-Howells*, p. 639.

2. That is, Harper & Brothers.

3. Howells refers to Garland's *A Son of the Middle Border*, which he reviewed in the New York *Times*, 26 August 1917; to Ernest Poole's novel *His Family* (1917; Howells had commented on *The Harbor* in the "Editor's Easy Chair," *Harper's Monthly*, April 1915); to Paul Kester's *His Own Country*; and to Abraham Cahan's *The Rise of David Levinsky* (1917). Cahan had been a friend since Howells praised *Yekl* in 1896. See Howells to Hitchcock, 13 July 1896, n. 1. Ten days later, on 30 September 1917 (RPB), Howells wrote again to Duneka about his feelings about Cahan's latest novel: "I am glad you like Cahan's book. Of course I thought it great, but I have had to tell him privately that there is too much harlotry in it, and that I may not write of it, though otherwise I should like toa [sic]—still, it is no worse in that [sic] Tolstoy's *Resurrection*. But I hate so much sexuality as has got into fiction. I am still very Victorian in my tastes. If I wrote of 'Levinsky' I should probably brace it with Poole's 'His Family,' another strong book, but also with too much lechery in it."

4. See Howells to Griffith, 19 August 1917, n. 1.

5. The chronicle written by Jean Froissart (ca. 1337–1410?) covers the history of western Europe from the early fourteenth century to 1400; the standard English translation is *The Chronicle of Froissart*, translated by Sir John Bourchier (London: D. Nutt, 1901–1903). Howells was most likely also reading Thucydides' *History of the Peloponnesian War* in the standard English translation by R. Crawley, first published in 1874. The most recent major work on the England of Edward III (1312–1377) was *England in the Age of Wycliffe* (1909) by George M. Trevelyan, whose father's work on the American Revolution Howells had read with interest. See Howells to Trevelyan, 5 February 1908. *The Newcomes* (1855) and *The Adventures of Philip* (1862) are novels by William Thackeray, whom Howells rediscovered at this time. See also Howells to Perry, 19 February 1917, n. 3.

13 NOVEMBER 1917, NEW YORK, TO MILDRED HOWELLS

Abbys House,[1]
Nov. 13, 1917.

Dear Pilla:

Glad that things have gone so well, and hope you will come back to the good old Blackstone in high spirits. Of course you will let us know which train to expect you on. Will it be the 3. o'clock?

It's pleasant to think of your finding such an old home at the Bellevue. We must cling to it in spite of the kitchen.

Be sure to collect our bonds at the New England Trust Co.

I am feeling much gayer if not better. I took John with me to see my good old Dr. Ewing,[2] and he pronounced me in a good way, with no more heart-kick than most sages. He voluntarily prescribed aromatic ammonia for gas in the tummy, and offered to give me a tonic, deciding on arsenic instead of strychnene, partly because, I think, he had it around. No caution about walking in the teeth of high winds, or climbing stairs, perhaps because he had a flight of twenty-four treads beside the steep stone steps outside.

All going well, here. Abby out with the boys just now. Weather fine but not hot.

Aff'tely
Papa.

You seem to have "boarded round" almost as much as an old time schoolmarm.

1. Howells had returned via Boston to New York about a week earlier, while Mildred remained at the Bellevue Hotel on Beacon Street. In her absence, Howells stayed with John and Abby's family before moving into the Blackstone, a residential hotel on East 58th Street.
2. Not identified.

19 NOVEMBER 1917, NEW YORK, TO FREDERICK A. DUNEKA

The Blackstone,
50 East 58th street,
Nov. 19, 1917.

My dear Duneka:

I hear you are still waiting to go South, and we expect to follow you after no great time. We expect to go only to Savannah, which we like greatly for its excellent hotel and its admirable people; we came to know nearly all of them this early spring. I have been immensely interested in the Mark Twain letters, and am expecting of course to write about them.[1] I think I have still something to say of him that they will help me say. He is the naturalest if not wildest man that I ever knew, and on some sides I knew him better than anyone else. His letters sparkle, or bristle with texts; and the difficulty will be to keep my sermon within bounds.

I saw Dressel North[2] the other day, and he told me of you with an affection that would have made me jealous if I did not want everybody to share my love for you. I hope the Southern roads will smooth themselves under your car wheels and that you will reach Miami in good shape. I used to bathe in the Miami in the *Boy's Town*, five times a day when the Southern Ohio summer got well heated. It is three times a river in Ohio, Great Miami, Little Miami, and Miami of the Lake; but

I suppose the Floridian sojourners think we Buckeyes borrowed the name from Florida.

My daughter and I have been in Boston since we closed at York Harbor, and here a fortnight nearly; we expect to start again about the 30th. She wishes her affectionate regards to Mrs. Duneka and you with my own.

Yours sincerely,
W. D. Howells.

1. Reviewing Albert B. Paine, ed., *Mark Twain's Letters* (2 volumes, 1917), Howells wrote in the "Editor's Easy Chair," *Harper's Monthly*, March 1918, that "while first of all a man, Mark Twain was lastingly a literary man. He did greatly and truly love his art, and his letters testify how greatly and truly he endeavored for excellence in it."

2. Ernest Dressel North originally worked for the Scribner rare book department, then from 1910 to 1950 was an independent dealer in manuscripts and rare books. Howells was at this time in correspondence with North, who acted as an agent for someone interested in buying the letters Clemens had written to Howells. On 2 November 1917 (KyU) Howells wrote that he probably did not "have a proprietary right in Clemens's letters," and that he would "like to be sure of his [Clemens'] daughter's approval, first, or before deciding anything." In another letter, 8 December 1917 (KyU), Howells again refers to this matter: "As I do not know the name of the proposed purchaser of these letters...I am obliged to say that if he is any sort of grafter, or mere profiteerer, or in any wise scandalous, the affair is off." Three months later, however, the deal seems to have fallen through, since Howells wrote to North on 27 February 1918 (KyU) that he supposed "the purchaser is of another mind about to taking [sic] them."

8 FEBRUARY 1918, MIAMI, FLORIDA, TO VAN WYCK BROOKS

31 Fort Dallas Park,
Miami, Fla., Feb'y 8, 1918.

Dear Mr. Brooks:[1]

I revere and admire Raemakers beyond words, and I should be proud to have something of mine go with anything of his. But I cannot write to order, and I can think only of a poem about the Lusitania, printed and consigned to oblivion in the *North American Review*, which *may* serve your purpose.[2] I think mighty well of the piece, but I cannot think of the name of it, or the month of its disappearance last year. The N. A. R. people can tell you, and I am sure they will let you have it.

Yours sincerely
W. D. Howells.

1. Van Wyck Brooks (1886–1963), historian and critic, was an interpreter of American literature and culture for half a century. His change of heart about Howells parallels a major change in his view of American literary development: Howells the "Puritan" editor-suppressor of Mark Twain's wild genius, in *The Ordeal of Mark Twain* (1920) becomes Howells the representer, integral and respected, of American life, in *Howells: His Life and World* (1959).

2. Louis Raemakers (1869–1956), Dutch political cartoonist, was noted for his vigorous anti-German cartoons in World War I. Howells' "poem about the Lusitania" had appeared as "The Passengers of a Retarded Submersible," *North American Review*, November 1916. A loose dialogue between the American people and a German submarine captain, the poem ends with the bitter words of the ghosts of the Lusitania. It was reprinted under the title "The Massacre of the Innocents" in Raemakers' book of cartoons, *America in the War* (1918). Later that year, on 5 August 1918 (transcription at InU), as the Allies' victory appeared imminent, Howells wrote again to Brooks, asking him to "somehow indicate that my poem on the Lusitania expresses the feeling of the time, but is now a shame lived down.... As it stands the poem requires the glorious retrieval of our former sufferance."

28 FEBRUARY 1918, ST. AUGUSTINE, FLORIDA, TO FREDERICK A. DUNEKA

Hotel Alcazar . . . .
St. Augustine, Fla. Feb'y 28, *1918*

My dear Duneka:

I thank you all my possible for "Ruggles of Redgap," which is one of the best studies of our life I have read for many a day, and a piece of humor worthy of Bret Harte in his prime. Do you know anything else by the author? I think I have got an Easy Chair topic out of it, and I should like to make my manners to him generally.[1] I find the book known to many here, and I wonder how I have skipped it, or missed it.

I talk much here with an old General Davis who is impassioned for everything about Fanny Kemble, and has collected a lot about her. He is an old fellow of my own age; and I met him at lunch some years ago, when he actually dozed between courses. Think of being frankly able to do that!

My daughter and I are reading *Great Expectations* aloud. Do you remember it? An amazingly meaty book, by far one of Dickens's best. It amazes me by its variety and fullness and makes me ashamed of ever slighting Dickens in my opinions.[2] We ought to have several lives—not so many as a cat, but far more than most men, so as to correct the mistakes of one in another.

The weather is just right here. I hope it's so at Miami, too. With our affection to you all,

Yours sincerely
W. D. Howells.

1. Writing about Harry Leon Wilson's *Ruggles of Red Gap* (1915) in the "Editor's Easy Chair," *Harper's Monthly*, June 1918, Howells felt that it was "full of guff and graft." Later that year, Howells and Mildred saw a film version of *Ruggles*, which Howells called "the very best movy of our lives." See Howells to Duneka, 25 April 1918 (RPB).

2. Howells was reading *Great Expectations* "for the second time in sixty years," as he put it in a letter to Duneka, 20 February 1918 (CCamarSJ). He had listened to his father reading Dickens aloud when he was a boy, and he wrote about Dickens throughout his career. But his sharpest deprecatory comment concerned Dickens' "insinuation" or "downright *petting*" of his characters and his "mannerism," in "Henry James, Jr.," *Century*, November 1882. See Howells to Gosse, 16 November 1882, n. 1.

13 MARCH 1918, ST. AUGUSTINE, FLORIDA, TO FREDERICK A. DUNEKA

St. Augustine, March 13, 1918.

Dear Duneka:

Decidedly but not very distinctly, Pip did marry Estella. I should have preferred more wedding-cake; but I suppose they looked upon that of Miss Havisham as a warning. When you get at the book again you will see.[1] We have just packed our copy for York Harbor.

It *was* cold, the other day, but it was delicious. Still I thought twice about advising St. Augustine for an inveterate Miamian like you, and I now advise against it!

We expect to go on to Savannah on Sunday, and our address will be the De Soto Hotel. I hope to keep writing you from point to point.

I always expect Providence to fail me with Easy Chair subjects; but after the Mark Twain letters, here comes Sidney Colvin's wonderfully comprehensive expansion of his life of Keats—a perfect feast.[2] It is the time of all others that I delight in most. Scribners ought to send it to you, and let you renew your friendship with Leigh Hunt, Charles Lamb, Hazlitt, Wordsworth, and all that goodly fellowship. I have spent a glad morning just cutting the leaves of the book.

With our love to Mrs. Duneka,

Yours sincerely,
W. D. Howells.

1. Howells and Duneka were reading *Great Expectations* as revised, in which Pip does marry Estella. Howells had written Duneka a few days earlier: "You remembered exactly the closing words... which we repeated after you from the book soon after getting your letter.... When I realized what a *great* book G. E. was I hung my head for shame to think what slighting things of C. D. I had once said." See Howells to Duneka, 8 March 1918 (RPB). Late in December, however, he found *Little Dorrit* and *A Tale of Two Cities* "awful stuff." See Howells to Duneka, 26 December 1918 (RPB).

2. Howells' review of A. B. Paine's edition of *Mark Twain's Letters* had just come out. His enthusiasm for Colvin's "expansion" of *John Keats*, an enlarged second edition (1918), is manifest in his "Editor's Easy Chair," *Harper's Monthly*, July 1918; he had commented on the original edition three decades earlier in the "Editor's Study," *Harper's Monthly*, October 1887.

1 APRIL 1918, SAVANNAH, GEORGIA, TO AURELIA H. HOWELLS

> *The De Soto*
> *Savannah, Georgia . . .*
> April 1st, 1918.

Dear Aurelia:

When I was in Miami some weeks ago I made a codicil to my will revoking the bequest of six thousand dollars to you which it contained.[1] My reasons for doing this were partly the difficulties attending the matter, and the heavy duties levied by our recent laws upon all bequests, and partly because the sum would have yielded you only three hundred dollars a year instead of the eight hundred which I now pay you, and which will be paid you, if you survive me, by John and Pilla from their inheritance. You will remember that your allowance from me was first $600, but when your stocks went bad I continued the income from them to its amount of $200, giving you $800 in all. This will be continued to the same result by the children, whom I consulted about the codicil. I am sure you will approve of it too, and I would have told you of it before if I had not been waiting to see them together and have them join me in writing you. Now it happens that John has come down here to do some pictures for a paper I am going to write about Savannah,[2] and I must not delay any longer.

> Your affectionate brother
> Will.

We both agree to what father has done and what he promises for us.

> John.
> Mildred

1. See Howells to Aurelia Howells, 10 June 1918, n. 1.
2. "Savannah Twice Visited," *Harper's Monthly*, February 1919, with six illustrations by John M. Howells.

1 MAY 1918, NEW YORK, TO SALVATORE CORTESI

> ...*130 West 57th Street*
> May 1st, 1918.

My dear Mr. Cortesi:[1]

Many old and young lovers of Italy here have heard with grief that Italians in Rome and elsewhere have credited the German slander that Americans care nothing for them except as they can make some selfish use of them. You who know us at first hand will not need to be set right in this matter, but if you know any Italians who do, will you say to them from an old American author whose literary life began with his "Venetian Life" that he has never known any American who does not love Italy with patriotic fervor and is not proud to claim fellow-citizenship with her sons in the ideal Republic which unites all the children of liberty. I entreat all Italians to believe in our honor of their name, and our devotion to their cause, which is *our* cause. I lived through the last four years of the Austrians at Venice, and it is the great sorrow of my old age that I see them again on the shores of the Lagoon while it is my strongest hope that I shall live to see them driven from them forever.

> Yours sincerely,
> W. D. Howells.

1. Salvatore Cortesi (1864–1947), after news reporting in the United States in the 1890s, was appointed head of the Associated Press in Rome in 1902. Howells had made friends with him during his last visit to Italy in the winter of 1907–1908. See *Life in Letters*, II, 380. Ernest Poole, a director of the Foreign Press Bureau in Washington, wrote John M. Howells on 23 May 1918 (MH) that the Italian embassy had issued a statement indicating that Howells' "letter to Cortesi received wide publication in Italy." To his son John, Howells wrote on 1 May 1918 (MH) that he could take up the question only through a letter to Cortesi. "I can't fire a long-range gun into the air, without launching more punk," he added; "I don't say that my letter isn't partly punk."

5 MAY 1918, NEW YORK, TO CURTIS BROWN

> ...*130 West 57th Street*
> May 5, 1918.

Dear Mr. Curtis:[1]

Your letter with its enclosure came as a joyful surprise last night, and I beg to thank you for your check for $118.26 in payment of the Continental (English) rights of The Leatherwood God. I thought that the good Louis Conard[2] had gone under with all our works in the present "crush of worlds." Now I shall begin to believe with you that the war may end suddenly though here we are preparing to fight it for a thousand years on unbridled billions of Liberty Bonds.

I am very grateful to you for keeping my books in mind so constantly every way.

Yours sincerely
W. D. Howells

1. Curtis Brown—misnamed by Howells in the salutation—was an English publisher and literary agent.

2. Louis Conrad was a Paris publisher who secured the rights to *The Leatherwood God* through Brown.

8 MAY 1918, NEW YORK, TO BRAND WHITLOCK

...*130 West 57th Street*
May 8, 1918.

My dear Whitlock:

I duly received the beautiful medallion which you sent me,[1] and I wish to thank you for it after so many days as have elapsed since it came to me in Florida. It is truly classic.

We have been following your story of the Belgian crime,[2] and suffering as if the story were all new. In fact you have made it new; but I think your full and final record of it will be in fiction, in the novel which the hope and faith of us who went with you abroad to help you write will be effective in your art.* You are fit to have been the witness of the great things you have seen.

I am growing old almost day by day, and I cannot tell you fully what I feel. But sometime yet I hope to do so when we meet after the war I long to outlive.

Just now we are off for Kittery Point where we shall spend the summer with my son and his family.

Do give our love to Mrs. Whitlock and believe me in all affection and honor,

Yours sincerely
W. D. Howells.

*No one can be before you in that!

1. Many months earlier Whitlock wrote to Woodrow Wilson: "I am sending you by today's courier a medal presented to me by the gentlemen of the National Committee that has charge of the relief work in Belgium.... The medal has not been made public as yet ... but I am privately ... giving a few of them to intimate friends." See *The Letters of Brand Whitlock*, ed. Allen Nevins (New York: Appleton-Century, 1936), p. 213. Howells' "beautiful medallion" is surely the "medal" given to Wilson.

2. Whitlock's *Belgium: A Personal Narrative* was being serialized in *Everybody's Magazine*; it began in February and was published in book form in 1919. Other Whitlock pieces on "the Belgian crime" appeared in the *Delineator*, April, June, and July 1918. See *The Letters of Brand Whitlock*, p. 256; and David D. Anderson, *Brand Whitlock* (New York: Twayne Publishers, 1968), bibliography.

18 MAY 1918, KITTERY POINT, TO THOMAS S. PERRY

Kittery Point, May 18, 1918.

My dear Perry:

Thank you truly for the little book of passages from James's stories.[1] The things have an extraordinary gain in quality through their isolation from the context. One feels almost as never before what a great artist he is. The accusation of obscurity falls from their wonderful clarity. What a characteristic letter he writes the editor!

All the family here hope to see you presently and join me in love to you.

Yours ever
W. D. Howells.

1. *Pictures and Other Passages from Henry James* (1917), selected by Ruth Head. In his "characteristic letter" to the book's editor, taking much pleasure in the idea of the anthology, James wrote: "And I find ... a great deal of *intrinsic* possibility in the application of so practical a test as the little compendium you have so ingeniously conceived of such value as my writings may have to show" (p. vii). The "Preface" is dated 28 May 1916, after James's death.

10 JUNE 1918, KITTERY POINT, TO AURELIA H. HOWELLS

Kittery Point, June 10, 1918.

Dear Aurelia:

I have your letter telling me of your satisfaction with the codicil to my will, and of the arrangement I have made with the children for continuing the monthly payments instead of the bequest.[1] It is very gratifying to have your approval and that of Annie and Achille, and I thank you all; I did not suppose you would object, even if you did not outlive me.—I think a great deal about dying (as father used to do in his old age,) but somehow not with the alarm the thought used to give me when I was younger. There are things in my life which I would have different if I could; but I fear no punishment. The creator made me what I might become, and he will not forget it, though I cannot forget what I regret.—I am more unhappy about the war than anything else, and I long for peace through a victory of the right.—Meanwhile I write constantly, as always, but not to my satisfaction. I am conscious that I am wearing out, mind as well as body; my memory fails me distressingly; and I tend to obscurity in my expression. I have two longish stories well started but I cannot force them on.[2] I am always fancying that I can do so later, but probably I cannot. I read my novels of the past aloud to the family, and wonder that I could do them.—I enclose the picture of Howells's pretty little boy,[3] I dare say you have it, but you may like it again.—Pilla is in Boston teething as usual. We expect to spend August inland together. Our house at York Harbor is let for a rent that would seem very high if everything else was not so high.

With love to all

Your aff'te brother
Will.

1. The codicil, dated 15 February at Miami, Florida (typed document, MH), re-vokes a bequest of $6,000 to Aurelia Howells and bequeaths her $250. A year earlier, Howells had directed Mildred and John to pay Aurelia $800 a year. See Howells to John and Mildred Howells, 8 February 1917 (MH); also Howells to Aurelia Howells, 1 April 1918.

2. Howells published no further fiction. One of the stories was "The Home-Towners"; the other may have been "a torpid story" ten to fifteen thousand words long set in Boston in the 1880s. See Howells to W. A. Gill, 21 February 1919 (County Reference Library, Bristol).

3. The son of Howells Fréchette, William Dean Howells Fréchette (b. 1917).

13 JUNE 1918, KITTERY POINT, TO THOMAS S. PERRY

Kittery Point, June 13, 1918.

Dear Perry—

I found your pathos for the past at Newport very touching.[1] It was wonderful your being associated there with the James boys, and I wish I could have had such companionship in my time; I had it later with H. J. at Cambridge, of course.[2] I think a good deal of him lately, admiring his advent to the full fame which he was stinted from in his earlier life, almost his whole life; it is such a posthumous renown, with all this tardy generation bowing and genuflecting before his shade.

You wont suffer my enjoying poor old Clarke's life of Fiske;[3] but you can't help yourself. It is very simple, almost childish, and yet it brings that childlike spirit very sensibly back. Of course it blinks a lot that it would be infinitely better for setting in full light; but I suppose this was the bargain. I should like to talk it over with you, some time. I shall scarcely write of it; yet I may.

Yours aff't'ely,
W. D. Howells.

1. Probably the notes on James that Perry wrote for the benefit of Percy Lubbock in editing *The Letters of Henry James* (New York: Charles Scribner's Sons, 1920), I, 6–9. Howells read them aloud to his family at Kittery Point and wrote Perry on 25 June 1918 (MeWC): "I think you might well have made more."

2. See "Novel-Writing and Novel-Reading," in William M. Gibson and Leon Edel, ed., *Howells and James: A Double Billing* (New York: New York Public Library, 1958).

3. John S. Clark, *Life and Letters of John Fiske* (2 volumes, 1917). Perry had written a biography of Fiske in 1906, and Howells had been Fiske's next-door neighbor at 37 Concord Avenue in Cambridge, in the 1870s. See Cady, *Howells*, II, 161–62.

14 JULY 1918, KITTERY POINT, TO MILDRED HOWELLS

Kittery Point, July 14, 1918.

Dear Pilla:

There's nothing to add to yesterday's nothing today, except that dear little Jacky continues feverish, but angelic. He lies all day in bed, and plays with his "chil'ren," and his temperature goes up towards night. But he sleeps well, and the doctor thinks it is merely his stomach. There was never a more saintlike little soul. Even the hardy Bill feels his sweet influence. Last night B. got me in for reading one of his scientific magazines on rabbit-culture, and marking "just the important parts," so that he could more rapidly take it in. I also have mainly to provide our pair with clover. But I might as well, for otherwise I loaf the time away. At night I promise myself to work the next morning, but go to sleep over the newspaper. I am reading a most ridiculous life of Mary Wollestonecraft Shelley,[1] whom I would like to have mamma characterize. Last night I had one of my lost-ones dream. It was to arrange a second marriage between her and myself! The only second-marriage I could imagine for myself. Among the guests were the Shepards, Joanna her kind young self, and Gus with his hair and beard turned from white to the brown I first knew him in.[2] The master-spirit seemed to be an ancient Briton whose name* I forget. Mamma arranged getting a motor, which turned into a motor bus full of people to take us through the slush, to the hotel where we were to be married, but forgot the trunks, and we exchanged reproaches. All very realistic and probable. No more at present.

> Affectionately
> Papa.

*Something like Aristogerasio, a Latin form, evidently.

1. This was most likely Florence A. Marshall, *The Life and Letters of Mary Wollstonecraft Shelley* (2 volumes, 1889). Howells wrote T. S. Perry the same day (MeWC) that he had been "reading a long life of Mrs. P. B. Shelley, the woeful woman who wrote *Frankenstein* and lengthier and drearier and duller letters than I have not often suffered through."

2. Joanna Mead, a younger sister of Elinor Mead Howells, and her husband, Augustus D. Shepard, who had died, respectively, in 1914 and 1913.

27 JULY 1918, INTERVALE, NEW HAMPSHIRE, TO THOMAS S. PERRY

> *. . . The Bellevue*
> *Intervale, . . . New Hampshire* July 27, 1918.

Dear Perry:

Goethe *was* a wide-minded old Goat, as the unlettered would call him. Last summer our preciously lost friend lent me Eckermann,[1] which I read with the greatest instruction. Eckerman milks him into his mouth, and then gives his divine juice forth in a welter of Eckermannish, but not spoiled. I too read W. Meister in my hot youth, and almost read the Wahlverwandschaften, with a young wish to find it greater than it was.[2] Of course I know Faust, even in the second part (poor old Bayard Taylor's version is wonderful, but I read the first part in German) ;[3] largely though, I unknow the immortal Goat. You had better read the beautiful chapters on Weimar in my much ignored Their Silver Wedding Journey.[4]

Mrs. W. did one thing wonderfully well: the story of some one's dull adoptive daughter, who is adored and married by a young man as dull as she. Bores are often so; but Mrs. W. found out this case.[5] After much reluctance of H. J. from her pen this jewel shines afar.

We will contrive our meeting yet; such souls need each other once every summer. Pilla's tooth calls her to Portland where her einzige[6] dentist happens to be, but we shall be here a week yet. Meantime my best ricapito[7] is John, K. P.

> Yours ever
> W. D. Howells.

1. Helen Choate Bell, Howells' neighbor in York Harbor, had lent him Eckermann's *Conversations with Goethe.* See Howells to Perry, 23 August 1917. At the time of her death, Perry wrote a tribute to her, which appeared in the Boston *Evening Transcript,* 25 July 1918. See Virginia Harlow, *Thomas Sergeant Perry: A Biography* (Durham, N.C.: Duke University Press, 1950), p. 213. Howells also planned to write about her "or rather about the Boston which created her" for the *Atlantic,* as he informed Perry on 21 August 1918 (MeWC), but Ellery Sedgwick did not want the article for another three months. It was probably never written.

2. See Howells to Victoria Howells, 18–24 April 1859.

3. See Howells to Longfellow, 23 December 1870.

4. See Howells to Perry, 31 August 1917, n. 2.

5. Edith Wharton's story was "The Mission of Jane," in *The Descent of Man and Other Stories* (1914). She responded to Howells' request to print this story in his anthology *The Great Modern American Stories* (1920), stating: "It must be nearly thirty years ago that a very shy young woman sent you a handful of worthless verse, & received the kindest of letters in reply. She is very glad to think that any work of hers...may have partly liquidated her debt. [¶] I am proud to have 'Jane' included in the volume you are preparing, & especially proud that you should think she comes under the rubric of 'best.' "

6. German for "one and only."

7. Italian for "address."

14 AUGUST 1918, KITTERY POINT, TO FREDERICK A. DUNEKA

Kittery Point, August 14, 1918.

My dear Duneka:

You will think it hard that I should work this script on you, and I would not if I could change the type-plate without dashing my fingers so much.[1] I was extremely glad to hear from you, and I show it by trying to hear from you again in so promptly answering you.

I think you are more right about the two other magazines than the Harper,[2] which sometimes too easily suffers itself to be better. Still it is always honestly readable, and since it has gone into the war it has done so with dignity and importance. I fancy I am thinking with you in wishing to get out of the "Harper story," which I have heard you lament. Somebody ought to be born again, and write differently, but I must be honest and own that I don't speak from recent acquaintance with the stories. Every now and then you do hit it wonderfully, and you never fail disgracefully. This sounds more patronizing than I mean it to. I enclose a letter from my old friend Perry, who reads more than all other men, but has only just discovered our Red Gapper.[3] Could you get something from the R. G.? Probably it would be disappointing, though.

What you tell me of Wells[4] is interesting to touchingness, and makes me wish to try writing to him. Latterly, he had begun to replace you in my affections. I remember I used to come in sometimes, and in my eagerness to have two minutes with you, hardly notice him. He did not notice it, and he has always been good friends with me, except touching our beloved Red Gapper.

I have just told Mr. Hartman[5] of having written a reminiscential paper about a week's visit at the White House in Hayes's time. Hayes was my wife's cousin, and our visit was intimate, so that I think I came nearer to understanding that great and strangely fated man than most who met him; perhaps you remember I wrote his campaign life. I think my paper of rather unique interest, but not knowing how much you are doing on the magazine, I mention it to you mostly because I cannot bear not to. I don't know who will have authority to say me yea or nay.[6]

I am glad to hear your news of your boy, and all your family intelligence. My daughter and I regret the mountains,[7] but she is going back to them this afternoon, and I am staying on here, where I find myself very much minded to write about a lot of things.

Yours effectionately,
W. D. Howells.

1. See Howells to Duneka, 20 September 1917, n. 1.

2. Since Duneka's letter has not been located, it is unclear what comment he made about the magazines. Perhaps "the two other magazines" are the *North American Review* and *Harper's Bazar*, both published by Harper & Brothers.

3. Harry Leon Wilson, the author of *Ruggles of Red Gap*.

4. Thomas B. Wells of Harper & Brothers.

5. Lee Foster Hartman of Harper & Brothers.

6. The reminiscence of the Howellses' visit to the White House in 1880 had the provisional title "A Week in the White House," and Howells had intended to send it for comments and corrections to Webb C. Hayes, the former president's son (see Howells to W. C. Hayes, 1 July 1918; OFH), but did not actually do so until a year later. He did, however, send it to F. A. Duneka on 22 August 1918 (RPB), and Duneka replied on 26 August 1918 (MH) that the public was not interested in reading about Hayes, and that Howells' attempt to "rehabilitate" him clashed with the general view of Hayes as "a selfish robber, a man of narrow vision and of provincial manners." This response prompted Howells to write to Mildred Howells, 30 August 1918 (MH), that "Duneka spewed my White House out of his mouth because I praised Hayes and [he] wrote vulgar abuse of him which I cannot resent because he is sick. It's all right; the paper will easily sell." For Howells' final disposition of the manuscript, see Howells to W. C. Hayes, 12 October 1919. Howells' campaign biography, *Sketch of . . . Hayes,* appeared in 1876; for his comments about his visit to the White House, see Howells to R. B. Hayes, 17 May 1880.

7. Howells and Mildred had recently returned from an excursion into the White Mountains.

15 August 1918, Kittery Point, to Thomas S. Perry

Kittery Point, Aug. 15, 1918.

My dear Perry:

If you were that constant reader of The Easy Chair which you have somehow abused my fancy to the belief in you would have known months ago all about *Ruggles* of *Redgap* if not its author.[1] But I forgive your ignorance in this case to your knowledge in all others. Who publishes the Redgapper's other books, anyhow?

Here is a letter about a dream about me which may interest Mrs Perry if not you. Send it back.—But the best thing (not autobiographical) ever dreamed about me was by St. Gaudens. A lot of people on shipboard were betting on the distance of a very flaming planet in the eveny sky. Some thought it millions of miles off; but I went quietly down to my cabin, and came up with the shotgun which it seems I always had with me, and now aimed, by a realistic impulse, at the planet. I fired, and down dropped the planet. I said quietly, "There!" and went back with my shotgun. This is a true story and I have always been very proud of having a great genius dream the fact about me. I forgot to say that I had bet the star was no way off at all.[2]

No doubt you're right about the best culture for our Redgapper, but he wont get it. Nobody does.

Yours ever
W. D. Howells.

1. Howells had written about Wilson's novel in the "Editor's Easy Chair," *Harper's Monthly*, June 1918. He forwarded Perry's letter to F. A. Duneka on 18 August 1918 (RPB) with the comment: "The...letter is from my old friend Perry, whom I smashed on the nose for not knowing that I had written about our favorite classic of Redgap six months before he found it out."

2. Augustus Saint-Gaudens had recalled Howells' objecting to the ideal feminine figure in the equestrian statue of General Sherman that the sculptor was then working on—so Howells reported to Homer Saint-Gaudens, who was editing his father's reminiscences. "Apropos of my realism," Howells continued, "he told me a dream he had had about me. We were on shipboard together, and a dispute rose between the passengers as to the distance of a certain brilliant planet in the sky. Some said it was millions of miles away, but I held that it was very near; and he related that I went down to my stateroom and came up with a shotgun, which I fired at the star. It came fluttering down, and I said 'There! You see?'" See *The Reminiscences of Augustus Saint-Gaudens* (New York: Century, 1913), II, 61–62.

22 August 1918, Kittery Point, to The Board of Directors of the American Academy of Arts and Letters

Kittery Point, Maine, August 22, 1918.

Gentlemen:

I am sorry to say that I do not see a proper function for the American Academy in the judgment of German Culture. It does not seem to me that we can usefully or fitly treat this matter, and I shall not be able to contribute to the criticism suggested in your circular of the 17th inst.[1]

Very respectfully yours
W. D. Howells,
President.

The Board of Directors of the
American Academy.

1. In June, Howells had told R. U. Johnson, secretary of the Academy, that he could find much of his writing about the war in the *North American Review*, Hall Caine's *King's Book*, and Mrs. Wharton's *Book of the Homeless*. He also pointed out that "There is a prophetic sense of Germany throughout *Their Silver Wedding Journey*, and there is a clear confession of our love for France in my welcome to *Brieux*." See Howells to Johnson, 4 June 1918 (NNAL). But he evidently had no desire to condemn German culture and the German people.

14 September 1918, Kittery Point, to Thomas S. Perry

Kittery Point, Sept. 14, 1918.

Dear Perry:

Which of those blessed Bensons was Charnwood before he became a lord?[1] I have no Who's Who here but W. W. in America and W. W. in New York and neither avails to help me hide that ignorance of contemporary literature which a single ray from your universal intelligence will disperse.

I am reading a great many idle books, but now and then a good one, such as *Stop Boone*—a R. R. station and town in that Far West, which is finding itself out on the human terms.[2] I do not remember any study of raw but harmless youth better than this. I sent for all the other Red Gap books,[3] but at best they are only così così. The author is staying with Booth Tarkington at Kennebunkport, and expects too look me up, I believe. But success spoils all of us youth. How much I should like to take daily counsel of your age and infirmities!

Yours ever
W. D. Howells.

That is a good choice of things from H. J., which you sent me; but Middle Years is draughty and echoy.[4] All the same he was a great genius. He lived too long in England.

1. Upon Perry's suggestion, Howells was preparing a review of G. R. B. Charn-wood's *Abraham Lincoln* (1916) for the "Editor's Easy Chair," *Harper's Monthly*, December 1918. Godfrey Rathbone Benson (1864–1945), liberal politician and man of letters, became first Baron Charnwood in 1911; his brother was Sir Frank Benson, an actor and theater manager.

2. Homer Croy's *Boone Stop* (1918), a "fresh fiction" about a boy growing up in a Western whistle-stop town, became the subject, with three other books, of the January 1919 "Editor's Easy Chair."

3. See Howells to Perry, 15 August 1918, n. 1.

4. *Pictures and Other Passages from Henry James.* See Howells to Perry, 18 May 1918. *The Middle Years* had been published in November 1917.

21 SEPTEMBER 1918, KITTERY POINT, TO AURELIA H. HOWELLS

Kittery Point, Sept. 21, 1918.

Dear Aurelia:

I have just come in from being kodakked with the boys on the library veranda in a harvest-house picture of ourselves and all the squashes and pumpkins left of the year's crop in John's garden; the boys helped raise them, and the whole family has eaten of them. Yesterday we had corn-pudding from the almost last of the corn.—There have been no peaches, but the Baldwin apple-tree before my windows hangs down with unbroken strands of apples—one for every blossom, and all perfect because of the spraying against the coddling moths. Old Albert and Jacky have made in a mill of their own some excellent cider from the windfalls of the Gravenstein.

I must tell you how much I liked your version of Y. Doodle; it is better than the original, and I don't wonder your fellow-pupils admire it. All you tell me about the poor fellows is very interesting. I didn't know that food could be got to the Ally prisoners; we are going to try sending some. I am specially interested in the prisoner who studied Spanish; you must tell him how I struggled with it when I was a boy.

About a month ago I ordered the Daily and Sunday Sun for you. We had such bad luck with the Times that I did not try for that.

I have told you about my frequent dreaming of the dead, the earlier and later; and last night I had a long dream about going to housekeeping with Elinor in a new Cambridge house. It is always in some new place. I wish I had written these dreams down.

The summer has turned its back on us with many sunny looks at us over its shoulder. But there is no doubt of its going. It is leaving the fact and the hope of victory behind it, and that is the best it could do for us. I snatch furiously at each day's news, and after the American smash at Mihiel, I am now shelling Metz with the rest.[1] I don't see why we shouldn't take the place. But one has to hold one's breath in trust and doubt.

We have the Spanish grip about us—among the Navy Yard workers who now inhabit the Champernowns, taken over for them by the government; and one poor young girl has died, a daughter of the Coutts family who used to live in the Lady Pepperrell house, but had gone onto a farm.

John and Abby will be going early in October to Beloit Wisconsin, to inaugurate the tablet on John's monument to her grandfather and father. Her family founded Beloit and founded the college there.[2] Pilla and I shall wait their return here—about mid-October—and then go to Boston and New York. We are not sure just where we shall go in the South, but it looks rather like St. Augustine, Savannah being filled up by the housing of the shipbuilders; we wished to take an apartment. Perhaps we shall devolve on Augusta, Georgia.

I shall be glad to hear from Annie, and none the less so because I think I owe her a letter. With our love to all

> Your affte brother
> **Will**.

Sam has ordered his winter's coal—9 tons, and got in 3 of it.

1. Under the command of General John J. Pershing, American troops had won a first and decisive victory as an independent army at Saint-Mihiel on 12 September 1918. Although this was planned as a stepping-stone to an attack on the German forces at Metz, the Americans were ultimately ordered to assist the British in their successful effort to break through the Hindenburg Line.

2. Dr. Horace White, a physician and agent for the New England Emigration Company, brought the first permanent settlers to Beloit in 1836. His son Horace, Abby's father, graduated in 1853 from Beloit College, which was originally affiliated with the Congregational and Presbyterian churches. John Howells' memorial, including the plaque, is located in Horace White Park in Beloit.

7 NOVEMBER 1918, BOSTON, TO JOHN M. HOWELLS FAMILY

Hotel Bellevue,
Boston, Nov. 7, 1918.

Dear Abby, John and both the Boys:

Perry has just been in and we have been helplessly trying to rejoice together at the Peace![1] I can only hand my failure over to you dearest ones who will remember this glorious event and try to tell another generation how you felt. I am sure you have told the grandeur of it to your dear boys and bidden them remember it as the greatest thing in the history of mankind. I wish we could all have been together this wonderful day, but I am glad to have been in Boston for it, in the same air where our own part of the long battle for freedom began.

The pictures of the boys by one of them are astonishing and Bill must realize how glad I am of his skill; for Jack it is enough to exist as he does.

A great mass of people swarmed up to the State House where the governor came out and spoke to them.[2] Now the sun has set and the new moon which I saw last at Kittery Point is looking down again from a clear sky.

Love to all.
Fafa.

1. The actual armistice agreement was not signed until 11 November 1918, but Howells may have heard of the outbreak of revolution in Germany on 4 November and the departure from Berlin on 6 November of the German delegation for negotiating an armistice.

2. Samuel W. McCall (1851–1923), U. S. Congressman from Massachusetts (1893–1913), was Republican governor of Massachusetts (1916–1919).

10 FEBRUARY 1919, AUGUSTA, GEORGIA, TO THOMAS S. PERRY

The Hermitage Inn . . .
Augusta, Ga. . . . Feb'y 10, 1919.

My dear Perry:

I don't see why you complain of not knowing my address when here it is as plain as print can make it. To be sure we have been a month at Savannah, but we were a month before that at Augusta.

You are trying to be magnanimous toward a very dull book in praising the S. C. Book,[1] and it doesnt become you; it isn't natural. I, who am all generosity and good feeling, have kept myself from massacring the letter-press by lighting into the pictures. To be sure I have read the l. p. little or not at all; who could, but a born hypocrite and flatterer? In spite of all this I believe you about the Cobb book.[2] Who publishes it? Thanks.

Could you find me a good cheap second hand book treating topically and not too critically of American stories, short and good ones? A publisher wants me to select and do an introduction to a volume of them,[3] and in the decay of my memory I don't know which I like, but if I once saw the names of them, I should know like lightning. Do!

Also, I am asked to do an introduction to a new edition of Don Quixote;[4] and Pilla and I are reading the lovable book aloud together; but it doesn't seem the good old Jervas version. Could you send me that in a cheap form? Perhaps *Everyman's*.

We had a nice friendly time in Savannah; but this is the good air. Try for a fine old attack of bronchitis, and come down all of you, and join Mrs. Perry in getting triumphantly well of her influenza. I'm sorry to hear of her affliction from it. *I* have a cold that I brought with me from New York two months ago.

Pilla joins me in love to you all.

Ever yours
W. D. Howells.

1. Howells is perhaps referring to a letter from Perry now missing, but more likely to the manuscript of Perry's review of Edward W. Emerson, *The Early Years of the Saturday Club* (1918) that appeared under the title, "The Golden Age of Boston," *Yale Review* 8 (1918), 856–58. Perry contrasts the "former glory of Boston" with its present "fantastic reputation for priggishness." Howells, for his part, in the "Editor's Easy Chair," *Harper's Monthly*, May 1919, largely ignores the text and compares the quality of the picture portraits with the actual appearance of the originals as he knew them.

2. Probably Irvin S. Cobb, *Eating in Two or Three Languages* (1919) which was published in February and reviewed in April; though it might have been *The Glory of the Coming* (1918). Both were published by George H. Doran Company.

3. Horace B. Liveright had offered Howells $500 to select the best American short stories and write an introduction to the anthology. See Liveright to Howells 19 and 24 December 1918 (MH). *The Great Modern American Stories* was published in July 1920.

4. An abridged edition of the Charles Jarvis translation of *Don Quixote* was published by Harper & Brothers in 1923, "Edited by William Dean Howells / With an Introduction by Mildred Howells." Although Mildred Howells states unequivocally that her father "never wrote his intended introduction" (p. v), Howells' 21-page manuscript draft is located in the Beinecke Library, Yale University. The introduction for the 1923 edition extensively quotes from Howells' comments on *Don Quixote* in *My Literary Passions*, "The Country Printer," *Criticism and Fiction*, "Editor's Easy Chair," and *Familiar Spanish Travels*.

7 APRIL 1919, NEW YORK, TO MR. GOLDSTEIN

The Blackstone,
April 7, 1919.

Dear Mr. Goldstein:[1]

I cannot autograph the books you have sent me because I am old and tired and sick, and I beg you to send and fetch them away, for they crowd and incommode us. Personally I have no interest in first editions, which are always dirty and shabby, and bear nothing of their former owners' history to the present.

Yours sincerely
W. D. Howells.

1. Goldstein has not been identified. On 10 April 1919, Howells wrote again: "I must beg you to send at once for the books you have put here.... if they are not taken away by noon tomorrow I will return them at your risk." See Argosy Bookstore catalog (ca. 1956).

13 MAY 1919, BOSTON, TO ROSE KOHLER

Hotel Bellevue ...
Boston May 13, 1919.

Dear Miss Kohler:[1]

I wish I could claim the imaginative motive you attribute to me, but honesty obliges me to own that I used the name Inglehart for the Duveneck Boys because I thought I ought not to say Duveneck outright.[2] Inglehart was chosen by pure chance.

The life of Duveneck ought to be one of the most interesting and valuable of biographies. I knew him here and in Venice; and I knew his wife and father-in-law much better.[3]

Yours sincerely
W. D. Howells.

1. Rose Kohler was, presumably, writing a life of Frank Duveneck, the American painter; the biography, however, was never published.
2. The "Inglehart Boys" in Howells' *Indian Summer* (1886) were drawn from Duveneck's American students studying art in Munich, Florence, and Venice in the early 1880s. See *Indian Summer*, HE, p. 282.
3. For Elizabeth Boott Duveneck and her father, Francis Boott, see Howells to James, 25 December 1886, n. 10.

7 JULY 1919, YORK HARBOR, TO C. SYMON

York Harbor, Maine, July 7, 1919.

Dear Sir:

I beg to thank you for your kind letter notifying me that His Majesty the King of the Belgians has bestowed upon me the Broad Ribbon of the Order of Leopold II, and I desire to express my very earnest sense of the honor done me.[1]

At the same time I have to regret that as the citizen of a Republic I cannot receive this monarchical decoration, inestimably as I must prize the distinction of its bestowal by a prince so great and good as your sovereign.

Yours truly
W. D. Howells

Hon. C. Symon
Secretary of Legation.

1. Symon had written Howells from Washington on 26 June 1919 (MH) "that His Majesty the King of the Belgians has been pleased to bestow upon you the Broad Ribbon of the Order of Leopold II (Grand Cordon de l'Ordre de Léopold II) as a token of his appreciation of the devotion you have shown to the cause of Belgium."

19 AUGUST 1919, YORK HARBOR, TO THOMAS B. WELLS

York Harbor, Aug. 19, 1919.

My dear Wells:

Since I proposed the continuance of my autobiography as a serial and a book, I have been thinking it had better be called *Years of My Middle Life*; and I have put down a few heads from each of which many tails would dangle. In fact, these topics are only sparse suggestions, which would indefinitely enrich themselves in the working out.[1]

I should be glad to have you think the matter over soon, and let me know your mind about it.

I hope soon to let you have the paper on *Eighty Years and After*, which I am now in the mood of writing. It is to be, as I understand, not a reminiscence but a study of old age.[2]

What was the other thing we agreed on my doing?

Yours sincerely,
W. D. Howells.

1. The text of the synopsis appears in appendix B to *Years of My Youth*, HE, pp. 257–58; the manuscript is located in the Houghton Library, Harvard University.

2. "Eighty Years and After" appeared in *Harper's Monthly*, December 1919, and was reprinted posthumously in pamphlet form. See pp. 157–67.

20 AUGUST 1919, YORK HARBOR, TO BOOTH TARKINGTON

York Harbor, Aug. 20, 1919.

My dear Tarkington:

I thought you could not do another book as great as *Turmoil*, but I believe your *Mag-Ambersons* is even greater in certain ways.[1] It is very *even*, very close, very equal. Your Bibbs in the T. was a weakness, though true to our Midwestern poetry, but there is no weakness in the Ambersons. George and his mother are no truer than the rest, but they are wonder-true, and they are marvellously managed. The atmosphere is our native midwestern air. It is all very touching, and tragic, tragic. I hail you again triumphant. I have not got at the other book yet.[2]

Yours ever
W. D. Howells.

1. *The Magnificent Ambersons* (1918) was the second part of Tarkington's trilogy dealing with Midwestern city life. The other two parts were *The Turmoil* (1915) and *The Midlander* (1923); the trilogy appeared under the title *Growth* in 1927.

2. Apparently Tarkington, who was summering in nearby Kennebunkport, had sent Howells his most recent novel together with another book, not identified. Replying to this letter on 28 August 1919 (MH), Tarkington agreed with Howells' strictures about *The Turmoil* and then continued: "It is strange: we think we are aware of your lessons, taking advantage of what you showed us—and then, suddenly perhaps, we get a cold glimpse of what we have done, and see it smeared with those infernal old stencils! You long ago showed us how ridiculous they are—and we understood—and yet some devil slides them under our hands when we work." Apparently Howells felt that Tarkington had misunderstood his criticism, for he wrote on 4 September 1919 (NjP): "No, no! Bibbs was not a weakness of *yours*, but of *his own*. I knew of such people in my Mid-Western youth, and I liked seeing them again in him."

14 SEPTEMBER 1919, YORK HARBOR, TO MARY R. JEWETT

...York Harbor, Sept. 14, 1919.

Dear Miss Jewett:

Yesterday there came a box of your dear sister's and my dear friend's books, which I suppose came from you. At any rate I will thank you for it from a heart warm with reading in it many places. Just now I was reading to my daughter about that circus, and the lecture to young men,[1] and we were both between laughing and crying. What beautiful work everywhere! Nobody else has come near it.

I hope you will like my choosing for my "American Stories," that delicious sketch *The Courting of Sister Wisby*.[2] It has been hard to choose, and as a story this is slighter than some others, but the study of the supposed teller of it is all but incomparable—that dearest and sweetest old mullen-gatherer.

Sometime when you have time and can copy my letter to your sister suggesting the kind of work she should best do for the *Atlantic*, I should be very grateful for it.[3]

My daughter joins me in love. It was such a rare pleasure to see you.

Yours sincerely
W. D. Howells.

P. S. I shall have my say about your sister in my introduction to the book of stories.[4]

1. The circus and the lecture are in Sarah Orne Jewett's "The Circus at Denby," a double sketch of a New England "caravan" and a free lecture to young men—with no males whatsover in the audience. It is part of *Deephaven* (1877).

2. Mary Jewett approved Howells' choice for his anthology *The Great Modern American Stories*.

3. Howells' editorial letter to Jewett seems not to have survived; it may be the letter in which he refused her very early story, "Lady Ferry," making a judgment she would not herself accept. See Annie Fields, ed., *Letters of Sarah Orne Jewett* (Boston: Houghton Mifflin, 1911), p. 226. Having received the copy, Howells wrote Mary Jewett on 4 October 1919 (MH), referring to it as "that queer, priggish letter which I wrote your dear sister fifty years ago; but in spite of its queerness and priggishness I am proud of having divined the true bent of her beautiful gift in it, and however superfluously advised her aright."

4. Howells commented on the "beautiful art, the gentle nature-love, and the delicate humor" of Sarah Orne Jewett and characterized "The Courting of Sister Wisby" as a study "richer than a story." See George Arms et al., eds., *Prefaces to Contemporaries* (Gainesville, Fla.: Scholars' Facsimiles & Reprints, 1957), pp. 194–95.

14 SEPTEMBER 1919, YORK HARBOR, TO CHRISTOPHER MORLEY

... York Harbor, Me., Sept. 14, 1919.

Dear Mr. Morley:[1]

I thank you for your very interesting letter. I know nothing of a Columbus edition of the "Rubaiyat" but I am retroactively proud of it.[2] I had not read Omar Khayyam in Columbus, or until I went to live in Cambridge, at about the date of the Columbus edition—or several years earlier.

Yours sincerely
W. D. Howells.

1. Christopher Morley (1890–1957) published more than fifty books of fiction, poetry, and travel and was a noted bibliomaniac.

2. The "Columbus edition" was the *Rubaiyat of Omar Khayyam, The Astronomer-Poet of Persia, Rendered into English Verse* (Columbus, Ohio: Richard Nevins, 1870). This was in fact the "Second Edition," as claimed. See A. G. Potter, *A Bibliography of the Rubaiyat of Omar Khayyam* (London: Ingpen and Grant, 1929).

3 OCTOBER 1919, KITTERY POINT, TO LILIAN W. ALDRICH

. . . Kittery Point, Me., Oct. 3, 1919.

Dear Mrs. Aldrich:

Pilla told me of the generous leave you gave me to "use anything" of Aldrich's in my collection of *Favorite American Stories,* but I should like your specific permission to include "Marjorie Daw"—publishers do like so to make a row if they think you are hooking any of their stuff. Will you give me your written authority?[1]

You see I want Aldrich's most precious jewel, for I wish to write something characterizing the quite new kind of thing he did in that story; I mean in my introduction.

I hope to get on to see you while I am here, which will be for 8 or 10 days yet. We closed up at York Harbor on Tuesday.

Yours sincerely
W. D. Howells.

I am an awful old dodderer and get about with great pains if not expense.

1. Ferris Greenslet of Houghton Mifflin refused Howells permission to reprint "Marjorie Daw" in *The Great Modern American Stories* because the Aldrich story was "one of our most choicely guarded pieces of literary property" and because granting permission to Boni & Liveright might set a costly precedent. See Greenslet to Howells, 14 October 1919 (MH). Howells' second choice was "Mademoiselle Olympe Zabriskie," which, as he explained in the preface, "I reproduce here, not as the better but the best his publishers can allow his latest editor who was his earliest." He hoped some time to tell of his relation to Aldrich "as a most favored and desired contributor with the young under-editor, and all our joyous lunching and joking . . . ." See George Arms et al., eds., *Prefaces to Contemporaries* (Gainesville, Fla.: Scholars' Facsimiles & Reprints, 1957), pp. 195–96.

12 OCTOBER 1919, KITTERY POINT, TO WEBB C. HAYES

...Kittery Point, Maine October 12, 1919.

Dear Colonel Hayes:

When I shall presently have burnt the MS. of my "Week in the White House," that will be the end of it, for I shall not touch the subject again, though I feel all the generosity of your offer to help me retrieve what seem to you its injurious shortcomings.[1] I had let the matter go too long, and had forgotten much of the history of the time, as a man of eighty-one must. I thank you for keeping me from wronging, as you feel it, even the lightest facts in my recollections of one of the purest and noblest men who ever lived. It is very touching to learn of his purpose of honoring me with the public appointment he had in mind for me, and I duly value that memorandum which you have sent me from his diary.[2]

You may be sure that I remember the pleasant beginning of our acquaintance in Cambridge, and I shall be glad of the meetings which I hope are to come.

I am here for a few days since closing our house at York Harbor, but tomorrow I go with my daughter to Boston, and then New York, and South for the winter.

Yours sincerely
W. D. Howells.

1. After having received Duneka's negative opinion of "A Week in the White House" (see Howells to Duneka, 14 August 1918, n. 6), Howells sent the manuscript to Webb Hayes together with a letter of 23 August 1919 (OFH). He explained that Rutherford Platt, a nephew of the former president, may have disapproved because Howells reported in his essay that the president had responded to Elinor's assurance "Well, you'll soon be out of it," with "Yes, out of a scrape, out of a scrape." But the "political references," "inaccuracies," and lack of "personal touch" in Howells' paper dismayed Webb Hayes, and on 7 October 1919 (OFH) he offered Howells specific criticism and materials for rewriting the reminiscence. So, between Duneka's prediction of the public's lack of interest in the subject and Webb Hayes's dissatisfaction, Howells destroyed the paper, a fact confirmed by Mildred Howells in *Life in Letters*, II, 391.

2. The memorandum copied for Howells read simply "Wm D. Howells Minister to" without specifying the country, and named Governor E. F. Noyes to France, and General James F. Comly to the Sandwich Islands. Presumably Hayes intended to appoint Howells minister to Switzerland, Germany, or Russia. Webb Hayes refers to the three men as his father's "dearest friends," whom he wished to appoint to diplomatic missions. But Howells may well have discouraged any such proposal for himself because he did not wish to endanger his father's consular appointments. See Rutherford B. Hayes Diary, volume 13, May 1876–February 1878 (OFH); W. C. Hayes to Howells, 7 October 1919 (OFH); *Twain-Howells*, p. 371; and Howells to Rogers, 7 April 1877, n. 3.

Hotel Bellevue
Boston Oct. 16, 1919.

My dear Garland:

I am waiting hopefully for *The Return of the Private*; and I wish you could send me some best story of Stephen Crane's, who ought to be in my book for the honor of it, and for our old time's sake.[1]

My affection to your family.

Yours ever
W. D. Howells.

1. No story by Crane appeared in *The Great Modern American Stories*. Garland's early enthusiasm for Crane had long before waned, and he may simply have passed over Howells' request. See Donald Pizer, "The Garland-Crane Relationship," *Huntington Library Quarterly* 24 (1960), 75–82; and James B. Stronks, "Garland's Private View of Crane in 1898 . . . ," *American Literary Realism* 6 (1973), 249–50.

Hotel Bellevue
Boston Oct. 30, 1919.

Dear Judge Grant:[1]

We had, for me, a delightful "visit," as the country folks say, yesterday; but why did you leave this terrible tooth-breaking book with me? I tried to bite into it at many places, and I have scarcely a bicuspid or grinder left in either jaw. Did the Education of H. A. begin or end with this awful study of old French?[2] All the same I thank you for your call.

Yours sincerely
W. D. Howells.

1. Howells knew Robert Grant chiefly as a Bostonian and fellow novelist. See Howells to Munro, 13 April 1909, n. 4; and Howells to Moody, 28 May 1900, n. 2.

2. Howells is here referring to Henry Adams, *Mont St.-Michel and Chartres* (privately printed 1904; published 1913), in which the author quotes and translates long passages of thirteenth-century French poetry. Earlier that year, in the "Editor's Easy Chair," *Harper's Monthly*, February 1919, Howells had written about *The Education of Henry Adams* (1906; 1918), contrasting Adams' education with W. H. Hudson's youth on the pampas of Argentina, in *Far Away and Long Ago* (1918).

1 NOVEMBER 1919, NEW YORK, TO HARRIET SPRAGUE

> *The Saint Hubert . . .*
> *New York* Nov. 1, 1919.

Dear Mrs. Sprague:[1]

I do not know whether I wrote that criticism of Whitman, or not, and I could not say without seeing it.[2] I do not like Whitman so much as most of his later admirers, but I try to be honest about him. I have written rather often about him, for or against, but I could not tell where or when. I am glad you liked the Garland review;[3] I tried to make it good.

> Yours sincerely
> W. D. Howells.

1. Dr. Neda Westlake, curator of the Rare Book Collection, University of Pennsylvania Library, identifies Harriet Sprague as a collector of Whitman who sold her Whitman materials to the library.

2. When Sprague sent the clipping or copy to Howells for confirmation of his authorship, he replied on 4 November 1919 (PU): "This sounds so very much like me, that I have almost no doubt that I wrote it." Dr. Westlake believes that the Howells essay referred to is the "Editor's Study," *Harper's Monthly*, February 1889, in which Howells had praised *November Boughs* (1888), calling them "innocent as so many sprays of apple blossom." But the authorship of the "Editor's Study" was an open secret, and Howells would most likely have recognized it at once by its format and title, even thirty years later. Sprague may have been collector enough to have found the New York *Saturday Press*, 11 August 1860, review of the third edition of *Leaves of Grass* (1860), "A Hoosier's Opinion of Walt Whitman," reprinted from the Ashtabula *Sentinel*, 18 July 1860. For a brief treatment of the Howells-Whitman relationship, see Jean Rivière, "Howells and Whitman after 1881," *Walt Whitman Review* 12 (1966), 97–100. The poem "To Walt Whitman" that Rivière cites is not, however, by W. D. Howells, but by William Hooper Howells. See David J. Nordloh, "A Mistaken W. D. Howells Ascription," *Serif* 11 (1974), 38–39.

3. See Howells to Garland, 22 July 1917, n. 1.

17 NOVEMBER 1919, NEW YORK, TO HENRY B. FULLER

> *The Saint Hubert . . .*
> *New York* Nov. 17, 1919.

My dear Fuller:

I have mislaid your last letter, and I have forgotten which story of yours I liked best among those you mentioned. Was it the last, with rather a long title, somewhat fantastic? If so, wont you send it me at Three Oaks, Augusta The Hill, Georgia.[1]

Yours ever
W. D. Howells.

Garland was here yesterday with his two fine girls.[2] The oldest is to do Iphigeneia in a school tragedy, Gilbert Murrays rhymed version. The youngest is charming, and chockfull of sense. Mrs. G. was not well. Garland has got well on his feet again, with no rheumatism in 'em. A good soul as ever lived.

1. At the end of this letter, Fuller noted: "On Nov. 20th sent to Georgia, vol. of 'Waldo Trench' and Memo. of 5 uncollected Stories." This is confirmed by Fuller's letter to Howells, 20 November 1919 (MH). Howells finally chose "Striking an Advantage" for inclusion in *The Great Modern American Stories*; he thanked Fuller on 5 December 1919 (MH), telling him that he would be in the "best collection of American stories ever made—that is the best in the world." Fuller's *Waldo Trench and Others* was published in 1908.

2. Constance and Isabel Garland.

22 JANUARY 1920, SAVANNAH, GEORGIA, TO THOMAS S. PERRY

De Soto Hotel
Savannah, Ga. . . . Jan'y 22, 1920

Dear Perry:

I can hazard a better guess than Phelps's why James should have "appealed to Englishmen rather than his own countrymen" in the case given.[1] His own countrymen never treated him decently in any case, and he had no reason to trust them. Never was a great writer so vulgarly hooted at and rejected by his own people. Some time I may blow out about it all.[2] By the way when does the leisurely Lubbock's life appear, if ever?[3]

I am sorry Mrs. Perry is so much better that she will not come to Augusta, for we may ultimately return there in the interest of my Nachkur,[4] and I could show you both about with a backache in every step.

Yours aff'tely
W. D. Howells.

1. Howells enclosed a clipping of William L. Phelps's review, dated "Yale University, New Year's Day, 1920," of a posthumous collection of early James stories, *A*

Landscape Painter (1919). The editor, Albert Mordell, as quoted by Phelps, believed it "strange that James should have chosen to appeal to English readers rather than to his own countrymen." Phelps explained the anomaly by arguing that American readers strongly preferred "cheerful terminations" and therefore disliked the tragic endings of all four stories.

2. Howells may already have begun his review of Percy Lubbock's *The Letters of Henry James* (2 volumes, 1920) and his essay, "The American Henry James," the last things he wrote. They appear in *Life in Letters*, II, 394–99.

3. Lubbock wrote no life of James; but James was the chief figure and exemplar in his *The Craft of Fiction* (1921).

4. German for "convalescence." Howells had torn a ligament in his back in late November or early December, as he wrote Perry on 30 December 1919 (MeWC): "I have been a whole month in bed, practically helpless, and am just today out of the hospital here, from an attempt to turn my chair under me."

22 JANUARY 1920, SAVANNAH, GEORGIA, TO HAMLIN GARLAND

De Soto Hotel
Savannah, Ga. . . . January 22, 1920

My dear Garland:

I wish you were coming here instead of Columbia which will be still six hours short of us. We are full of the most lovable weather, and can hardly keep from planting peas.

Poor Matthews! He merits all his pain if he will not have your doctor set him prancing as he has set you. I wish he could get at my back, which has been a month in bed with me. You know I had ruptured ligament?

What gayeties you tell me of! I have just got my dear **Don Quixote** copy ready and am going at the introduction.[1]

I have a two year old story on hand, but I doubt if it will ever grow up. It lives at St. Augustine, and I call it The Home Towners.[2]

I'm glad you are full of work, and that the editors want it out of you. Love to your dear girls.

Yours ever
W. D. Howells.

1. See Howells to Perry, 10 February 1919, n. 4.
2. See Howells to Mildred Howells, 31 October 1915, n. 1.

22 MARCH 1920, SAVANNAH, GEORGIA, TO MAXWELL E. PERKINS

...The De Soto
Savannah, Georgia March 22, 1920.

Dear Mr. Perkins:[1]

I am returning the Don Quixote cut to the quick. If you require a closer shave, I must beg you to employ a more ruthless hand.[2] I can always write an introduction which will suppose an untouched masterpiece, which indeed I would have left intact except for the omission of The Curious Impertinent.[3]

I hope none of you will be disappointed in my essay—above all Mr. Burlingame and Mr. Brownell, who you say hope to like it.[4]

I have done my best for you.

Yours sincerely
W. D. Howells.

The second cutting is that shown by the wavering lines.—I am still mostly in bed—all but two or three hours a day.

1. Maxwell E. Perkins (1884–1947) was an editor at Scribner's, who later became famous for his patience, his sensibility, and his candid advice to F. Scott Fitzgerald, Ernest Hemingway, Thomas Wolfe, and others.
2. In January, Howells had already returned his abridged version of *Don Quixote* to Perkins, who at first thought the cuts were satisfactory but later requested additional cuts so that the two-volume edition would total 190,000 words. See Perkins to Howells, 28 January and 17 March 1920 (copies at NjP).
3. A novel within the novel, in part 1, book 4, chapters 6, 7, and most of 8.
4. E. L. Burlingame and William Crary Brownell were editors with Scribner's. See also Howells to Perry, 10 February 1919, n. 4.

20 APRIL 1920, NEW YORK, TO EDWIN MARKHAM

The Saint Hubert...
New York April 20, 1920.

My very dear friend:

Till now I have felt it impossible, to write at all since I came to these two last weeks of my four months of bedridden helplessness from influenza, but I must, I *must*, try to tell you how deeply your words and your book have touched me.[1] I thank, I thank you, I thank you, I thank you. I wish there were words besides these hard little dry words; but such as they are, here they are. I thank and bless you. I shall read your book and love it, and then try to praise it aright.

In all affection,

Yours ever
W. D. Howells.

1. Markham's *Gates of Paradise* (1920) contains these dedicatory words: "I venture—with equal admiration and affection—to dedicate this my latest volume of verse to that lover of justice and brotherhood who has had the courage to take unprofitable risks—to that writer who wears the greatest honour and bears the greatest name in our contemporary letters—to William Dean Howells." This is Howells' last letter: he died on 11 May 1920.

Eighty Years and After

All my life I have been afraid of death. I think the like is true of every one, and I think it is also true that now, when old and nearer death, in the order of life, than ever before, I am less afraid of dying than when I was young and naturally far from it. I believe this again is true of all men, but it may not be at all true of others. Perhaps in age, as in sickness, when the vital forces are lowered we lose something of that universal and perpetual dread, until as observation if not experience teaches, we survive it altogether and make the good end common to the dying.

Apparently the fear of death does not always mount with the loss of faith in a life hereafter, but sometimes the contrary. Until I was thirty-five years old I had no question but if I died I should live again; yet the swift loss of that faith, through the almost universal lapse of it in the prevailing agnosticism of the eighteen-seventies and eighties, was a relief from that fear. I had hitherto felt that being a sinner, as I did not doubt I was, I should suffer for my sins after death; yet, now that the fear of hell was effectively gone, a certain stress was lifted from me which had weighed upon my soul. When I was a well-grown boy I used to pray before I slept at night that I might not die before morning and that I might not go to hell, but neither of my petitions had been inspired by the wise and kind doctrine of Swedenborg which I had been taught from my earliest years, and so I must suppose that my terror was a remnant of the ancestral, the anthropoidal fear which once possessed all human life.

In age, in youth, most people believe in God because they cannot deny the existence of a cause of things. The universe did not happen of itself though we may, in middle life, say so sometimes. Even then I felt that there was a Creator of Heaven and Earth, but I had not the sense of a Father in Heaven, though I prayed to Him every night, by that name. I had not the sense of loving him, though I feared him because I knew myself a wrong-doer in my thoughts and deeds, and imagined him a just judge. The fear of his judgment has passed from me more and more as I have grown older; but at no time have I thought irreverently of him or spoken so of him. Still I have not affectionately prayed to him outside of the scriptural words. I have not praised him in the terms of flattery which must, if he is the divine consciousness we imagine him, make him sick at heart. I do not say this is the case with other old men, but I note it in my own case with whatever humility the utmost piety would have.

My fear of him has not grown upon me; neither do I think it has lessened, as it seems to me my fear of death has. There is apparently no reason for this diminishing dread, and I do not account for it as a universal experience. There seems to be a shrinkage of the emotions as of the forces from youth to age. When we are young life fills us full to the verge of being, and leaves us no vantage-point from which we have any perspective of ourselves. For instance I cannot recall inquiring what I was at twenty, thirty, forty, fifty, and hardly at sixty, as I am now inquiring what I am at eighty-two, though I have always been keenly interested in the analysis of life and character. But experience grows with age, and the study of it may be the last stage of introspection, though hardly, I should say, could it prevail till ninety or after.

The greatest and most dramatic shrinkage of consciousness is of course that which follows from the cooling of the passions, and is something apparently quite physical. Love at its best means marriage, and is altogether the most beautiful thing in life. It is never self-consciously ridiculous, though often ridiculous enough to the witness. Its perversion is the ugliest thing in life and the shamefullest, but for a day, for an hour of its bliss, one would give all one's other years; yet it does not escape the imperfection which mars everything. The best of existence, the home and the children, proceed from it; without it there can be no death and the rending of the dearest ties and the anguish of grief come from love too; the grave as well as the home awaits it.

There are faults which age redeems us from, and there are virtues which turn to vices with the lapse of years. The worst of these is thrift, which in early and middle life it is wisdom and duty to practice for a provision against destitution. As time goes on this virtue is apt to turn into the ugliest, cruellest, shabbiest of the vices. Then the victim of it finds himself hoarding past all probable need of saving for himself or those next him, to the deprivation of the remoter kindred of the race. In the earlier time when gain was symbolized by gold or silver the miser had a sensual joy in the touch of his riches, in hearing the coins clink in their fall through his fingers, and in gloating upon their increase sensible to the hand and eye. Then the miser had his place among the great figures of misdoing; he was of a dramatic effect, like a murderer or a robber; and something of this bad distinction clung to him even when his specie had changed to paper currency, the clean white notes of the only English bank, or the greenbacks of our innumerable banks of issue; but when the sense of riches had been transmuted to the balance in his favor at his banker's, or the bonds in his drawer at the safety-deposit vault, all splendor had gone out of his vice. His bad eminence was gone, but he clung to the lust of gain which had ranked him with the picturesque or histrionic wrong-doers, and which only ruin from without could save him from, unless he gave his remnant of strength to saving himself from it. Most aging men are sensible of all this, but few have the frankness of that aging man who once said that he who died rich died disgraced, and died the other day in the comparative penury of fifty millions.

Few old men have the strength to save themselves from their faults, perhaps because they have no longer the resilience of youth in any sort. It would be interesting to know when this ceases in mind or body; but without calling other dotards to witness I will record that physically it had ceased in me half way through my seventies, as I once found when I jumped from a carriage at the suggestion of the young driver who said he did not like the way the horse was acting. I myself saw nothing wrong in the horse's behavior, but I reasoned that a driver so young must know better, and I struck the ground with the resilience of an iron casting of the same weight.

Yet any time within the seventies I should say that one still felt young in body if not in mind; after that, one feels young oftenest in spirit; a beautiful morning will go far to find the joy of youth in the octogenarian, as a gloomy sunset will find the pathos of it. I imagine, in fact, that youth lurks about in holes and corners of us as long as we live, but we must not make too free with it. We may go a good long walk in the forenoon, and feel the fresher; but we must not be tempted to another walk in the afternoon, lest the next morning find us fully as old as we are. Exercise is not for age unless it is the carriage-exercise which used to be prescribed by the physicians of the rich; certainly not motor-exercise, which is almost as bad as walking-exercise. A stick helps out, but it will not do so much as it promises on an uphill way. In the summer, for instance, I live in a valley with the sea at either end of it, and I can traverse the intervening meadows with refreshment or at least without exhaustion; but in front there has grown up since I was seventy a hill which was not there before and is as surprising as the effect of some recent volcanic upheaval. When I begin to climb this strange acclivity I find my stick a very lively leg, but as I mount, it falters and goes lame; and before I reach the top I think I should almost be better without it. Before a certain time in my later seventies I was a quite indefatigable pedestrian, but one night, coming out of a theatre in Boston, I boldly crossed the Common towards my hotel on Beacon Hill till it began to rise under me. There I began to sink under it, and before I reached the top I despaired in a deadly fatigue which was probably in part the effect of sitting unmoved through several hours in the theatre. I should like to warn all octogenarians to beware of resting too much; there is such a thing as that and it is a very serious thing.

After sixty one must not take too many chances with one's self; but I should say that the golden age of man is between fifty and sixty, when one may safely take them. One has peace then from the different passions; if one has been tolerably industrious one is tolerably prosperous; one has fairly learned one's trade or has mastered one's art; age seems as far off as youth; one is not so much afraid of death as earlier; one likes joking as much as ever, and loves beauty and truth as much; family cares are well out of the way; if one has married timely one no longer nightly walks the floor with even the youngest child; the marriage ring is then a circle half rounded in eternity. It is a blessed time; it is indeed the golden age, and no age after it is more than silvern. The best age after it may be that between eighty and ninety, but one cannot make so sure of ninety as of seventy in the procession of the years, and that is where the gold turns silver. But silver is one of the precious metals, too, and it need not have any alloy of the baser ores. I do not say how it will be in the years between ninety and a hundred; I am not yet confronted with that question. Still all is not gold between eighty and ninety as it is between fifty and sixty. In that time, if one has made oneself wanted in the world, one is still wanted; but between eighty and ninety, if one may still be wanted, is one wanted as much as ever? It is a painful question, but one must not shirk it, and in trying for the answer one must not do less than one's utmost, at a time when one's utmost will cost more effort than before. This is a disadvantage of living so long, but we cannot change the conditioning if we wish to live.

There is always the question whether one does wish to live, but for the averagely happy or unhappy man, I should say yes, yes, yes. We could ignore the fact that there are some men so unhappy beyond the vast average that they cannot wish to live. These kill themselves, but speaking without the statistics I do not believe these are often people of eighty and after. Apparently life is seldom so unbearable with these that one almost never hears of their suicide.

The young mostly think the old are subjectively dull because they seem objectively dull, but they may often seem so because youth, not life, is uninteresting. I have known only one octogenarian who was not interested in any phase of life, who no longer cared to hear or tell of a new thing, who turned from books as jadedly as from men. This might have been because he had known the best of both to satiety. If one is of the reading habit as this sad sage was of, one has, by eighty and after, read most of the best books. In my own case, though, I have not been a measureless consumer of literature; I have devoured so much of it that every now and then when I propose myself some novelty, I cannot find the desired freshness in books which I have read only two or three times before, or even never before. Yet, not counting the latest poetry and fiction, I have ignored many of the things which most people have read—some very signal things, in fact. I have been rather fond of reading things many times over; they do not tire: certain passages of Shakespeare which I got by heart when I was a boy—say Henry V's heartless snub of Falstaff when the new King must cast his joke-fellow off, or things out of Macbeth, or Othello. Tennyson does not bear re-reading like Keats, though long as much my favorite; and Heine does not, though he was once my greatest favorite. Yet within my eighty-second year I have read *Don Quixote* with as much zest as in my twelfth year; and the other day I read Milton's "Lycidas" with as rich a woe as the first time.

Literature is a universe where we poor planets swim about as if we were each no greater than the Earth which is wellnigh lost in its own little solar system. The question should be of one's continuing interest in public questions, and of one's value in treating of them. If I were boasting here of senility or its signal usefulness I would allege that of the octogenarian who seems to me the first of those publicists among us in addressing the sense and conscience of his countrymen since the German war upon mankind began.

The attitude of amaze in comparative youth at mere superannuation is one of the hardest things which the old have to bear from their juniors, far harder than the insult of Hamlet's mockery of Polonius. Every old man knows the truth about physical age, and it can only hurt him the more to be told that he is looking better than ever, to be forced to smirk in the acceptance or refusal of the false homage offered his years in the effort to discount them for him. Let us alone, I say, and we can bear our burden; do not add the weight of your gross kindness to it. We know that we have wonderful alleviations and even advantages; we are at least not dead, and there we are at least equal with younger men, for at the end of the ends no grade of juniority can claim more.

I have met many old people and I am glad that when I was younger I did not wish to praise their youthfulness or exalt their abounding health and vigor. When I once sat next to Emerson and heard him asking his other next hand neighbor who I was when I had just told him who that neighbor was, I did not praise his wonderful memory. I must have been saved by somehow realizing that time would do all the needful remembering of him and eternity for him. Loss of memory is almost the first infirmity of noble minds and I am proud to recall that when I was little more than thirty I clung to the hand of a fellow-citizen and tried for his familiar name, a name as idle as could well be. I had it as soon as our backs were turned, and I have never since lost it, or been

the richer for it. I was young then, but when I was really beginning to
be old I found myself at Rome, in returning to the use of my earlier
Italian, often failing of a word before I realized that I had first failed
of the English of it. Now I wander in a whirl of lost words which I can
find only by first defining their uses to myself. Then the name wonderfully appears and I keep it a longer or shorter time; but meanwhile I
have suffered. The worst case of forgetfulness that I remember was the
name of a tree, that tree which looks an evergreen but is really deciduous,
the ——— There it is gone again! No, I have it! *Larch, larch, larch!* How
could I have forgotten it? It never was *serge*, at all! Tolstoy says that
remembering is hell, and nothing can be more terrible than remembering everything, as those newly arrived spirits do in the life to come,
when their inner memories are explored for the things which have
been dropped into their outer memories and comfortably forgotten. But
if it is a blessing to forget, what a torment it is to fail of the thing we
want to remember!

Titian outlived his ninety-nine years and kept on painting almost to
the last. I have not found any critic to say how well he continued to
paint, though I daresay there is more than one such critic. I can well
believe that he wrought as greatly then from his exhaustless soul as in
his prime. At ninety-nine he was working hard at Venice, in the intimacy
of another Venetian master, the great sculptor and architect Sansovino, who was, however, only ninety-three. I used to view his Renais-
sance work with as great pleasure as my subservience to Ruskin's Gothic
tyranny would let me, but I did not try to distinguish the later work in
it from the earlier, and I cannot say from my personal knowledge that
his mastery held out to the last. It is only now that from the Encyclo-
pedia Britannica I have learned that "his masterpiece, the bronze doors
of the sacristy in St. Mark's," was done when he was eighty-five, and
that at eighty-eight "he completed a small bronze gate with a graceful
relief of Christ surrounded by angels." Titian and he lived in great
jollity together, and were of a gaiety which is rather characteristic of the
old, though their younger friends are apt to think otherwise. Sansovino
was not of his friend's unfailing health, but he knew how to ward off
an attack in his latest years, when Vasari tells us "he retired to a dark,
warm place," and remained there till perfectly restored. It seems worth
trying.

As old as Titian when he died was the great Admiral Andrea Doria,
who refused a crown from Genoa and kept her a republic after he saved
her from her enemies by his victories; but I do not know when he won
his last battle any more than I know when Titian painted his last
masterpiece. The Doge Enrico Dandolo was a blind nonagenarian when

he led his Venetians to the assault of the Byzantine walls, but his exact age is something the reader must learn from history.

The most distinguished American nonagenarian whom I have personally known was our eminent citizen, John Bigelow, and I recall with lasting pleasure hearing him give in the Century Theater at New York his recollection of an interview, fifty years earlier, with Alexander Dumas—a charming characterization of the mighty mulatto, done with delicate humor and friendly criticism and delivered with unfaltering force and grace.

There is a common superstition of old people's severity, and even surliness, which I should here like to combat, for I have oftenest found age kind and sweet. I have not known so many nonagenarians as to have lost count of any, and I recall one dear lady whom I first saw when I was still twenty-nine and met a second time when I was thirty and she ninety-seven. "You remember Mr. H., mother?" her daughter suggested. "Yes," she chirped in answer, "but he won't remember *me*." Think of one's not remembering a lady of ninety-seven! After an interval of more than half a century, I met my second nonagenarian, who was indeed only ninety-five, but who came tripping downstairs to greet me in his parlor like a light-footed youth of thirty-five and who said, as if to excuse his delay, that his wife was not very well, though only ninety. Soon afterward she died and then he died too; but that day he was as much alive as need be. His face showed few marks of age, though his eyes, which were bright, were narrowed to little more than a fine gleam. It was in Cambridge and of course we talked books with the back-thought in my own mind that I must not tire him. Will the reader believe that before I was aware I *did* tire him? I am so fond of talking books! I shall always be ashamed of that inadvertence, though I almost rushed away. At seventy-three I could still rush a little.

Once in Boston, long before that, I lunched with a brave gentleman of ninety-four who was still in the office-practice of the law, and went to his office every day. He did not brag of this, but his son did in a proud aside to me. As to octogenarians there is simply no end to them; they swarm, they get in one's way. I recall notably the first I met on my way to Europe. I had left my father at home in his eighty-eighth year; he had always been alive and I did not think his age strange; but my fellow-voyager had perhaps never been very much alive, and I observed him with question whether people were usually so dull at eighty. Now I do not think they usually are; they seem rather a sprightly generation, and rightly resentful of the sympathy of people who regard them as infirm and in the need of being told that they are looking wonderfully well, and younger than ever. So, perhaps, they are; but why rub it in?

When I met this octogenarian I am speaking of I was making the first of five or six successive transatlantic voyages in ten or twelve years—after remaining homebound for nigh twenty years; now I hope, as soon as the terms of universal peace are fixed, to begin going to Europe again. "I cannot rest from travel," as Ulysses says in the words of Tennyson. It involves some risks; but is not it the only escape from death, for the time being? Yet if you wish to escape promptly you must not delay beginning to go, or it will cost you a certain suffering. When I began to go, between my sixties and seventies, I loathed the terms of perpetuity presented in the run from the country to the city, where I was to sail, with the railroad ticketing and checking, and then the transferring of baggage to the steamer: I saw the whole loathly perspective from the starting-point; and yet I knew that England was my goal; and now I know, if I did not then, that English travel is pure joy. There is no other travel like it, though American travel is a little like it in its unhampered movement. As for the continent—France, Germany, Italy—it is purgatory which you plunge into or out of in the going to or from that heaven of English travel; in this you begin to rest from the moment you begin to move.

Among the things that the octogenarian must guard against is that solitude which is liable to grow upon him through the fault of other octogenarians. I do not know that they are apt to die out of proportion to other mortals; but certainly they seem to die more noticeably and to leave their contemporaries lonelier than people who have not lived so long. Perhaps this is an effect of the stir which is made about their dying at such an advanced age—as if having lived so long they ought to have lived longer. But I cannot say what is to be done about it, if anything; the solitude is inevitable; and yet, I cannot pretend that I miss other old people much. This is possibly because we octogenarians are not so much in the habit of seeing one another as septuagenarians and sexagenarians are. Perhaps there is a remote feeling of relief when we hear of one another going; we realize that those others were often rather dull company. Still, we are lonelier, till the solitude accumulated upon us ceases to be a conscious fact. I have no remedy to suggest unless it is the rather mechanical device of cultivating the acquaintance of the young. But then the young are often so dull, too, and they cumber one with kindness, more than the old; you do not see *us* helping the old on with their overcoats, or putting them chairs. The best thing would be to be born of a copious generation, with lots of brothers and sisters, and no end of cousins. There is comfort in the next of kin, such as comes from no other propinquity, though there is now and then a pain-ful sense of responsibility for our blood-relations if they are rather fitter for the kingdom of heaven in their pecuniary circumstances than for the best society of a democratic republic. If they are somewhat silly one feels that one would rather have them criminal.

Quite apart from these digressions, and only because his case comes into the chapter of octogenarian loneliness, I wish to speak of a very gentle old man whose acquaintance I made in sharing with him a wayside seat several years ago when we were still within our seventies. We began at once with those intimate topics which strangers enter upon so promptly, and he told me that he had left his farm, and was passing his widower-years in the family of his son, where they were all very kind to him. He casually mentioned that he always went to bed at six o'clock, and when I showed some surprise at this he explained that he did not wish to disturb the wonted course of the family life, or to put his children and grandchildren to the trouble of entertaining him. He seemed to imply that he was less lonely in withdrawing from them, than if he had kept about with them. He sweetly touched upon differences in the young and old which no good will or affection could annul. "But," he added, "there is an old lady coming to visit us, and then I shall keep about. We shall have more to say to each other and be more sociable." I ventured to ask how old this lady was, and he said sixty; he did not seem to think the space between this and his eightieth year any great matter. In fact, upon reflection I could not feel it so, either, considering how far the sympathy of women can go in bridging such intervals.

I recall that when I was a very small boy—small, but of fixed opinions— I unspeakably preferred old ladies to old men, as I saw them about our house in the character of guests, for the day or the dinner. They were mostly of Quakerly guise and cult, apparently, but the one old gentleman who visited us was of our small sect and perhaps came for the comfort of the little-friended doctrine which we shared with him. He must have stayed overnight, for I have still the vision of his movable teeth in the tumbler of water where he kept them while he slept, and where they remained while he scraped a sweet apple for luncheon before the noonday dinner. He was somehow dreadful to me for these facts, and I contrasted him in my mind with those old ladies, to their infinite advantage.

I have carried these my preferences through life, and I still regard old ladies as angelic, insomuch that I have never seen one that I did not revere. I do not know when they begin to look old to other eyes, but to mine they never look old as old men look. Very likely some of them may once have been silly, and some naughty, but they do not show it, while all the goodness and wisdom of their youth has grown upon them. I should like to touch here, but barely touch, the thought of the dear and lovely lady which has all this time been in the back of my mind as a supreme proof of the highest praise that could be given to aging woman.

She was of the finest modernity in her love of the best things in literature and life, and could no more err in taste than in truth or the beauty which is one with it. She is gone now, who was so lately here in such perfection of mind and soul that it seems as if she could never have left us who were priviledged to share the bounty of her wisdom and grace.

If I have praised the loveliness of age in women, I must not forget that the most lovable of all the octogenarians I have known was my own father. He died immortally young at eighty-seven, and, until paralysis muted his laugh, was the blithest among us. Yet once he touched a matter that must often weigh upon the hearts of the old. At eighty-two he grieved that he could do nothing to help in his own support, and tried to think of something. I could only remind him that his whole good and useful life had worked for him, and was working still, and I hope this comforted him a little.

There is a matter so personal to people at all times of life that I must not fail to speak of it in the case of people in their eighties, and that is dreaming. It was once held (and may still be held) that dreams are of such instantaneousness that they might be said to take no time at all in their lapse; but if the psychologists no longer contend for this I may say that I have spent a large part of my life in the conscious cerebration of sleep. There have been nights of mine almost as busy as my days in even more varied experiences, among persons from the other world as well as this; and it is so yet, but I think that I do not dream so much as formerly, though less than a week before this writing I dreamed of occurrences where my father and mother, dead for near twenty and fifty years, figured no more nor less lovingly than certain entire strangers.

A few paragraphs back I treated of failing memory, especially in the reluctance of this or that word to come when we wanted it, though it was ready enough when not wanted; and now I should like to inquire of other old men whether they were equally forgetful in other matters. Of course we all forget where we have put things and are astounded to find them in places where we would like to be sworn we never put them. I have not happened to see dotards of my acquaintance going about crowned with the spectacles which they were ransacking the house for and almost cursing and swearing in their failure to find, though I have heard of them often; and I have myself wandered in parallel oblivion till I had to abandon the search in despair. Yet if I have been charged by myself or others with duties, I never forget them; and I should like to think that no fellow-dotard of mine has failed in the like point. I should like to know also whether women who increase in years, but who age no more than the angels, are equally subject to forgetfulness with old men. Do they so infallibly fail of the word they want? Let no trifler enter here with "a fool-born jest" to the effect that this would be impossible in the nature of things. I have indeed seen some of them carry their lost spectacles on top of their caps; but I doubt if they ever forget the burden of their errands, for otherwise how should they so confidently charge us men with them, and so justly inculpate us if we fail in them?

In the rashness which I have never paid dearly enough for yet I am here, at the end of my sheet, as the old time letter-writer used to say, tempted to hold that the first failure of memory to give us the name of the person who has lost it, is the first token of death, the first falling leaf of autumn, the first flake of the winter's snow. But who knows? Whence is death, and out of what awful void or whither? All along the line of living, from the moment of birth when we first catch our breath and cry out in terror of life, death has set his signals, beckoning us the way which we must go. Kind Science knows them but will not let us believe they are what they are, and Nature laughs them to scorn, because she is our fond mother. "Oh, that is nothing, is it, Science?" she cries at our alarm, and Science echoes, "Nothing at all, Nature; or if it is anything it is proof of superabounding vigor, of idiosyncratic vitality." Very likely; but quite the same, all the men born of women must die in a destined course; every man of eighty and after must die as certainly as the newborn babe, or often sooner, or if not, certainly in the event. It will not avail against the fact whether we pray and praise, or whether we eat and drink; the merciless morrow is coming. But why call it merciless? No one knows whether it is merciless or not. We know that somewhere there is love, the love that welcomed us here, the love that draws us together in our pairing that our children may live, the love in our children which shall see that their fathers and mothers do not die before their time even if their time shall be delayed till eighty and after.

Appendix

THE letters selected for inclusion in this appendix are part of the Fréchette Collection in the Alfred University Library, Alfred, New York. The editors of these volumes learned of the existence of close to one hundred Howells letters in that collection too late to include any of them in their proper chronological context in the preceding volumes. The fourteen letters selected for this appendix (in addition to three letters from the Fréchette Collection added to the first part of this volume) have been annotated sufficiently to establish connections with earlier letters and footnotes. We are grateful for receiving permission to print these letters and thereby bring this publication project as up to date as is possible in an ongoing process of discovering letters and documents that shed light on the life and career of William Dean Howells.

10 JANUARY 1856, JEFFERSON, TO WILLIAM C. HOWELLS

Home, Jan'y 10, 1856.

Dear Father—
Your letter came to hand this morning; and found me, with the last packages of the mail done-up, ruefully contemplating some dozen columns of governor's message, and wondering how it was all to be got in. I am glad you wish me to make a synopsis of it. I think one *can* be made in very little space; and I shall try to prepare such an one.[1]

I have not yet got Spooner's address, but will say all about it you could ask when it comes.[2] In passing, I think we have a good letter from you in the Sentinel;[3] and I dare say the paper will be greatly benefitted by letters the capitol this winter. It will give eclat to it, and interest readers more than mere sketchy telegrams.

I am doing all I can in the way of getting up a good paper for next week; but I dread to *spread* myself much, lest I should be found like Peirce, "awful thin."[4] Do not take the barrenness of this week's "issoo" badly, for I have been up so many nights hand-reeming that I can almost do without sleep; and acting as *assistant-engine* on both sides of the paper, I had not a fair chance, editorially.

There is a pretty big hole, father, in the house and hearts that you have left; but we are all very proud of your success, and do not let ourselves think we feel badly because you are away.

Do not fear but Joe and I will get along well; and remember me to les bons hommes, Harris and Lawrence,

Your affectionate son
Will.

1. Governor William Medill's message to the opening session of the Ohio legislature, delivered on 7 January, appeared in the Ashtabula *Sentinel*, 17 January, with the following introduction: "THE GOVERNOR'S MESSAGE Whose 'slow length' would fill a dozen columns of the *Sentinel*, we herewith place before the reader in as few words as may be, keeping the spirit, while we sometimes throw away the letter of the text."

2. Thomas Spooner's address to the state convention of the American party was a ringing endorsement of the antislavery position; it was reprinted under the heading, "ADDRESS OF PRESIDENT SPOONER, Office of the President, State Council of Ohio, Cincinnati, Jan. 3, 1856," in the *Sentinel* of 24 January. Spooner was elected as delegate to the national party convention in Philadelphia.

3. The *Sentinel* of 10 January has two items in the column, "Letters from the Capitol": one is dated "Columbus, Jan. 7" and the other "8 p.m. Jan. 7." Signed "W.C.H.," they give an account of the opening session of the legislature and comment on the state convention of the American party.

4. A reference to President Franklin Pierce, then in his last year of office. His State of the Union address appeared on the front page of the *Sentinel* on 10 January. As active Republicans, the Howells family would make disparaging remarks about a Democrat who had endeared himself to Southerners by supporting the Compromise of 1850.

14 JANUARY 1861, COLUMBUS, TO AURELIA H. HOWELLS

Columbus, Jan. 14, 1861

Dear Aurelia—

Father and I have been somewhat uneasy at not hearing from home since he came to Columbus, but quiet ourselves with the belief that all is well, or we should hear quickly enough.

I meant at the time I scratched you that bit of a note, to tell you how proud I was of a sister who could so cleverly review a book as you did "Harrington."[1] Your success surprised me the more, because I do not know that you have read much criticism; you applied correctly the rules of the art, and what has been the result of patient study and labor with me, has been with you inspiration. I am very ambitious for you. I think that our whole family has genius—that you girls particulary have genius. You might all write. Why couldn't you, as well as the Brontës?[2] The first thing is to value yourselves, neither too much nor too little. The latter is to be chiefly regarded. It is not in the Howells nature to value itself too highly. The meek generations before us have taken care of that. But what I would have you be, is truly egotistical. The more a man makes of himself, the more he honors his Creator. The sentiments of egotism and pity are the same. But I wont be metaphysical if I can help.

I hope you will write all the time. Why not attempt a story? Miss Prescott is not older than yourself[3]—I do not fear but either of you girls could do as great things. Learn this lesson from her—to be original. Don't imitate anybody's style. It is not fatal to genius, but it is foolish— it is idle.

I understand all your drawbacks and troubles. But everybody has them. If you choose, you can make them everyone a triumph.

Sometimes I think it is a pity that you cannot see the world, and learn what to esteem and to admire, but perhaps your own instincts are better guides than experience. I have been sorry to see you deceive yourself, for instance, with regard to the anti-slavery people. They are all earnest and brave and true, I believe; but you have endowed the individuals with the grandeur of their cause. The truth is, however, except John Brown Sen'r, Wendall Phillips and one or two others, the aggressive abolition movement, has not produced great minds.[4] You are altogether in error about such people as Redpath and Hinton.[5] They are not great, at all.

I don't mean to lecture you—but I don't write so often and so much that you need object to what I say here. There are many other things to be added, but I haven't time to put them down.

You must write to me constantly. Never mind if I don't answer. I am only practicing an exalted selfishness—but I will answer. Tell me whatever you are doing, either in reading or reading, and when you have a story, or sketch or what not, send it to me.

I am not very well—am in fact threatened with a secondary attack of diphtheria. Give my dear love to all.

Your affectionate brother,
Will.

1. Howells' comments here suggest that the review of William Douglas O'Connor's abolitionist novel, *Harrington* (1860), which appeared in the *Ohio State Journal*, 26 November 1860, was written by Aurelia rather than by Howells. See Howells to W. C. and M. D. Howells, 31 October 1861, n. 5.

2. Charlotte (1816–1855), Emily (1818–1848), and Anne Brontë (1820–1849), English novelists and poets.

3. Actually, Harriet Prescott, born in 1835, was seven years older than Aurelia. By 1861 she had already established her reputation as a successful and popular novelist, which she continued to develop after her marriage in 1865 to Richard S. Spofford.

4. See Howells to W. C. Howells, 6 November 1859.

5. James Redpath (1833–1891), an outspoken abolitionist journalist who had been associated with the New York *Tribune* and the St. Louis *Democrat*, was at this time editor of *Pine and Palm*, a weekly newspaper advocating black emigration. In 1868 he established the Boston lyceum bureau and subsequently Redpath's lecture bureau. For Richard J. Hinton, see Howells to W. C. Howells, 7 September 1861, n. 4.

20 MAY 1864, VENICE, TO WILLIAM C. HOWELLS

Venice, May 20, 1864.

Dear father—

I don't know how to tell you I've got your letter with that news which seems to break my heart.[1] I wish he could have lived till I came home—I'm coming home so soon, now. But his death has made this world less and another more to me, and I do not doubt the goodness of God. As yet I can only speak of him as gone—I cannot realize that he will not meet me with the rest of you. Now we shall never all sit down together at home again—I keep thinking this, but I can't understand it. I pity you who have the bereavement present with you, and I send my dear love to you all. Do not be sad thinking of my grief, but write me very often and tell me of my dear Johnny's last hours, and tell me how poor mother bears this heavy sorrow. I've just got your letter—this to Sam was written yesterday.[2] Good-bye,

Your affectionate son,
Will.

Elinor would write also, but we both feel that it is beyond our power to relieve you;[3] and I cannot hope to express my own grief.

1. Howells' youngest brother, John, had died on 27 April. See also Howells to Anne Howells, 20 June 1864.

2. See Howells to S. D. Howells, 19 May 1864.

3. Following Howells' postscript is a note in Elinor Howells' hand: "My dear Father: / I *must* just write a word to assure you of my sympathy for you all in this great affliction, and especially for my poor mother. My dear husband bears the blow in a truly Christian spirit, but it nearly breaks his heart. He had high hopes for Johnny. Now our one idea is to go home as soon as possible and may God keep the rest till we come! Mr. Howells is going to take this to the post office himself so I must end. / Your affectionate daughter / Elinor".

1 JUNE 1864, VENICE, TO WILLIAM C. HOWELLS

Venice, June 1, 1864.

Dear father—

Your first letter since that saddest one to Elinor, came to-night, bringing a kind of relief, although it could bring me only repetition and confirmation of most sorrowful tidings. I say confirmation, for all this story of my dear brother's sickness and death, has only seemed to me like a wild rumor, which I might reasonably hope to have contradicted. And I think I shall never fully realize our loss, till I go home, and feel the absence which you know now. But I have spoken of this before, and I will not distress you by dwelling more upon it. The relief your letter brought was freedom from a fear that your health or dear mother's would give way. I am glad that you are all so well, though so unhappy. I shall see you again, and soon, I hope; and then I shall take up my share of the common sorrow, which here is a dreadful shadow only.—I feel somehow that I shall thus lighten your regret, in willing to do so.

Yesterday we found a letter of dear Johnny's—the last he ever wrote to me. It was dated at Cleveland in last October, and it told all the poor boy's little hopes and plans. He and Henry Wade were rooming together,[1] and they had learned to fence. Johnny was going to take Latin next term, and he wrote how fond he was of German. The letter is that of a bright-hearted, good boy—and as I read it, the thought of his untimely death gave all its boyish manner and gossip, and even the blunders, a pathos that I cannot speak of. My love for him was mixed with the fondest pride, and I always looked with the greatest eagerness for news of him in the letters from home. They have brought me the last that I shall hear, till my own summons comes, when I hope that we shall not be so far asunder, but that I shall hear him speak of immortal fulfillment of all earthly promise.

Our dear little girl[2] grows in health and beauty every day, and I do wish you could see her now, for it does not seem that she can continue so sweet and gracious. I think if dear mother and the girls had her with them, they might take their hearts from sorrow for a little while, in looking at her face of heavenly goodness. Her features are perfectly proportioned and regular, and she has grave, tender eyes of blue, that gaze with constant surprise on the unfolding mysteries of this world.— We have just had her vaccinated, and she has borne the feverish sickness of vaccination with the utmost amiability—never crying at the touch of the lance, nor being at all peevish with the sores. Her teeth have not begun to come yet, but she breakfasts with us every morning, sitting up at table, and eating bread and milk and strawberries. Everybody—Italians and all—about the palace, calls her Baby, and the servants never pass her without a kiss or a joke. In the street, she is followed by a chorus of "Ah! carina! che bei occ'i! che bella puteja!" ("Ah little dear! what beautiful eyes! what a beautiful girl!")

I am glad to hear that you will try to get poor Sam discharged.—A sick man, he can be of little use to the army, but to you now, he will be of unspeakable comfort. There is good stuff in him, and his rude experiences have brought it out. Poor fellow! how keenly his affectionate heart must feel this sudden stroke!—And you, dear father, you say nothing of yourself, when you speak of the grief of the others. It is like you—dear, dear father! I look so often now at my own child, and wonder—Will she love me with that entire love and honor when she is grown a woman, that I feel for my father, now I am a man? And I scarcely dare to hope so great a thing for my future.

I have often spoken lately of our return home. This will be about Christmas, though circumstances may delay it a little.[3] I feel deeply your kind offer of help, but I think I shall get something to do, without great trouble, and at any rate there is no use lingering here any longer.

I wish you would tell me in your next—your answer to this—some things of Johnny's last hours—what he said and did, and whether he knew he should not get well.—With dear love to all,

Your affectionate son,
Will.

1. Probably the son of Charles H. Wade, a farmer in Ashtabula county, Ohio, and the brother of Decius S. Wade.
2. Winifred Howells was then six months old.
3. The Howellses actually did not return to the United States until July 1865.

1 NOVEMBER 1874, CAMBRIDGE, TO ANNE T. HOWELLS

...The Atlantic Monthly....
Cambridge, Mass. Nov. 1, 1874.

Dear Annie:

I still do not agree with you about the conclusion of your story,[1] because it makes the whole look theatrical and forced, and produces a final huddle of events. However, it is your story and not mine, and having once stated my opinion, I'm quite ready to send it on to the Galaxy. I only want to hear from you on a point on which I am qualified to speak as an editor. I *know* that if Mr. Church[2] gets your MS. with an explanation that you will want to revise parts of it in case of acceptance, *he wont read it.* Editors have far too much material offered them to trouble themselves about unfinished work, and I advise you to write to Mr. Church, on getting this letter of mine, and tell him that it has taken longer than you expected to complete your story, and that you still have some last touches to give it, but that you'll send it soon. I will return your MS., and you can revise it; or if you so decide you can send me a line, and I'll forward it to Church as it is.

My expedition to Newport was partially successful and I came back pretty free of my cold, but I'm very sensitive and sneeze at the slightest provocation. The weather, however, continues wonderfully fine and that's in my favor. How divine the landscape must look from Durham Terrace, this morning! I think you are to be greatly envied your life in so beautiful a place as Quebec. There's more inspiration in it than one realizes at the time. I should like to know what your Quebec story is.[3]—Father's last Sentinel letter was good, and I'm glad he seems to be so much interested in the odd things he sees.[4]—Did his government orders turn out all right?—I return the sketch of the log-cabin—thinking he may want it, with thanks. It's quite the Eureka pattern of a palace.[5]— The play that I translated for the Western actor is a great success, he writes me, and he hints now at an original tragedy from me![6] Vic may yet be all to go on the stage as leading lady in one of my dramas!

Elinor wrote you girls during the week. She joins me in love to all.

Your affectionate brother
Will

1. "Reuben Dale," *Galaxy*, December 1875–April 1876. See Howells to Anne Howells, 21 October 1874.

2. Francis P. or William C. Church, editors of the *Galaxy*.

3. Possibly a reference to Annie's plans for writing "Le Coureur des Bois," *Scribner's*, May 1876, the setting of which is French Canada, but not specifically Quebec. More likely, Annie was already contemplating the story that eventually became "Pauvre Elise." See Howells to W. C. Howells, 31 December 1882, n. 1 (appendix).

4. For W. C. Howells' "Familiar Letters to the Editor," written from the vantage point of the American consul in Quebec, see Howells to W. C. Howells, 18 October 1874, n. 3.

5. Apparently W. C. Howells had sent a picture of a log cabin, which reminded Howells of the cabin at Eureka Mills, Ohio, where the family had lived in 1851. It may have sparked Howells' idea to write an account of that experience in "Year in a Log-Cabin" (1887) and again in *New Leaf Mills* (1913). See *Years of My Youth*, HE, pp. 38–56.

6. For Howells' arrangement with Charles R. Pope for a translation of Ippolito d'Aste's play *Sansone*, see Howells to W. C. Howells, 9 July 1874, n. 4. Pope had written Howells from Little Rock on 20 October 1874 (MH), reporting that the play had been performed fourteen times in Memphis, and requesting "the subject of your projected play."

17 JANUARY 1878, CAMBRIDGE, TO ANNE H. FRÉCHETTE

... *The Atlantic Monthly.* ...
Cambridge, Mass. Jan. 17, 1878.

Dear Annie:

It is a long time since I have written to you, but perhaps for that reason I have thought of you the oftener. That is the way I pay off most of my correspondents: I think of them, and I don't write. Now that we have eaten up the Galaxy,[1] I have such a horrible indigestion of contributions that I don't know what to do; and I have no longer any one to help me with them, or the proofs. In fact I am doing all the editorial work, now; and trying to write a story, and getting out a series of autobiographies besides.[2] So you see that if I were naturally the best correspondent in the world, I couldn't help some sins of omission.—Elinor insists that in your last letter to me (which I've mislaid) you asked some question about sending a contribution somewhere; but I think she must be mistaken. If she was right, and you will let me know how I can be of use, I shall of course be very glad.—We are now very much taken up with the small house we are building on Belmont Hill. It is about two miles and a half from Cambridge, and it commands a most superb view that nothing but the feebleness of the human eye prevents from ending in Africa. As it is we see Minot's Light, five miles down the harbor. Our idea is to let our Cambridge house (this being no time to sell) and to live for some years at least in Belmont.—Perhaps they have written you from Quebec that my play[3] had been brought out as near Boston as Worcester. I went over there to see it, and was most agreeably surprised to find myself quite exterior to it. I sat it out like any other spectator. They played it uncommonly well; and I was especially pleased with the way in which Constance was done. I was introduced afterwards to the young lady (she is only 22), and was astonished to find her quite a meek, plain little thing, and not the tall, acquiline beauty I had seen upon the stage. She seemed a good, nice girl, and she was going to hurry home and spend a spare day she had with her mother in Boston. It seemed to me a slavish life that she and all the others of the company were leading. Barrett comes here with the play in March, and will give it for a week at the Museum.—The family are all very well, and are in the usual futile excitement over their various interests. I have begun a new story,[4] and Pil has a Japanese doll; she calls it Hop Sing (after a Chinese washerman in Boston) but I haven't named my plaything yet. The children are all in school, this winter, you know, and are really a good deal occupied with their different lessons. Still we have a quiet hour in the evening, which we give to the works of Jules Verne.[5] Remember me affectionately to your husband. In fact we all send love to both of you.

Your aff'te brother
Will.

1. For the merger of the *Galaxy* into the *Atlantic*, see Howells to W. C. Howells, 6 January 1878, n. 2.
2. For the series of "Choice Autobiographies," see Howells to T. W. Higginson, 2 July 1877.
3. *A Counterfeit Presentment*.
4. *The Undiscovered Country*.
5. At this time, Jules Verne (1828–1905) was at the height of his popularity, with the publication of *Twenty Thousand Leagues Under the Sea* (1870) and *Eighty Days Around the World* (1872).

31 DECEMBER 1882, FLORENCE, TO WILLIAM C. HOWELLS

Hotel Minerva,
Florence Dec. 31, 1882.

Dear father:

I have let a Sunday pass without sending off my usual cut-and-dried letter, and I fancy that this may be almost a relief to you, for I feel the dullness whilst I'm writing. I am no talker, except when socially goaded into it, and letter writing is something like talking. How charmingly Annie does both! We are always glad of every scrap you send us from her, and we keep her letters carefully, and shall bring them back to you. I have just finished reading her Pauvre Elise, which I like extremely for its simple and unaffected reality. It is pitched in exactly the right key, and there is not a false note in it.[1]

We have now been more than three weeks in Florence, and we are slowly getting used to the mild, lifeless air. After the vigor of the Swiss air, it has no support in it, and at first, when I had walked half an hour, I became sick at the stomach. Nearly every one takes quinine, at some time or other, for though there is no positive malaria, there is a great deal of debility.—I dislike more and more all that relates to life in Europe, and the Americans who come over here to live seem to me for the most part very trashy people, without real interests or duties. They fade gradually into a mental and moral nothingness, to which the most disagreeable conditions at home are preferable. Some poor old things who have been away from home twenty-five years, are really like paper bags, for dryness and vapidity; I feel almost ashamed to be here, when I see what merely being here comes to. Of course, I only see the outside of these people.

I have met an old Swedenborgian minister, who has been stranded here ever since 1855, and who tells me that now he never expects to return. He is a Mr. Ford, of New Jersey, and he seems a kind, good old man. He came to call on me, and I hope to see him again. I wondered whether you knew anything of him.

Our cousin, Howell Howells,[2] has sent me his fotograf, from which you can see that personal beauty is not his foible. I also enclose his last letter, which touches upon some family matters that may interest you. He seems a good fellow, and I know that you will willingly tell him "what you know about farming." I'm afraid he's cooking up some sort of disappointment for himself.

John writes you a letter whose pomposity will amuse you; but you will see that he is using his eyes, and learning to use his pen. What the creature will finally become, I don't know, and he has no idea, as yet. Just now he is at the climax of a voice that breaks into three or four pieces whenever he speaks, and of a dignity that is almost insupportable. Day after to-morrow he begins with a tutor in Latin and mathematics.— Pilla gets quietly on in her old way, dashing off dozens of imaginative drawings every day. She has got through with saints, and is now doing clowns—in honor of a circus in the next street. Winny and Elinor are well, and all join me in love to all.

Your affectionate son
Will.

1. "Pauvre Elise" failed of publication in the major magazines but appeared both in the small New York weekly, *Our Continent*, and in the Ashtabula *Sentinel*. See James Doyle, *Annie Howells and Achille Fréchette* (Toronto: University of Toronto Press, 1979), p. 64.

2. Many of the distant relatives in the large Howells family are referred to by Howells as "cousins"; Howell Howells appears to be such a distant relative.

30 MARCH 1890, BOSTON, TO WILLIAM C. HOWELLS

Boston, March 30, 1890

Dear Father:

I want to tell a dream that I had about Winny, yesterday morning. I have dreamed several times about her since she died:[1] directly after, when I was wild to have some assurance that she still existed, and when she seemed to come to prove it. At one of these times, I took her cheeks between my hands, and said: Have you come back to poor Papa? and cried over her.

A few months ago I seemed to find her standing in her mother's room, in a gray dressing gown she often wore. Elinor said, "Here's Winny," and I took her in my arms and held her close and long. When I let her go far enough to speak, she said in a glad way, "Then you *do* love me?" and I choked out, "O, *love* you!" That was all.

But this last time the dream was longer. The night before, I had to go back from the room where I sleep to my study, and I lit a match in front of a large photograph of Winny, that stands on a desk. It is a sad face, and frowning from the strong light thrown upon her by the photographer, when it was taken. But as I saw it by the match light the melancholy face seemed to smile at me; and I had the thought of this in my mind, I suppose when I fell asleep, for when I saw her in my dream, just before I awoke in the morning, she had a smile on her face. We seemed to be in some sort of hotel; and Elinor and I were sitting at a small table set for four, when Pilla and Winny came in together, as if to breakfast. I said to Elinor, "Why here's Winny!" and I took her hand, which was slight but not thin, and had a warmth which I recognized as that of health. Neither Elinor nor Pilla seemed surprised, though I kept saying to them, "Here's Winny! Don't you see? It's Winny!" She was dressed in a dark blue, which she sometimes wore, and she was girlish and slender, but looked strong; this impressed me; and she had a humorous, half-teasing gayety, which was peculiar to her when she was with Pilla, and that was always so pretty in her. I knew that it was her spirit, and I began at once with what is so much in my mind about her. Throughout our talk, she had a surprised air, mixed with something puzzled and amused as if she wondered at my curiosity about something which was to her very plain and simple, and yet that she was not wholly free to speak of. "Are you happy there, Winny?" I asked. "Yes," she said. "At first I was lonesome, and cried." Then she laughed and said, as if joking at the form of the verb that she used, "but I haven't *weeped* since." I was holding her hand, glad of its warmth and strength after so much sorrowful sense as I used to have of her sickness; and now I looked very earnestly into her face and said, "Is it interesting, there?" I was aware that I asked this because all the accounts of the other life have made it seem dull. She answered, "Yes," in a way as if she would like to explain. "But not like here?" I went on. "No," she said, and she still kept that look, so like her, and so pertinent to the moment; and then the dream changed. She and Pilla were sitting on a window sill, somewhere. I introduced some young man to Winny. "This my daughter who is dead; this is her spirit." She slightly acknowledged the introduction, as if there were nothing strange in the affair; and then we were going up hill, as if to our house at Belmont, and I put my hand on her waist behind, to help her, and said, "I don't suppose you need that now." "No," she said "I am well," or something like that; and then the dream ended.

It was fantastic in its changes; but otherwise it was perfectly real; and it was true to Winny, in the sort of wise reticence it showed in her. I felt all the time that she could have told me fully every thing I wished to know, if it had not been against counsel that she knew the good sense of, but which she was free to disregard if she would. She apparently hesitated between her wish to gratify me, and her knowledge of what was best for me.

This dream has somehow given me courage and consolation. I could not say why, for I can account for it in a perfectly natural way. I feel as if I might dream again of her, as if I might continue that very dream. But of course I have no warrant for such a feeling. However, I have written fully out for you.

W. D. H.[2]

1. See Howells to W. C. Howells, 4 March 1889.
2. The extant version of this letter is a manuscript copy in W. C. Howells' hand. Following the initials, "W. D. H.," is a short note: "I have copied this dream for myself. It seems most natural to me, and the most probable view of the world of spirits and what its appearance would be to us, and just what would occur at a casual meeting of those concerned in this dream. / Wm. C. H."

30 JUNE 1899, KITTERY POINT, TO ANNE H. FRÉCHETTE

Kittery Point, June 30, 1899.

Dear Annie:

In the subscription trade, they count the author's percentage on the actual price of the book; but in the regular book-trade, *never*, to my experience or knowledge. *Of course*, your publishers sell your books to the trade at 40 off, and very likely more; but you have nothing to do with that; it is the regular discount, and all publishers do the same. It is their duty, as it is the universal custom, to pay the author a percentage on the *list price*. So, if your book were listed at a dollar, and they sold it at 60 cents, they ought to pay you 10 cents, and not 6 cents.[1]

They speak you so fair that I think they expect you to insist upon your due, but I should insist very mildly, and assume if possible that they intend to treat you fairly. You can refer to the universal custom of the book trade, to which you do not know an exception—*I* certainly don't—and imply that it is quite different in this from the subscription book business. But I need not preach tact to *you*!

I would not think of changing publishers. They are all alike, and make the most shameful blunders. Harper's got out "Christmas Every Day" a fortnight before Christmas, when it ought to have been out two months earlier.[2] Ticknor & Fields, in spite of the great popularity in the Atlantic, published Their Wedding Journey in a first edition of 1500, which went before noon; they had no more ready till after New Year's. So it goes.[3]

Perhaps your people really mean well. Give them the benefit of the doubt.

With love to all,

Your aff'te brother
Will.

1. After nearly twenty years Annie had revised her serialized novel, *Reuben Dale*, in the early 1890s and tried unsuccessfully for several years to find a publisher for it. See James Doyle, *Annie Howells and Achille Fréchette* (Toronto: University of Toronto Press, 1979), p. 91.

2. *Christmas Every Day* was published in book form by Harper & Brothers on 7 December 1893; it had earlier appeared in *Saint Nicholas*, January 1886.

3. Actually the publisher of *Their Wedding Journey* (1872) was James R. Osgood & Co., the successor firm to Ticknor & Fields and Fields, Osgood & Co.

16 July 1899, Kittery Point, to Anne H. Fréchette

Kittery Point, Me., July 16, 1899.

Dear Annie:

Your admirable, your exactly fit, little sketch came just as I had closed my last letter, and I could not speak of it. Now I wish to say that it is thoroughly artistic—as good as Maupassant in form; and most simply pathetic. I sent it at once to Alden, and I can only hope that it will strike him as it does me.[1]—I wish I could have a good talk with you, and go over some of your things, with the notion of comparing points of view. But if you could hit on a number of simple subjects, and treat them with the quiet and self-restraint of this sketch, I believe you would make an impression. You have a lovely talent, and I have always lamented that you could not have had luck equal to it. Of course your conditions have been hard, and your experiences discouraging; but it is not too late, yet.

I am working away with my usual perseverance, but I hardly know whether I am working to good effect. As my years increase, my patience dwindles, and I am afraid that I no longer am able to refine upon my performance. I do not fear imperfection as I used; I let things go. If I were only 40 again! But I shall much sooner be 80; my milk is spilt, and I cannot cry it up again.—I am writing on a lecture about "Heroes and Heroines," and, to my surprise, I have to push it.[2] Can you remember many of them? It is wonderful how few have stuck in my crop.—You must make this pass for a letter to Aurelia. With love to all,

Yours affectionately
Will.

1. Henry M. Alden was sufficiently impressed with "A Widow in the Wilderness" to accept it for publication in *Harper's Monthly*, December 1899.

2. For Howells' dissatisfaction with his lecture on "Heroes and Heroines," see Howells to Elinor Howells, 29 October 1899, n. 1.

17 JANUARY 1904, NEW YORK, TO HOWELLS FRÉCHETTE

48 West 59th st.,
Jan'y 17, 1904.

My dear Howells:

I did not think I should be so long answering your very welcome letter of last November; but I am apt to think too well of myself in every way.

You wrote me from Ottawa, when you were wavering about Detroit, and now Vevie tells me you are in New Foundland. I had hoped I might serve you somewhere in the States, for though I am not myself in the Steel Trust, I am "the intimate friend of the intimate friend of the intimate friend" of one of the greatest steel magnates (or magnets),[1] and I thought of suggesting the high gifts of my nephew as being disponible; but just then the trust became of the strength of its weakest link, as you very well know. So I was left with my good intentions on my hands. Perhaps I may yet get rid of them.

In the meantime you are not unprovided for, thanks to that "brafer Mann" whom Heine celebrates.[2] He is your best stay, and more efficient than the well-meaningest uncle. You have got pluck and talent and industry, and you know how to make friends with chance. Our breed has frayed out in so many instances that I will not claim for it the credit of qualities which I am so proud of in you: I assign them frankly to your Norman blood.

Your sister is again in New York, and she dined with us Friday night when I asked her your address, which I instantly forgot, so that I am sending this to your father's care. We are all in very good case, except John who grows more and more dyspeptic. Pilla is uncommonly well, and your aunt Elinor who shares my sense of you, is an example to old ladies.—I cannot report so well of that book of mine which you kindly liked: "Letters Home," seems inclined to remain where charity begins, and is almost entirely of domestic consumption.[3] However there is another novel, opening in the North American Review which promises more publicity.[4] If you see that periodical you can see the first chapters of my novel and I hope you will make an effort to like it.—If you are not too vexed with me, I wish you would write me something about your present life. We all join in love to you.

> Your aff'te uncle,
> W. D. Howells.

1. Most likely a reference to Andrew Carnegie, whom Howells first met in 1892. See Howells to W. C. Howells, 7 February 1892.

2. The passage proves once again how well Howells knew and remembered Heine. It refers to a poem in the section "Heimkehr" (no. 64) of *Buch der Lieder*, where Heine sarcastically remarks that the only mentor one can trust is oneself:

> Aber bei ihrem Protegieren,
> Hätte ich können vor Hunger krepieren,
> Wär nicht gekommen ein braver Mann,
> Wacker nahm er sich meiner an.

> Braver Mann! er schafft mir zu essen!
> Will es ihm nie und nimmer vergessen!
> Schade, dass ich ihn nicht küssen kann!
> Denn ich bin selbst dieser brave Mann.

(But despite their proffered protection / I could have died of starvation, / If a good man had not come / Bravely to take care of me. // My good man gave me food! / I will never forget his kindness! / Too bad I cannot kiss him, / Since I myself am this good man.)

3. *Letters Home*, an epistolary account of New York, was published in 1903.

4. *The Son of Royal Langbrith* was serialized in the *North American Review*, January–August 1904.

27 MAY 1908, LONDON, TO ANNE H. FRÉCHETTE

> 40 Clarges Street,
> May 27, 1908.

Dear Annie:

I have just got your letter with its sad, expected news.[1] Before you get this an earlier one will have reached you, acknowledging the letter in which you warned me of what was coming. We have so often said that life meant only useless suffering for poor Henry, and wondered that he had outlived those who could have survived more to some clear end, that I am surprised at feeling his death a real bereavement. You know that I had not your continual contact to keep me in thought of him; but in those years since his ghostly quiet came upon him, I have deeply realized a sort of angelic charm in him. The beauty of his younger face was translated into a spiritual loveliness surpassingly pathetic, and it makes its appeal to me now almost as if I were with you in his presence. Of what or where he is we know nothing; I hope, but without giving myself the pain of trying to imagine him in his new place. But Aurelia in regard to her change, almost as great as his, is touchingly and most sensibly with me. I know that you will plan for her what is best, and I have no anxiety, only the deepest pity, for her. When you have arranged something, you will let me know and let me help. Your dear boy[2] must be at no charge in any way appreciable; if he wants to give some little sum out of the kindness of his good heart, that is very well; but he and all of you have given out of proportion already in ways beyond money; I must give the money, and I now enclose a check in addition to the one I sent the other day, which I hope will help you over all present needs.

We are all very well; even Elinor has pulled up since we came to England, and Pilla is of course happy and hearty. She joins her mother and me in sympathy and love to each of you.

> Your aff'te brother
> Will.

1. Annie's letter is not extant, but she evidently informed Howells of the death of their brother Henry. See also Howells to Aurelia Howells, 23 May 1908.
2. Howells Fréchette.

3 APRIL 1910, NEW YORK, TO ANNE H. FRÉCHETTE AND AURELIA H. HOWELLS

> *...130 West 57th Street*
> April 3, 1910.

Dear Girls:

This is a glorious morning for us. After a most discouraging week, Elinor pulled up Friday night, and slept well; yesterday she let herself be pushed into her *bange*, at the front, and last night was the best she has had for the whole six weeks since she took to her bed. She breakfasted splendidly, and then demanded the English news—you know she despises ours. She is cheerful, and hopeful, and entirely rational. We go round knocking on wood, however.

I read her in the afternoon Achille's and Vevie's letters, and she enjoyed them to the last word. I think, as she does, that Achille's is delightful, and most delicately expressive of an amusing and touching personal relation to an interesting ethnical fact. If you don't make use of him in literature, Annie, you will be no true wife. His refinement, his poetical nature, brought bump up against that Parisian chauvinism, how charming!—I envy you your house-selling experiences,[1] but I know just how Mr. Purr felt at the gross indignity offered him; of course he suffered it in the general interest; nothing else could have saved that wretched child.[2]

Today John and Abby are at Kittery Point, confound them! John went on to Boston to rest his poor back, and K. P. was so near! Incidentally he has had a corset made for him by a famous Boston surgeon, which is to cure his back.

Elinor was touched by Annie's allusion to those drives in the Park, and I by her remembrance of our kind old sordid Jews. I wish I could see them again.—Yesterday I found Billie in the Park, and had Sabina push him down to the courrousel.[3] He stood on the wooden horses a while, and then whinnied, to certify their nature to us. As yet, he does not care for human speech; but he speaks the language of ducks, dogs and horses like a native; and every day he grows in sweetness and dearness. With our love to you both,

> Your aff'te brother,
> Will.

1. See Howells to Anne Fréchette and Aurelia Howells, 10 April 1910, n. 4.
2. Howells' allusions are unclear.
3. Billie is Howells' grandson and Sabina, presumably, the nurse.

29 APRIL 1911, NEW YORK, TO ACHILLE FRÉCHETTE

> Hotel Wellington,
> April 29, 1911.

My dear Achille:

Your kind letter for my birthday came to me in the last weeks of our dream-life at Bermuda, and I am just now waked up enough to thank you for it. I have heard, since, that your promise of recovered health has kept itself, and I shall expect yet to find you of my girth.

The dream-life of Bermuda rather tended to develop that, especially as for the first time I kept my carriage. The climate saps the human leg, and for some weeks I could only roll in and out of our carryall. But that changed in time, and the sojourn was in every way successful. If you and Annie fancied going into eggs and chickens, Bermuda would be the ideal place for you, except that it is *not* cheap. Every New York blizzard sends a chill down over the sea, and a change in the market here is instantly felt in the prices there.

We are to be here only till Mid-May, and as our flat is let, we are in a hotel before going to Kittery Point. We are in a gale of theatres, and we are so near John's that I can keep round after Billie every day. This fills life so full, that I leave literature out rather more than I used, though I have been drubbing away at a story of our early family experience in Ohio.[1] Annie knows of it.

We all had the greatest pride and pleasure in Vevie's acceptance at the salon.[2] What a little worker she is, and with what authority to work! I have never known any such joy as came to me from my children's work, and you and Annie have had your share of the like.

Some one has written me from Paris to take part in the Théophile Gautier commemoration—a Mr. Henri Boucher—and I am glad because he was a favorite of my youth, though it is hard to imagine what my part will be.[3]

I have no idea when you think of returning. Have you? And will it be to Canada, or to our poor republican province of Canada? With Pilla's love and mine to you all

Yours affectionately
W. D. Howells.

1. *New Leaf Mills.*

2. Marie Marguerite Fréchette, Howells' niece, had been studying art in Paris since 1909; she joined her parents and her aunt Aurelia in Lausanne, Switzerland, probably early in 1911.

3. Théophile Gautier (1811–1872), writer and literary theoretician, strongly influenced the development of nineteenth-century French poetry—especially the reaction of the symbolists against romanticism—with his theory of "l'art pour l'art" and his insistence on pure poetic form. Boucher, who has not been identified, evidently made preparations for Gautier's one hundredth birthday commemoration.

TEXTUAL APPARATUS

Introduction

THE letters selected for inclusion in these volumes of Howells correspondence are printed in clear text in the form reproducing as nearly as possible their finished state. The record of the alterations which took place during composition and which are evidenced on the pages of the manuscripts is presented in the textual apparatus which follows, in combination with the record of editorial emendations. The letters have been editorially corrected only in specific details and only when the original texts would make no conceivable sense to the reader. Thus Howells' few eccentricities of spelling and punctuation and his occasional mistakes and oversights have generally been retained. However, inadvertent repetitions of letters, syllables, or words—usually a result of moving the pen from the end of one line to the beginning of the next—have been emended and recorded in the apparatus. In cases where the actual manuscripts are not available and transcriptions or printed versions of letters have served as the basis for printing here, errors in those materials have also been retained, since the actual source of the error—Howells, the transcriber, or the printer—cannot be identified.

Except where extraordinary conditions have made it impossible, the following procedures have been followed step-by-step in the preparation for publication of the text of each letter, whether the extant form of it is the original document or an unpublished or published transcription. First a clean, typed transcription of the final form of the extant material is prepared from a facsimile of it. Then duplicate copies of this prepared transcription are read and corrected against the facsimile by the editor of the volume and by one of the editors of the letters series. At the same time drafts of the apparatus material are prepared, recording all cancellations, insertions, revisions, and illegible words or letters in the text, as well as possible compounds, end-line hyphenated, which must be resolved as hyphenated or unhyphenated forms. These drafts of the apparatus also include questions about proper interpretation of textual details. The corrected and edited transcriptions and accompanying apparatus are conflated at the Howells Center and any discrepancies identified and corrected. At this stage transcriptions and textual apparatus are completely reread against the facsimile of the original. The resultant material is next checked by a different editor against the original holograph, copy, or printing; he verifies all details, answers insofar as possible all remaining questions, and indicates matter in the original which has not been reproduced in the working facsimile. This completes the process of preparing printer's copy.

At this point the texts of the letters—though not the corresponding apparatus—are set in type. The typeset texts are proofread once against the facsimiles of the original documents and once more against the prepared printer's copy; necessary corrections are made in both typeset text and apparatus, and the apparatus is keyed to the line numbering of the typeset texts. After correction by the printer of the typeset text and the setting in type of the textual apparatus, these materials are proofread in full once more against the printer's copy, and the apparatus is proofread again separately. At every point at which revises are returned by the printer they are verified against the marked proofs.

This procedure—involving as many different people as possible from among the editors of the volumes, the series, and the Howells Edition staff—has been adopted to guarantee that the printed texts are as accurate as the combined energy and attention of a group of trained and experienced editors can make them. It will, we hope, warrant our statement that the errors, oversights, and possibly unidiomatic readings of the texts are those of the original documents and not of the editors. Further, since even the detailed textual record presented in this apparatus cannot fully indicate the physical condition of the letters, the editorial materials prepared during the assembly of these volumes are all being preserved, and can be consulted by anyone who wishes to see them—at the Howells Center at Indiana University as long as it is in operation for preparation of texts for "A Selected Edition of W. D. Howells" and in a suitable public depository thereafter.

The editorial considerations and procedures outlined above underlie the actual presentation of the letters printed in these volumes. Each letter is introduced by an editorial heading identifying the date and place of composition and the name of the correspondent to whom it is directed. The date and location identified in this heading may be different from those provided by the letter itself, since the content of the letter or other pertinent evidence can indicate that those details are inaccurate. When such cases arise, they are discussed in appropriate footnotes.

The translation of the ranges of handwritten and typewritten material and printed stationery into the stricter confines of the printed page obviously demands the adoption of certain formal and stylistic conventions. Regardless of their arrangement or placement on the original page, inside addresses are presented in one or more lines above the single line containing the place of origin and date provided in the letter. This format is followed regardless of the placement of the dateline at the beginning or at the end of a letter. When handwritten or printed letterheads provide more elaborate information than basic identification of place of origin and date, the additional information is omitted and its absence signaled by the appropriate placement of ellipses. The use of capitals or a combination of capitals and small capitals in printed letterhead forms has been reduced here to capitals and lowercase letters. In the printing of letters and datelines in the present text, italic type is used to indicate matter which occurs in the original part of printed stationery, and roman to indicate portions supplied by Howells himself. The distinction between print and handwritten or typed portions of heading information can be significant in that a printed letterhead in particular does not necessarily indicate that the letter itself was written in that place. If Howells supplied location information different from that of a printed letterhead, the printed letterhead is considered simply a mark on the paper and has been ignored in the presentation of the text.

The beginning of the body of the letter after the salutation has been consistently set off by a paragraph even if Howells continued on the same line or used any other unconventional spacing. Similarly, the positions of the complimentary close (e.g., "Yours ever") and the signature in relation to the body of the letter have been standardized without regard to Howells' widely varying usage. The relative spacing of the indentations of paragraphs has been normalized to conform to the typography of these volumes; this principle has been applied also to unindented paragraph breaks which occur in the originals. The interruptive or appositive dash within sentences and the transitional dash between sentences (the latter almost the equivalent in sense of the paragraph break) have been set in standard typographical form, and relative length not indicated. The long *s* of Howells' youthful hand has been set consistently in the ordinary typographical form. Underlined words have been set in italics without regard to the position or relative length of the underlining; when the form of the underlining indicates, however, that Howells clearly intended to emphasize only part of a word (e.g., *every*one), then only that part has been italicized.

When texts are derived from machine-printed rather than handwritten telegrams, the full capitalization used there has been reduced to capitals and lowercase letters, with an appropriate note in the textual apparatus. The same procedure has been followed for letters typed on typewriters using only capital letters. Where texts are derived from copies of now-missing letters rather than from manuscripts, any typographical peculiarities of those forms—indentation, employment of capitals and small capitals in proper names, and so on—have been altered to conform to the

format of the present edition. But only this strictly typographical altera-
tion has been enforced; the errors in spelling and punctuation and the
revisions and cancellations within these materials have all been considered textually significant and a potentially accurate record of the
originals upon which they are based.

Postscripts which follow upon the signatures in the original letters are
placed in the same position in the printed text, but marginal notes and
postscripts placed eccentrically are printed where they seem to belong
within or after the body of the letter, and their original locations indicated by editorial notes in the apparatus to the letter. The presence or
absence of page and leaf numbering or the location of such numbering
on the original pages has not been recorded.

In the preparation of the texts and apparatus, those marks, and those
marks alone, in the text of the letter which could be interpreted as slips
of the pen have been ignored. All other marks, including wiped-out
words or letters, erased material, incomplete words either canceled or
uncanceled, and random letters, have been recorded. Illegible words or
letters are identified in the apparatus by the abbreviation *"illeg."*

The presentation of this information in the apparatus demands the
use of certain symbols and abbreviations to conserve space. The record
for each letter is introduced by the same editorial heading that introduces
the item in the text proper. Then follows a note on the number of
pages (i.e., sides of individual sheets or of segments of sheets created by
folding which have been written on). Next is provided an abbreviated
indication of the kind of text and the presence or absence of authorial
signature (A.l. = Autograph letter; A.l.s. = Autograph letter signed;
T.l. = Typescript letter; T.l.s. = Typescript letter signed; A.n. =
Autograph note; A.n.s. = Autograph note signed; T.n. = Typescript
note; T.n.s. = Typescript note signed). If the authorial text is of a kind
not represented by these eight abbreviations, it is described fully (e.g.,
"Mostly in autograph of Elinor M. Howells"; "Telegraph form written
in Howells' hand"; "Typed telegram"). If the text is based on a transcribed copy, that fact is noted together with information about the
source of the transcription, if known; if the transcription is a published
text, the author, title, and other bibliographical information are provided
—in the cases of both published and unpublished transcriptions the number of pages of text is ignored as textually irrelevant. This information is
followed in turn by the standard abbreviation for the library in which
the original document or extant transcription is located,[1] or by the short-
form designation for a private collection.

1. The system of abbreviations used in this edition is that described in *Symbols of American Libraries*, 10th ed. (Washington: Library of Congress, 1969).

Following this heading appears the record of the internal revisions and cancellations in the letter document and any emendations made by the editors. All such revisions, even in typed letters, may be assumed to be by Howells, unless otherwise noted in the apparatus. Each entry in this record begins with the citation of the number or numbers of the lines in the text of the printed letter in which the cited material occurs. This numbering is based on the count of full or partial lines of type, and begins with the first line of the document, whether that be inside address, date, or salutation; it does not include the formal editorial heading which precedes each letter.

Sentences, phrases, words, or parts of words inserted into the running text of the document are indicated in the record by placement within vertical arrows, ellipses being used to abbreviate passages of four or more words. Thus:

↑evade↓   with↑out↓   ↑directly ... exchange.↓

No distinction is made between words inserted above the line and those inserted below it or manuscript revisions fitted into typescript lines, and the color of ink or the medium (pencil, pen, typewriter) used for corrections or additions is not described. The presence or absence of a caret or other conventional symbol for the insertion of the material is not recorded. When a word has been written over some other word or part of a word, that fact is indicated by the use of the abbreviation "*w.o.*" (for "written over") following the final reading and preceding the original. Thus:

parties *w.o.* party   people *w.o.* ple

Words canceled in the original are indicated by placement in pointed brackets in the context of citation of sufficient words from the text of the letter (either before or after the canceled words or phrase) as printed in this edition to identify its location. Thus:

went ⟨to⟩   ⟨we went⟩ I walked

An italic question mark within brackets following a word indicates a degree of uncertainty about the interpretation provided. The combinations of these various symbols and abbreviations should be self-explanatory: e.g., ↑⟨this⟩↓ indicates that the interlined word "this" has been canceled.

All editorial revisions are signaled in the apparatus by a left-opening bracket (]); preceding it appears the reading of the text as printed in this edition, and following it the reading of the original. When the editorial revision involves only the emendation of punctuation, each curved dash (∼) following the bracket stands for a word preceding the bracket. When it has been necessary to supply words, letters, or marks of punctuation missing in the original not because of oversight or error in composition but because of the present physical condition of the document—badly faded ink, deteriorated or torn paper, blots, or water-spots—the reconstructed portions are signaled by being placed between vertical lines: Thus:

af|te|r |the| commit|tee| met

Virgules (slashes) are used to indicate the end of a line of writing in the original document. All other editorial comments, including descrip-tion of the placement of postscripts and marginal notes or the presence in a document of notes or comments in another hand believed to be contemporary with the composition or receipt of the letter, as well as information about specific textual details not covered by the basic system of symbols and abbreviations outlined here, are provided in italic type within brackets.

In addition to the textual record which follows, this edition of letters contains a section headed "Word-Division," consisting of two separate lists: one, List A, indicates the resolution of possible compounds occurring as end-line hyphenations in the original documents, and the other, List B, the form to be given to possible compounds which occur at the end of the line in the present text. A description of the keying system em-ployed in these lists and the process by which editorial decisions about the resolution of such end-lines were reached is provided in the head-note to that section.

C. K. L.

D. J. N.

Textual Record

---

4 January 1912, New York, to Frederick A. Duneka. 1 p. A.l.s. MWA.
  8 ↑in good time.↓

18 January 1912, New York, to Frederick A. Duneka. 2 pp. A.l.s. MWA.
  4 that *w.o.* the

19 January 1912, New York, to Joseph A. Howells. 2 pp. A.l.s. OFH.
  8 ⟨f⟩ therefore   14 taxicab⟨,⟩   17 ↑out↓   21 your *w.o. illeg.*
30 ⟨a⟩ a   29–35 the drifts.... Will. [*in left margin, first two pages*]

29 February 1912, New York, to Sylvester Baxter. 2 pp. A.l.s. CSmH.
  10 ⟨I⟩ notion   11 his gray *w.o. illeg.* gray   14 buon *w.o. illeg.*
15 ↑that↓   15 account⟨*illeg.*⟩   22 me *w.o. illeg.*

February 1912, New York, to Armando Palacio Valdés. Location of MS.
unknown. *Life in Letters*, II, 311.

16 March 1912, New York, to William H. Taft. 2 pp. A.l.s. DLC.
  [*In upper left corner, first page, stamped*: ASWD / MAR 19 1912;
in pencil: by the President; *in upper right corner, stamped*: THE
WHITE HOUSE / MAR 19 1912 / RECEIVED]

17 March 1912, New York, to Henry James. 3 pp. A.l.s. MH.
  4 ↑an↓   8 have *w.o.* b   11 ↑in↓   16 sharing *w.o.* our
17 men ⟨to men⟩   22 some *w.o.* many   24 print *w.o.* pride
24 for *w.o.* in   26 ⟨the⟩ an   27 ⟨to⟩ which   29 elect ⟨*illeg.*⟩
29 board *w.o.* t   30 ↑the↓ President   32 twenty ⟨for 20⟩
34 knew it *w.o.* knew,   36 leave *w.o.* have   41–43 his.... beauty,

[*in margin, third page*]   43–44 and . . . . Indians. [*in margin, second page*]   45–48 Pilla . . . . Howells. [*in margin, first page*]

25 March 1912, New York, to Thomas Hardy. 2 pp. A.l.s. Dorset County Museum, Dorchester (England).

8 you ↑have↓   12 go⟨,⟩ of its *w.o.* :⟨,⟩

25 March 1912, New York, to Eden Phillpotts. 2 pp. T.l.s. (location unknown, photocopy at InU).

26 of *w.o.* If   29 my [*in Howells' hand*]

22 June 1912, Kittery Point, to Joseph A. Howells. 3 pp. A.l.s. MH.

    11 ↑has↓ taken   27 made; ⟨and⟩   37 ever⟨*illeg.*⟩
37 boy is *w.o.* boy *illeg.*   41 Magazine *w.o.* magazine

27 June 1912, Kittery Point, to Elizabeth Jordan. 2 pp. A.l.s. NN.

    5 character⟨s⟩   6 ↑range↓   8 The diners *w.o.* The dinners
9–10 commercial diners *w.o.* commercial dinners

13 August 1912, York Harbor, to Frederick A. Duneka. 1 p. A.l.s. MWA.

    7 and *w.o.* in

15 September 1912, York Harbor, to Edith Wyatt. 2 pp. A.l.s. ICN.

    10 ↑rather↓

6 October 1912, York Harbor, to Albert B. Paine. 2 pp. A.l.s. CSmH.

    7 book. ⟨*illeg.*⟩   12 man"⟨*illeg.*⟩ is

14 October 1912, New York, to Frederick A. Duneka. 1 p. A.l.s. MWA.

        8 fifty *w.o.* forty   9 *Storage w.o. Story*

23 October 1912, Kittery Point, to Frederick A. Duneka. 2 pp. A.l.s. NN.

    10 justice|.| 10 ↑even↓   11 it *w.o.* is   12 Clemen⟨'⟩s's
16 ↑Boss↓   16 ⟨played⟩ ↑paid↓

17 November 1912, New York, to Frederick A. Duneka. 2 pp. A.l.s.
George Arms, Albuquerque, N. M.

12 ⟨lef⟩ level   12–13 is lived *w.o.* as lived

10 December 1912, New York, to Frederick A. Duneka. 3 pp. A.l.s.
George Arms, Albuquerque, N. M.

7 ↑(for 2 weeks)↓   10 and] and and   10 am *w.o. illeg.*
17 much] much much

17 January 1913, Cambridge, to Anne H. Fréchette. 3 pp. A.l.s. MH.

2 1913 *w.o.* 1912   10 to⟨*illeg.*⟩ selling   12 ↑you↓   26 ↑her↓
27 get *w.o.* let   27 ↑to↓ do   31 ↑her letter for↓   33 Aff'tly *w.o. illeg.*

5 February 1913, Cambridge, to James F. Rhodes. 2 pp. A.l.s. NSyU.

4 My *w.o. illeg.*   8 through *w.o.* three

8 February 1913, Cambridge, to Henry James. 3 pp. A.l.s. MH.

5 I have] I have I have   13 Scudder [*Howells first crossed the d's,
then canceled his mistake*]   15 go *w.o.* you   17 ↑us↓   17 ↑still↓
25 ↑haired↓   29 glad *w.o. illeg.*   30 us ⟨if⟩   31 ↑their↓   36 work.] ∼
42–43 Of . . . . picture. [*in margin, first page*]

23 February 1913, Cambridge, to Aurelia H. Howells. 3 pp. A.l.s. MH.

18 ⟨*illeg.*⟩ know   19 try↑ing↓   22 1828 *w.o.* 1826
23 dentistry *w.o. illeg.*   27 ↑well↓

2 March 1913, Cambridge, to Frederick A. Duneka. 1 p. A.l.s. MWA.

29 March 1913, Cambridge, to Frederick A. Duneka. 2 pp. A.l.s.
George Arms, Albuquerque, N. M.

4 ↑to↓   11 ⟨"My *w.o. Times*⟩ "My

31 March 1913, Cambridge, to Lilla C. Perry. Location of MS. unknown.
Life in Letters, II, 327–28.

8 hand [*probably a misreading of* head]

22 April 1913, Cambridge, to John J. Chapman. 2 pp. A.l.s. MH.

    4 ↑a↓

22 April 1913, Cambridge, to Mildred Howells. 2 pp. A.l.s. MH.

    7 ⟨W.⟩ 130   7 W. *w.o.* 5   12 Sedgwick *w.o.* Swe   13 say *w.o.* so
18 beat *w.o.* best   19–21 The . . . . It [*in margins, second page*]
20 That *w.o.* it   21–23 wont . . . . K.P. [*in margin, first page*]

3 May 1913, Kittery Point, to Perry D. Popenoe. Location of MS. unknown. Typescript copy at MH.

3 May 1913, Kittery Point, to Annie A. Fields. 2 pp. A.l.s. CSmH.

    9 doors *w.o.* days   10 on *w.o.* in   12 the *w.o.* this   12 ⟨of⟩ of ↑this↓

23 May 1913, Kittery Point, to Waldo R. Browne. 1 p. A.l.s. ICN.

15 June 1913, Kittery Point, to William A. Gill. 3 pp. A.l.s. Avon County Reference Library, Bristol.

    5 ↑feel↓   15 friend ⟨ab⟩   27 Leaf *w.o. illeg.*   28 public⟨illeg.⟩
31 fa! *w.o.* fa?

17 June 1913, Kittery Point, to John M. Howells. Location of MS. unknown. Typescript copy at MH.

9 August 1913, Stratford-on-Avon, to Henry James. 2 pp. A.l.s. MH.

    4 an⟨d⟩   4 ↑do↓   9 ⟨*illeg.*⟩ must   10 the *w.o.* this ↑real↓

15 August 1913, Stratford-on-Avon, to Henry James, Jr. 1 p. A.l.s. MH.

24 September 1913, York Harbor, to Frederick T. Leigh. 2 pp. A.l.s. MH.

    10 story *w.o.* storage   11 ↑a good↓   16 him *w.o. illeg.*

28 September 1913, York Harbor, to Brand Whitlock. 3 pp. A.l.s. OOxM.

    10 Rome *w.o. illeg.*   12 at *w.o. illeg.*   19 to] to to

16 October 1913, Boston, to Samuel S. McClure. 1 p. A.l.s. InU.

    [*In upper left corner, in another hand*: Preserve this!]

22 November 1913, Lakewood, New Jersey, to S. Weir Mitchell. 3 pp. A.l.s. PU.

19 December 1913, Boston, to Hamlin Garland. 2 pp. A.l.s. CLSU.

 14 ↑when↓ 17 her⟨e⟩

19 December 1913, Boston, to Thomas S. Perry. 1 p. A.l.s. MeWC.

12 January 1914, Boston, to John M. Howells. Location of MS. unknown. *Life in Letters*, II, 330–31.

18 January 1914, Boston, to Bertha Howells. 2 pp. A.l.s. NN.
 6 ⟨y⟩ with 11 Cincinnati *w.o.*) 14 ↑(Howel)↓ 19 At *w.o.* In 26–27 Lloyd-George . . . Wales. [*in margin, first page*]

1 February 1914, Boston, to Lee F. Hartman. 2 pp. A.l.s. ViU.

 11 here and *w.o.* here *illeg.* 20 ⟨with⟩ from 20 ↑no↓

3 February 1914, Boston, to Frederick A. Duneka. 1 p. T.l.s. MWA.

 4 I *w.o.* i 6 continuing *w.o.* continued 6 I *w.o.* i 8 ↑the↓ 9 complete *w.o.* completi 9 works *w.o.* worgs 11 I *w.o.* i 12 ↑one,↓ 12 weighty *w.o.* weeghty 14 had *w.o.* tad 15 was *w.o.* aas 16 ⟨i⟩ I 18 Easy *w.o.* easy 18 st⟨i⟩rike 18 from *w.o.* fron 20 Boston *w.o.* Bostin 21 I *w.o.* i 22 country *w.o.* *illeg.*

9 February 1914, Boston, to Laura Mitchell. Location of MS. unknown. *Life in Letters*, II, 332–33.

10 March 1914, Boston, to Henry B. Fuller. 2 pp. A.l.s. MH.

 10 ↑though usual↓

6 May 1914, York Harbor, to Frederick A. Duneka. 2 pp. A.l.s. George Arms, Albuquerque, N. M.

 4 suggestions *w.o. illeg.* 5 ↑together↓ 6 rest⟨.⟩" 21 More . . . anger. [*in margin, first page*]

8 May 1914, York Harbor, to Thomas S. Perry. 2 pp. A.l.s. MeWC.

 12 ⟨writt⟩ read

12 May 1914, York Harbor, to Aurelia H. Howells. 3 pp. A.l.s. MH.

6 ↑not↓   8 safely [*Howells canceled the cross on* t, *changing* safety *to* safely]   10 mine.] ∼,   28 ↑Irish↓   29 ↑there↓
40 Annie ... it. [*in margin, first page*]

13 May 1914, York Harbor, to Frederick A. Duneka. 2 pp. A.l.s. MWA.

1 13 *w.o.* 11   10 it over *w.o.* it,   13 ↑P.S.↓

15 June 1914, York Harbor, to Annie A. Fields. 2 pp. A.l.s. CSmH.

1 June *w.o. illeg.*   6 saw⟨*illeg.*⟩   8 preceding *w.o.* preceeding
20 daughter- *w.o. illeg.*   21–25 of .... Howells. [*in margin, first page*]

21 June 1914, York Harbor, to Aurelia H. Howells. 3 pp. A.l.s. MH.

5 ⟨you⟩ ↑we↓   9 had *w.o.* have   19 verge of] verge of of ⟨*illeg.*⟩
22 ⟨*illeg.*⟩ here   31 amount *w.o.* number   35 *huc*"] ∼'

23 June 1914, York Harbor, to Thomas S. Perry. 2 pp. A.l.s. MeWC.

3 this *w.o.* the

12 July 1914, York Harbor, to Thomas S. Perry. 1 p. A.l.s. MeWC.

5 It *w.o. illeg.*

23 July 1914, York Harbor, to Fred L. Pattee. 1 p. A.l.s. PSt.

5 advantage *w.o. illeg.*   9 no⟨t⟩   9 affair.] ∼:

28 August 1914, York Harbor, to Booth Tarkington. 1 p. A.l.s. NjP.

3 read⟨er⟩

11 September 1914, York Harbor, to Barrett Wendell. 1 p. A.l.s. MH.

5 since *w.o.* ,

13 September 1914, York Harbor, to Anne H. Fréchette. 5 pp. A.l.s. MH.

2 Aurelia [*canceled and* Annie *written above in another hand*]
16 wrote *w.o.* wrote,   25 Pilla⟨s⟩   25 ↑Icelandic epic↓
34 lunch-getting *w.o.* sunch-getting   34 ↑lunch-↓giving

40 shouldn't *w.o.* shoult   40 ⟨f⟩ like   41 our *w.o. illeg.*
46 ↑of↓ writing

23 September 1914, York Harbor, to Frederick A. Duneka. 2 pp. A.l.s.
George Arms, Albuquerque, N. M.

14 pathos *w.o. illeg.*   15 ↑(*not* seduction.).↓

6 November 1914, Boston, to Brander Matthews. 1 p. A.l.s. NNC.

7 ↑my↓

8 November 1914, Boston, to Robert U. Johnson. 2 pp. A.l.s. NNAL.

4 ↑one↓   17 ↑speech of↓   23 ↑not↓

14 November 1914, Boston, to William R. Thayer. 2 pp. A.l.s. MH.

12 ⟨*illeg.*⟩*when*   13 saw ⟨*illeg.*⟩   13 ↑the↓ Panama
16 won *w.o. illeg.*   16 fit *w.o. illeg.*   19 ↑himself↓   26 so.] ∼

29 November 1914, New York, to H. A. McCaleb. 1 p. A.l.s. NN.

4 most ⟨*illeg.*⟩

29 November 1914, New York, to William E. Dean. 2 pp. A.l.s. MnHi.

9 ↑for us↓   10 Germans] German's   23–24 I .... past. [*in margin,
first page*]

15 December 1914, Asbury Park, New Jersey, to Thomas S. Perry. 2 pp.
A.l.s. MeWC.

3 ↑ever↓   4 accuse] accuse accuse

6 January 1915, Asbury Park, New Jersey, to Mildred Howells. 2 pp.
A.l.s. MH.

1 1915 *w.o.* 1912   3 Fields *w.o.* Pil

9 January 1915, Asbury Park, New Jersey, to Booth Tarkington. 2 pp.
A.l.s. NjP.

5 the⟨y⟩   8 to *w.o.* so   12 great *w.o.* yo

9 January 1915, Asbury Park, New Jersey, to Frederick A. Duneka. Location of MS. unknown. *Life in Letters*, II, 343–44.

21 January 1915, New York, to Frederick A. Duneka. 1 p. A.l.s. RPB.

  4 use⟨d⟩

30 January 1915, New York, to Frederick A. Duneka. 2 pp. A.l.s. RPB.

  11 novel; ⟨"⟩   14 Whitlock *w.o.* him

9 February 1915, New York, to Frederick A. Duneka. 3 pp. A.l.s. RPB.

  1 St. *w.o.* Str.   4 ↑to↓   22 ↑not↓   25 blossom *w.o.* prosper
25 ↑anew.↓

6 March 1915, St. Augustine, Florida, to Frederick A. Duneka. 2 pp. A.l.s. RPB.

  5 blamed *w.o. illeg.*

21 March 1915, St. Augustine, Florida, to Thomas S. Perry. 2 pp. A.l.s. MeWC.

  9 obelisk⟨s⟩   19 ↑tonight↓   28 *We . . . door [*at top of first page*]

15 April 1915, Asbury Park, New Jersey, to Sarah M. Piatt. Location of MS. unknown. *Life in Letters*, II, 347.

23 May 1915, York Harbor, to Aurelia H. Howells. 3 pp. A.l.s. MH.

  4 ⟨where⟩ ↑as↓   8 Stokwells *w.o.* stokwells   18 ↑it↓ in   21 ↑not↓
28 but *w.o.* and   32 the [*added in margin*]

30 May 1915, York Harbor, to Sylvester Baxter. 1 p. A.l.s. CSmH.

  3 list⟨s⟩

2 June 1915, York Harbor, to Thomas S. Perry. 2 pp. A.l.s. MeWC.

29 June 1915, York Harbor, to Henry James. 3 pp. A.l.s. MH.

  14 now *w.o.* in   14 magazine *w.o.* magazines   16 ↑are↓
25 ↑by day↓   29 ↑I↓ wonder

1 July 1915, York Harbor, to Brander Matthews. 2 pp. A.l.s. NNC.

   7 ↑⟨Fillip⟩ *Filippo*, or↓   8 ⟨my-iss⟩ mine-issimo

21 July 1915, York Harbor, to Aurelia H. Howells. 3 pp. A.l.s. MH.
  12 on *w.o.* in   17 and *w.o.* or   21 ↑Institute↓   35 this *w.o.* the

24 July 1915, York Harbor, to Thomas S. Perry. 2 pp. A.l.s. MeWC.

   7 to? Not *w.o.* to: not   9 the knee] the know the knee   18 It⟨s⟩
19 her *w.o.* a   20–22 joins . . . . Howells. [*in margin, first page*]

26 October 1915, New York, to Paul Kester. 2 pp. A.l.s. NN.

   7 ↑way↓   12 ⟨y⟩our   14 but ⟨⟩⟩

31 October 1915, New York, to Mildred Howells. 2 pp. A.l.s. MH.

   9 ↑do↓   13 without *w.o.* within   13 ⟨f⟩ used

2 November 1915, New York, to Mildred Howells. 3 pp. A.l.s. MH.

   7 ↑that↓ ⟨t⟩he   11 be⟨f⟩   23 1500 *w.o.* 1100   25 3550 *w.o.* 3500
38 has *w.o.* was

10 November 1915, New York, to Hamilton W. Mabie. 2 pp. A.l.s. DLC.

   4 that *w.o.* the

7 December 1915, New York, to Frederick A. Duneka. 2 pp. A.l.s. RPB.

   15 ⟨kep⟩ khaki   16 under *w.o.* I am   16 which *w.o.* what
19 Author *w.o.* author   19 ↑free↓

15 December 1915, New York, to Henry James, Jr. 1 p. A.l.s. MH.

   7 however *w.o.* *illeg.*

26 January 1916, St. Augustine, Florida, to Kate D. Wiggin. 2 pp.
A.l.s. NN.

26 January 1916, St. Augustine, Florida, to Henry James. 2 pp. A.l.s. MH.

   2 26 *w.o.* *illeg.*   9 this *w.o.* these   12 ↑as my senior↓

11 February 1916, St. Augustine, Florida, to Sinclair Lewis. 2 pp. A.l.s. CtY.

    4 took *w.o.* r   6 good, better, best [*Howells underlined* good *once,* better *twice, and* best *three times*]   9 Palm *w.o.* F   10 We *w.o.* I

16 February 1916, St. Augustine, Florida, to Thomas S. Perry. 3 pp. A.l.s. MeWC.

    2 1916 *w.o.* 1917   6 ⟨viny for⟩ vine   6 wild ⟨here,⟩ 9 woman *w.o.* wood   9 four⟨*illeg.*⟩   9 ↑she↓   10 We *w.o.* He 12 so *w.o. illeg.*   13 ⟨up⟩ at   15 ↑-out↓   16 nap *w.o. illeg.* 17 These *w.o.* They   18 amidst *w.o.* in   21 folks *w.o.* foes 29 him *w.o.* his

7 March 1916, St. Augustine, Florida, to Frederick A. Duneka. 2 pp. A.l.s. RPB.

    7 better. ⟨; and deliver it within a month, ↑or two.↓⟩

17 March 1916, St. Augustine, Florida, to Frederick A. Duneka. 2 pp. A.l.s. RPB.

    11 April *w.o.* E

18 March 1916, St. Augustine, Florida, to Frederick A. Duneka. 1 p. A.l.s. RPB.

    5 that *w.o.* it   7 ↑have↓   7 be *w.o.* been

23 March 1916, St. Augustine, Florida, to Frederick A. Duneka. 2 pp. A.l.s. RPB.

    5 ↑on↓   6 ↑in that case↓   8 the paper] the the paper 12 ⟨cl⟩ calling

25 March 1916, St. Augustine, Florida, to Hamlin Garland. 2 pp. A.l.s. CLSU.

    4 whose *w.o.* word   4 could *w.o.* wo

2 May 1916, New York, to Albert Mordell. Location of MS. unknown. Typed copy at InU.

5 yours] your   7 that . . . agreed] that you had not that you had not agreed   9–10 [illegible word] [*notation made by original transcriber*]

6 May 1916, New York, to Editor, New York *Evening Post*. Location of MS. unknown. New York *Evening Post*, 8 May 1916.

16 June 1916, York Harbor, to Waldo R. Browne. Location of MS. unknown. *Life in Letters*, II, 362.

4 July 1916, York Harbor, to Aurelia H. Howells. 3 pp. A.l.s. MH.

[*Above dateline*: *W. D. Howells.* ⟨*130 West 57th Street*⟩]
6 ↑them↓   8 This *w.o.* It   15 writing *w.o. illeg.*   16 ↑me↓
20 ↑continues↓   35 their *w.o.* they

6 July 1916, York Harbor, to Henry E. Krehbiel. 2 pp. A.l.s. NN.

[*Above dateline*: *W. D. Howells.* ⟨*130 West 57th Street*⟩]
2 Krehbiel *w.o.* Krebiel   6 Fabain [*possibly* Fabarin]
7 somewhat *w.o.* somehow   7 disgustedly *w.o. illeg.*

8 August 1916, York Harbor, to Thomas S. Perry. 2 pp. A.l.s. MeWC.
8 Whack *w.o.* whack   10 ⟨*illeg.*⟩ sentiment   10 man *w.o. illeg.*
15 tired *w.o.* tr

25 August 1916, York Harbor, to Paul Kester, 2 pp. A.l.s. NN.
5 ⟨afr⟩ arriving   6 of ⟨of⟩   7 ⟨her⟩ our

10 September 1916, York Harbor, to Thomas S. Perry. 2 pp. A.l.s. MeWC.
3 ↑round↓   10 much *w.o.* my

8 October 1916, Kittery Point, to Hamlin Garland. 2 pp. A.l.s. CLSU.
9 ⟨and⟩ where   11 ↑no↓

8 October 1916, Kittery Point, to Lawrence Gilman. 1 p. A.l.s. CtY.

13 October 1916, Kittery Point, to Thomas S. Perry. 2 pp. A.l.s. MeWC.
14–15 sickness *w.o.* soc   15 of⟨f⟩   17 ⟨thing⟩ time *w.o.* , ⟨but⟩

28 October 1916, Kittery Point, to R. F. Wormwood. Location of MS. unknown. Typescript copy at MH.

October 1916, Kittery Point, to Henry B. Fuller. 2 pp. A.l.s. MH.
  16 ⟨g⟩ conditions

19 November 1916, New York, to Frederick A. Duneka. 2 pp. A.l.s. RPB.
  10 ↑everywhere↓   11 me] me me   17 that ⟨I do not suppose that⟩ the
18 ↑is↓   21 ⟨condit⟩ continued

23 December 1916, St. Augustine, Florida, to Frederick A. Duneka. Location of MS. unknown. *Life in Letters*, II, 365–66.

31 December 1916, St. Augustine, Florida, to Anne H. Fréchette. 3 pp. A.l.s. NAlf.
  6 ↑even↓   13 ⟨but⟩ still   21 badly ⟨for⟩   24 ⟨intel⟩ ignorantly
25 ⟨them⟩ us   32 on *w.o.* in   40 ⟨*illeg*⟩ among

21 January 1917, St. Augustine, Florida, to Mary R. Jewett. 1 p. A.l.s. MH.
  3 remembering *w.o.* remembeing

10 February 1917, Savannah, Georgia, to Hamlin Garland. 1 p. A.l.s. CLSU.
  4 '8os *w.o.* '88s

19 February 1917, Savannah, Georgia, to Thomas S. Perry. 2 pp. A.l.s. MeWC.
  5 ⟨*illeg.*⟩ occasion   8 ⟨be⟩ English   9 ↑its↓   9 layout *w.o. illeg.*
12 ⟨sp⟩ supper   18 readings] ∼.   20 could ⟨of⟩

28 February 1917, Tryon, North Carolina, to Thomas S. Perry. 2 pp. A.l.s. MeWC.
  4 ⟨pr⟩ blame   5 you much *w.o.* you.   9–10 subscription *w.o. illeg.*
14 ↑we↓

18 March 1917, Augusta, Georgia, to Hamlin Garland. 2 pp. A.l.s. CLSU.
  8 ⟨made⟩ ↑to make↓   15 ⟨w⟩but   15 ⟨ca⟩ must   21 ↑in↓

12 April 1917, Atlantic City, New Jersey, to Paul Kester. 2 pp. A.l.s. NN.
　7 ↑whole↓　9 ⟨th⟩ your　10 black *w.o. illeg.*　12 where ⟨you⟩

13 June 1917, York Harbor, to Aurelia H. Howells. 2 pp. A.l.s. MH.
　5 I'v⟨'⟩e　7 at *w.o. illeg.*　16–17 ↑of the fighting↓
30 (*though . . . francs) [*in margin, first page*]

29 June 1917, York Harbor, to Thomas B. Wells. 1 p. T.l.s. NNC.
　3 than *w.o.* that　4 Bloodroot. *w.o.* Bloodroot,
5 multiplies *w.o.* muctiplies　5 enough *w.o.* enoggh
6 handsome *w.o.* tandsome　7 was] uas　7 books *w.o.* boogs　9 ↑to↓
9 hopes *w.o.* some　[*opposite first page, in an unknown hand*:
Publication of / "A Hazard of New Fortunes"/"Son of Royal Langbrith"/
by / *Boni & Liveright* / 6¢ roaylty / equal division / between author /
and Harper and / Brothers. / June 26, 1917.]

29 June 1917, York Harbor, to Hamlin Garland. Location of MS. unknown. *Life in Letters*, II, 384–85.
　1 1917] 1919

10 July 1917, York Harbor, to Sarah M. Piatt. Location of MS. unknown. Typed transcription by W. M. Gibson of an earlier typed copy by Cecil Piatt at InU.
　1–2 York . . . Piatt: [*not transcribed by copyist in this form; date and place of origin at top of page*]　3 We] "~　7 lost [*original typescript reads* last; *emendation by W.M.G.*]　18 poethood [*original typescript reads* porthood; *in W.M.G. copy* authorhood? *added in brackets*]
19 no [*original typescript reads* as; *emendation by W.M.G.*]
22 illegible word [*original typescript reads* interest; *in W.M.G. copy* ??garbled *added in brackets*]　22 My [*original typescript reads* Thy; *in W.M.G. copy* my? *added in brackets*]　24 meandering [*W.M.G. added* ? *in brackets*]

22 July 1917, York Harbor, to Hamlin Garland. 1 p. A.l.s. CLSU.

19 August 1917, York Harbor, to William Griffith. Location of MS. unknown. Typescript copy at MH.
　23 exegeses] exigeses

23 August 1917, York Harbor, to Thomas S. Perry. 2 pp. A.l.s. MeWC.

4 his *w.o.* he   5 sends *w.o. illeg.*   8 ↑over⟨*illeg.*⟩↓
17 auto↑bio↓graphy   19 it⟨s⟩   24–25 He . . . them. [*on back of envelope*]

31 August 1917, York Harbor, to Thomas S. Perry. 2 pp. A.l.s. MeWC.

1 August *w.o.* S   14 ↑have↓   14 been a *w.o.* be a

13 September 1917, York Harbor, to Alexander Harvey. Location of MS. unknown. Typescript copy at DLC.

20 September 1917, York Harbor, to Frederick A. Duneka. 2 pp. T.l.s. RPB.

4 can't *w.o.* caa't   5 have *w.o.* haee   7 walking *w.o.* welking
11 thing *w.o.* tiing   11 te↑m↓pts   13 Review↑,↓⟨s⟩   14 Yo↑u↓
14 Poole's] Poole'r   15 ⟨Ke⟩ Kester's   19 spoken] rpoken
20 Jus↑t↓   20 I'm *w.o. illeg.*   21 Polyponessian *w.o.* Polypenessian
21 Edward *w.o.* Eaward   23 have read *w.o. illeg.* read
23 her *w.o. illeg.*   23 ⟨*illeg.*⟩"Philip;"   24 d↑u↓st
25 ↑d↓ug *w.o. illeg.*   25 bushels *w.o.* pushels   26 corn-patch *w.o.*
cornipatch   26 I *w.o.* i   28 go-/⟨*illeg.*⟩ment's
30 daughter *w.o.* deughter

13 November 1917, New York, to Mildred Howells. 2 pp. A.l.s. MH.

2 13 *w.o.* 14   6 train⟨s⟩   12 aromatic *w.o. illeg.*
16 ⟨th⟩ treads

19 November 1917, New York, to Frederick A. Duneka. Location of MS. unknown. *Life in Letters*, II, 376–77.

8 February 1918, Miami, Florida, to Van Wyck Brooks. Location of MS. unknown. Typed transcription at InU.

1–2 31 . . . 1918. [*not in this form in copytext; date, street, and place at top of page*]

28 February 1918, St. Augustine, Florida, to Frederick A. Duneka. 2 pp. A.l.s. RPB.

4 ↑you↓   13 Think] Thank

13 March 1918, St. Augustine, Florida, to Frederick A. Duneka. Location of MS. unknown. *Life in Letters*, II, 379.

1 April 1918, Savannah, Georgia, to Aurelia H. Howells. 2 pp. A.l.s. (with signatures by John and Mildred Howells) NAlf.

7 difficulties *w.o.* difficulty   7–8 ↑attending the matter,↓   8 ↑heavy↓
13 went *w.o. illeg.*   14 ⟨their⟩ its   17 ↑you↓   18 ⟨had⟩ ↑have↓
20 ↑must↓

1 May 1918, New York, to Salvatore Cortesi. 2 pp. A.l.s. Polly Howells Werthman, Kittery Point, Me.

13 children *w.o. illeg.*   17 ↑to↓

5 May 1918, New York, to Curtis Brown. 1 p. A.l.s. ViU.

6 God⟨s⟩   9 ↑for↓   11 ↑books↓   [*at bottom of page, in another hand*: 5/21/18]

8 May 1918, New York, to Brand Whitlock. 2 pp. A.l.s. OOxM.

5 for ↑it↓   8 all ⟨true⟩ ↑new *w.o. illeg.*↓   8 it ⟨true⟩ ↑new↓
9 final *w.o.* finat   10 ⟨write⟩ help   18 ↑me↓   22 *No . . . that!
[*in left margin, first page*]

18 May 1918, Kittery Point, to Thomas S. Perry. 1 p. A.l.s. MeWC.

3 stories *w.o.* sh

10 June 1918, Kittery Point, to Aurelia H. Howells. 2 pp. A.l.s. MH.
3 with ⟨my⟩   16 out, *w.o. illeg.*   16 body *w.o.* m   22 like ↑it↓
23 inland *w.o.* int

13 June 1918, Kittery Point, to Thomas S. Perry. 2 pp. A.l.s. MeWC.

2 Perry— *w.o.* Perry I   3 touching. *w.o.* touching,   7 to *w.o. illeg.*
7 ↑the↓   7 ⟨o⟩from   11 childish *w.o.* stu

14 July 1918, Kittery Point, to Mildred Howells. 2 pp. A.l.s. MH.

6 is *w.o. illeg.*   7 hardy *w.o. illeg.*   7 Bill *w.o. illeg.*
11 it in *w.o.* it.   13 ⟨It⟩ I am   23 ⟨fr⟩exchanged

27 July 1918, Intervale, New Hampshire, to Thomas S. Perry. 2 pp. A.l.s. MeWC.

2 27 *w.o.* 17   9 ↑a↓   10 Of *w.o.* I   13 Their Silver] Tilver ↑Silver↓ [*Howells apparently wrote* Silver, *then began to write* Their *over it, adding a second* Silver *above the line*]

14 August 1918, Kittery Point, to Frederick A. Duneka. 2 pp. T.l.s. RPB.

1 ⟨GL,⟩ ↑14,↓   3 on ⟨y⟩   4 change *w.o.* chanke   4 dashing] dasbing 4 my *w.o.* mn   5 I show *w.o.* i show   11 you] yiu   13 recent *w.o. illeg.* 14 stories *w.o.* stohies   15 sounds *w.o.* soundr   16 letter] let⟨te⟩ letter 17 ↑all↓   21 replace ⟨me in yo⟩   22 used *w.o.* ured   22 ↑in↓ my 23 eag-/erness *w.o.* eage/erness   25 our *w.o.* ous 26 Hartman *w.o.* H.rtman   27 time *w.o.* tim.   28 and *w.o.* aad 29 most *w.o.* mout   30 him⟨.⟩;   30 ⟨kremeber⟩ ↑remember↓ 30 campaign *w.o.* cagpaign   32 mention *w.o.* meotion   32 ↑mostly↓ 33 ⟨w⟩ will   33 authority *w.o.* asthority   34 ⟨o⟩to 34–35 intelli-/gence *w.o.* intellige/gence   36 afternoon] afternion 37 much] m much

15 August 1918, Kittery Point, to Thomas S. Perry. 2 pp. A.l.s. MeWC.

3 Easy *w.o.* C   4 to *w.o.* is   4 ⟨of your⟩ ↑in↓   4 ↑have↓ 5 not *w.o.* aut   11 ⟨plant⟩ planet   11 ↑in the eveny sky.↓ 12 Some⟨*illeg.*⟩   16 ⟨*illeg.*⟩ true   17 the *w.o.* it   17 ↑fact↓ 18 bet *w.o.* but   19 ⟨Reg⟩ Redgapper

22 August 1918, Kittery Point, to the Board of Directors of the American Academy of Arts and Letters. 1 p. A.l.s. NNAL.

1 August *w.o. illeg.*   4 does *w.o. illeg.*

14 September 1918, Kittery Point, to Thomas S. Perry. 2 pp. A.l.s. MeWC.

5 New *w.o.* new   7 ⟨wl⟩ will   9 that *w.o.* the   19 genius *w.o.* man

21 September 1918, Kittery Point, to Aurelia H. Howells. 4 pp. A.l.s. NAlf.

8 apple-tree⟨s⟩   8 ↑before my windows↓   16 Ally *w.o.* ally 30 we *w.o.* was   41 ⟨I⟩ we   48 Will *w.o.* W. D   48 Sam ... it. [*in margin, fourth page*]

7 November 1918, Boston, to John M. Howells Family. Location of MS. unknown. *Life in Letters*, II, 383.

10 February 1919, Augusta, Georgia, to Thomas S. Perry. 2 pp. A.l.s. MeWC.

   5 sure ⟨it is⟩   8 C. ⟨C.⟩   8 ↑who↓   9 ⟨fel⟩ feeling   14 ↑hand↓
15 ↑ones?↓   19 ⟨introduction to a ⟨*illeg.*⟩ new⟩ edition ⟨to⟩
20 lovable *w.o.* love   21 ⟨go⟩ good   21 that *w.o.* the   23 ↑is↓
24 Try ⟨it⟩   24 ⟨of⟩ all

7 April 1919, New York, to Mr. Goldstein. 1 p. A.l.s. NN.

13 May 1919, Boston, to Rose Kohler. 1 p. A.l.s. NN.

   5 ⟨*illeg.*⟩ obliges

7 July 1919, York Harbor, to C. Symon. 1 p. Autograph draft signed. MH.

   7 Republic *w.o.* republic   8 ⟨any⟩ ↑this↓   9 the *w.o. illeg.*
9 ⟨from⟩ ↑its bestowal by↓

19 August 1919, York Harbor, to Thomas B. Wells. Location of MS. unknown. *Life in Letters*, II, 387.

20 August 1919, York Harbor, to Booth Tarkington. 1 p. A.l.s. NjP.

   6 Midwestern *w.o.* Mid Western

14 September 1919, York Harbor, to Mary R. Jewett. 2 pp. A.l.s. MH.

   4 I suppose *w.o. illeg.* suppose   5 warm *w.o. illeg.*
6 reading *w.o. illeg.*   .10 *Wisby.* ⟨"⟩   16 for⟨,⟩

14 September 1919, York Harbor, to Christopher Morley. 1 p. A.l.s. PHC.

   4 ⟨Cob⟩ Columbus   5 Khayyam *w.o. illeg.*   5 until ⟨*illeg.*⟩

3 October 1919, Kittery Point, to Lilian W. Aldrich. 2 pp. A.l.s. MH.

   3 gave ⟨to⟩

12 October 1919, Kittery Point, to Webb C. Hayes. 1 p. A.l.s. OFH.

   14 ↑of↓   18 Boston *w.o. illeg.*   19 South *w.o.* south

16 October 1919, Boston, to Hamlin Garland. 1 p. A.l.s. CLSU.

 2 16 *w.o.* 11

30 October 1919, Boston, to Robert Grant. 1 p. A.l.s. MH.
 4 ⟨")for 6 a bicuspid *w.o. a cuspid*

1 November 1919, New York, to Harriet Sprague. 1 p. A.l.s. PU.

 6 admirer⟨'⟩s

17 November 1919, New York, to Henry B. Fuller. 2 pp. A.l.s. ICSo.

 5 ↑it↓ [*at bottom of second page, in Fuller's hand*: on Nov. 20th sent to Georgia, / vol. of "Waldo Trench" and / Memo. of 5 uncollected Stories]

22 January 1920, Savannah, Georgia, to Thomas S. Perry. 1 p. A.l.s. MeWC.

 4 should] "∼ 7 ↑no↓ 12 ↑ultimately↓

22 January 1920, Savannah, Georgia, to Hamlin Garland. 2 pp. A.l.s. CLSU.

 4 ↑of Columbia↓ 8 ⟨I⟩ ↑he↓ could

22 March 1920, Savannah, Georgia, to Maxwell E. Perkins. 1 p. A.l.s. NjP.
 4 ⟨cut⟩ quick 4 you⟨r⟩ 6 always *w.o. illeg.* 7 ↑indeed↓
8 The *w.o.* the 9 I *w.o.* Th 10 ↑Mr.↓ Brownell, ⟨Mr.⟩

20 April 1920, New York, to Edwin Markham. 1 p. A.l.s. NNWML.
 4 ↑at all↓ 5 ⟨o⟩f↑rom↓ 8 these *w.o.* be 8 hard *w.o. illeg.*
9 as they *w.o.* as these 9 here they *w.o.* here there
[*at end of letter, in another hand*: To Edwin Markham]

"Eighty Years and After"

 The copy-text for this edition of "Eighty Years and After" is Howells' 39-page manuscript (which includes four typed pages), now the property of Professor William White Howells. Howells made extensive changes, presumably in the now lost secretarial typescript and in proofs, before the essay appeared in *Harper's Monthly,* December 1919. In so far as the variants from the manuscript in the printed essay appear to be authorial, they have been accepted into the present text. In the following list they appear to the left of a left-opening bracket; to the right of it is given the rejected reading of the copy-text. The only other possibly relevant published form of "Eighty Years and After" is an eight-page pamphlet, without publisher's imprint or date, but with a slip tipped in before page [1]: "Reprinted from Harper's Magazine, 1919 / By courtesy of the editors." It differs from the *Harper's* text in only two minor details—a typographical error and an omitted comma—and has no authority, since it was most likely reset and printed after Howells' death. A copy of the pamphlet is located in the library at Northwestern University (814.4 H859e).

157.2	I think] I say this because I think
157.2–3	every one, and I] every one, but whether it is true of every one, or not it is very true of me. I
157.3	now, when old] now when I am old
157.5	far] farther
157.6	but it] but I may easily be mistaken; it
157.6–7	Perhaps . . . sickness,] In sickness
157.7	that] this
157.9	to the] to all the
157.10	Apparently . . . mount] I do not believe the fear of death mounts
157.11	sometimes] almost
157.12–13	again; . . . loss] again. Rather the swift and total loss
157.13	faith, through] faith was a relief from that fear, through
157.14–15	eighties, . . . I had] eighties. I had
157.15	did not] did and do not
157.16	yet . . . fear] and now that this fear
157.17	was . . . certain] was gone, effectively if not entirely, a certain
157.18	soul. When] soul from the beginning, though I still felt myself a sinner and suffering for my sins. ¶ When
157.19	morning and that] morning, that
157.20	hell, but neither] hell, that I might not have my leg cut off. ¶ The terror of this last was injected into my life-

long dread by the experience of a poor young fellow only a few doors off in the dreadful days before the mercy of anaesthetics. Neither

157.20	petitions] prayers
157.23	fear] horror
157.24	life.] life, and which still prevails in the Christian world.
157.25	In . . . believe] I fancy that the old believe
157.27–28	may . . . . the sense] may say so sometimes in earlier life; but I have never had the sense
157.29	name.] name in the words of his Son.
157.30	I had not] I have never had
157.30	him, though] him, at any time of my life, though
157.31	deeds,] ~;
157.33	older; but at] older. At
157.34	spoken so of him] spoken of him so
157.34	Still I have] Still I could not honestly say that I love him, and I have
158.3	have.] have me.
158.4	me;] ~,
158.5	lessened] grown less
158.6	do not] cannot
158.7–8	shrinkage . . . from] shrinkage of all the emotions from
158.9	vantage-point] vantage
158.10	recall] imagine
158.12	eighty-two] eighty-odd
158.12	I have always been keenly] I was always keenly
158.14	introspection] intellectuation
158.15–16	after. ¶ The] after. Luigi Cernaro lived to be ninety-nine, but he was only eighty-two when he wrote *The Advantages of a Temperate Life*, and this was not a psychological inquiry, but the record of his hygienic experiments, and their lessons. ¶ The
158.17	the passions] all the passion
158.19	life.] life however less or other it may be.
158.21–22	of its bliss, one] of it one
158.22	years; yet] years, if one could have it back; yet
158.25	grief come] it comes
158.26	too;] ~:
158.26–27	awaits it. ¶ There] awaits it. ¶ Men cannot speak for women in this, but old men can speak better than

young men of that spiritual knowledge which comes from it. This knowledge is one of the things that follows length of years, and is a foretaste of heaven if the souls of women take their minds with them into the world imaginably beyond this. Their bodies wither and weaken away; but their minds remain young with a wisdom past all youthfulness. ¶ There

158.27	us from] from vileness
158.28	thrift] frugality
158.31	ugliest . . . shabbiest] ugliest, or cruellest or shabbiest
158.33	to the deprivation] and for the deprivation
158.33	the remoter] those further
158.33–34	race. In] race who are not weakened in their claim upon him by their folly or their fault. In
158.35	clink] clinking
158.36	fall through] fall from
158.37	the miser] he
158.38	misdoing] misdoers
158.38	was . . . like] was like
158.40	paper currency] the crisp currency of the banks
158.41	bank] notes
158.42	the sense] this sense
159.1–2	favor . . . gone out] favor recorded in the book returned from his banker, all virtue had gone out
159.6	from it.] from.
159.6	of all this] of this
159.7	man . . . that] man who said twenty years ago that
159.9–10	from . . . because] from any fault, because
159.10–11	youth . . . . It] youth. It
159.13	seventies . . . when] seventies when
159.17	ground with] ground well on both feet with
159.19	Yet] But
159.20–21	young . . . beautiful] young only in mind; though a beautiful
159.21–22	octogenarian . . . it] octogenarian, and a standardized sunset of sad coloring will find the grief of it
159.22	imagine, in fact, that] imagine that
159.27	age] ~;
159.30	so much] as much
159.30	an uphill] any uphill

159.30–31	summer, for instance, I] summer I
159.31	valley] hollow
159.31	end of it, and] end, and
159.33	exhaustion] resting
159.35	strange] novel
159.36	it falters] it lags, and falters
159.36–38	lame . . . . Before] lame; I notice the same thing in the stick of my neighbor the Admiral; but before we reach the top I think we would almost be better without our sticks. ¶ Before
159.39	night,] ~
159.39	a theatre] a Tremont Street theatre
159.39	Boston,] ~
159.40	Common . . . till] Common till
159.41	me. There I] me towards my hotel on Beacon Hill. Then I
159.42–160.1	top . . . effect] top I thought I should die. My deadly fatigue was the effect
160.2	much; there] much. There
160.5–6	man . . . . One] man was between fifty and sixty. One
160.9	earlier; one] earlier, perhaps because one is too gladly busy to think of it; one
160.10	as much;] more than ever;
160.11	way;] ~,
160.12	with even the] with the
160.12–13	the marriage . . . half] marriage is then a ring half
160.17	But silver is one] Yet silver is also one
160.21	time,] ~
160.22	oneself] one's self
160.22	wanted; but] wanted. But
160.23	ninety,] ~
160.26	than before] than ever before
160.26	This . . . living] This is one of the disadvantages of living
160.27	we cannot] one cannot
160.27	we wish] one wishes
160.28	live, but] live, and
160.31	they cannot] they do not or cannot
160.33	after. . . . unbearable] after. Life is so seldom unbearable
160.34–35	suicide. ¶ The] suicide. But the
160.35	are subjectively dull] are dull subjectively

160.38	in any phase of life] in life
160.38–39	tell of a new thing] tell new things
160.39	men. This] men. But this
160.40	known] read
160.40	If one is of] If one of is of
160.42	though,] ∼
160.43	literature;] ∼
161.3	Yet,] ∼
161.4	many of the things] most of the books
161.4	read—] ∼:
161.5	signal . . . . rather] signal things, like the Aeniad of Virgil, like the Cid, like Burton's Anatomy of Melancholy though I must have read Keats's Ode on Melancholy well almost once for every year of my Eighty-two. I am never tired of that, or of any of his odes. I am rather
161.7	boy—] ∼,
161.9	re-reading like] re-reading nearly like
161.10	favorite;] ∼,
161.10–11	Heine . . . . within] Heine does not. Within
161.13	read Milton's "Lycidas"] read *Lycidas*
161.13	as rich a woe as] as great *angenehmer Schmerz* as
161.13–14	time. ¶ Literature] time, or more. ¶ But what is the use? Literature
161.15	greater than the Earth,] better than an Earth
161.17–18	If . . . boasting] If I were I were boasting
161.18	or its] and its
161.19–20	in addressing . . . German] in treating of the great curse which has befallen our time in the German
161.21–22	mankind began. ¶ The attitude] mankind. No other American at least has addressed the sense and conscience of his countrymen with such force of reason, from first to last; no other octogenarian, to say the least, has redeemed age from the reproach of mere phenomenality. The attitude
161.25	about physical age] about age
161.28	effort . . . . bear] effort discount them. Let us alone, and we can bear
161.33	and . . . when] and when
161.35	I once sat] I sat
161.37	was, I did not praise] was, I am glad I did praise

161.42	tried for his] tried to recall his
162.2	myself . . . to] myself in returning at Rome to
162.3	Italian,] ~
162.3	word before] word in it before
162.5	myself. Then] myself, as Emerson used to do. Then
162.6	appears and I keep] appeared and I kept
162.6–7	time . . . suffered] time, which; but meanwhile I had suffered
162.7	case . . . was] case was
162.8	tree . . . which] tree which
162.10	it?] ~!
162.10	all! Tolstoy] all! ¶ Tolstoy
162.13	when their] when as Swedenborg tells, their
162.13	the things] those things
162.14	forgotten. But] forgotten: the things they have *wished* to forget! But
162.16–17	remember! ¶ Titian] remember! That is a curse common to all who outlive their psalmist's limit. ¶ Titian
162.17	ninety-nine] twenty-nine
162.18–19	he . . . there]he painted, though no doubt there
162.19–163.12	critic. . . . known] critic. I fancy there are miracles of that coloring which he wrought in his mastership at that wonderful Venetian school where Michelangelo thought it such a pity to find no drawing. If so it came from his unexhausted soul, and if there are like miracles in other cases, they must be from like sources. He had ninety-nine birthdays Here but his hundredth came as the first. Yonder. I have not known
163.16	"Yes," she chirped] "Yes," the undying spirit in her sweetly chirruped
163.20	youth . . . said] youth of say thirty-five. He said
163.21	delay,] ~
163.21–22	wife . . . . Soon] wife who was only ninety was not very well. Soon
163.22	afterward] afterwards
163.29	away. At seventy-three] away; at seventy three
163.30	that,] ~
163.34	swarm, they get] swarm and get
163.34	recall] remember
163.35	Europe.] ~;

163.35	eighty-eighth] eighty-eigth
163.35	year;] ~,
163.39	they usually are; they] they are. commonly They
163.40	rightly] sufficiently
163.40	who regard] who seem to regard
163.41–42	well . . . . So] well. So
164.2	transatlantic] Transatlantic
164.2	years—] ~,
164.3	years; now] years. Now
164.4	fixed,] ~
164.6	is not it the] is not it is the
164.8	suffering. When] suffering. I remember that when
164.9–10	perpetuity . . . run] perpetuity as the run
164.10–11	city . . . railroad] city I was to sail from, as they were implied in the railroad
164.11	and then the] and then then the
164.12	steamer:] ~.
164.13–14	now I know,] I know now,
164.16	continent—] ~,
164.16	Italy—] ~,
164.16–17	purgatory which you] purgatory you
164.18	travel; in] travel. In
164.26	such an advanced age—] such advanced an age,
164.27	longer. But I] longer. I
164.29	miss . . . much] miss them much
164.29	possibly] perhaps
164.30	one another] their
164.32	those others] they
164.37–38	helping . . . chairs] helping one another on with our overcoats, or putting chairs
165.1	the best society] the society
165.1	republic. If] republic. Or, if
165.3	digressions,] ~
165.4	octogenarian loneliness] octogenarian solitud loneliness
165.8	and he told me that] and after several meetings he mentioned that
165.10	him. He] him. Then he
165.12	or to put] or put
165.15	them. He] them. Then he
165.15–16	differences in] differences of

165.16	annul.] ~,
165.17	added,] ~
165.17	lady] ~,
165.20	think the] think that the
165.21	so, either, considering] so, considering
165.22	bridging] abridging
165.22–23	intervals. ¶ I recall] intervals. A woman of sixty might feel too young in the company of a woman of eighty, but with a man of eighty, she would feel he herself of his age just as would feel herself of the age of a man of forty. ¶ I recall
165.23	boy—] ~,
165.23	small,] ~
165.23	opinions—] ~,
165.27–28	visited . . . shared] visited us may have come for the comfort of our unfriended religion we shared
165.32	the noonday] our noonday
165.34–35	advantage. ¶ I have] advantages. The lovableness of all old ladies began with my two grandmothers, my Welsh grandmother and my Pennsylvania-German grandmother, equally dear to me, the one for something celestial in her dleicate caps, and her large, deepset blue eyes, and the other for the smell of her clay pipe which she had learned to smoke in her pioneer days, where she would have hardly taken up cigarettes. I had only one grandfather, and I did not cover him with the dislike I felt for the old gentleman I have mentioned, but I was afraid of him, both for the tender severity of his looks, and for the doubt which I somehow knew he felt as to my fate hereafter in my tenure of doctrines where the only hell was of a sinner's own choosing, and probably in such a case was bad enough in all conscience. ¶ I have
165.35	my] early
165.39	it,] ~
165.40	youth has grown upon them.] youth grows upon.
165.41	touch,] ~
165.42	all this time] all time
165.42–43	as . . . woman.] as the proof of all the praise I should like to give aging womanhood.

166.1	the finest modernity in] the modernity of the angels in
166.2–3	beauty ... it] beauty of it
166.3	gone now, who] gone who
166.3–4	such perfection] the perfection
166.4–5	seems ... left] seems as if could not have left
166.6–16	grace. ¶ If .... little. ¶ There] grace. ¶ There
166.17	speak of] touch upon
166.19	instantaneousness] instancity
166.20	lapse] occurrence
166.20	psychologists] psychologers
166.21	cerebration] cerebrations
166.25	and it is so yet] this is so yet
166.27	lovingly ... entire] convincingly than a number of entire
166.27–28	strangers. ¶ A few] strangers present. It would be interesting, but probably not very important to know if other octogenarians dream much or in the same kind. What I do think rather significant is that my dead when they come to me are frankly of another world though they are as much at home in this as I am, or as those strangers who frequent our circle. I should really like sometimes to make the acquaintance of the probability of this. ¶ A few
166.30	wanted] needed
166.31	matters] things
166.34	not] never
166.36	find, though] find; but
166.38	Yet] But
166.39	duties, I] duties or cares, I
166.40	mine has failed] mine failed
166.42	but who age] but age
166.42	angels,] ~
166.43	so infallibly fail] so poorly, so madly, fail
167.2	have indeed seen] have seen
167.4	errands,] ~;
167.5	confidently] infallibly
167.5	with them] with ours
167.7–8	I am here] I I am here
167.8	sheet, as] sheet (as
167.8	letter-writer] letter-writers
167.8–9	say, tempted] say) tempted

167.9	give us the name] give us the word, or the name
167.13	living,] ~
167.14	breath . . . terror] breath in the terror
167.16–17	Nature . . . mother] Nature with her nose in the air, laughs them to scorn, (but that is because she is our fond mother)
167.17–18	Science?" . . . and] Science?" and
167.18	Nature;] ~!
167.19	is proof] is a proof
167.20	but quite] and all
167.20–21	women . . . every] women have died, or shall die in a fixed course, and every
167.22	babe . . . certainly] babe; perhaps sooner, even, or perhaps not, but certainly
167.23	avail . . . whether] avail whether
167.24	drink;] ~,
167.25–26	that somewhere there] that there
167.26–27	here . . . live] here, the the love that drew us together that our children might live

Appendix

10 January 1856, Jefferson, to William C. Howells. 2 pp. A.l.s. NAlf.

5 ↑wondering↓ ⟨what⟩   5 ↑all↓   9 ⟨got⟩ ↑have↓   10 ⟨for⟩ ↑in↓
17 acting *w.o. illeg.*   19 that *w.o.* when   20 have *w.o.* were
20 have ⟨to⟩   20 left; *w.o.* be,   20 let ⟨th⟩

14 January 1861, Columbus, to Aurelia H. Howells. 5 pp. A.l.s. NAlf.

7 ⟨*illeg.*⟩ so   9 applied ⟨the⟩   25 ⟨the⟩ idle   30 sorry ⟨than⟩
32 you⟨r⟩   35 ↑great↓

20 May 1864, Venice, to William C. Howells. 2 pp. A.l.s. (with addition by Elinor M. Howells) NAlf.

10 ⟨h⟩ who   11 ↑very↓

1 June 1864, Venice, to William C. Howells. 4 pp. A.l.s. NAlf.

12 ⟨so⟩ glad   12 ↑all so↓   12 ⟨hap⟩ unhappy   15 ⟨somethin⟩ somehow

27 ⟨spirit⟩ speak   32 might *w.o. illeg.*   33 ⟨fact⟩ face   36 ⟨Wash⟩ We
46 ↑he↓   51 ⟨f⟩ often   52 entire ⟨trust⟩ ↑love↓   58 ⟨but⟩ ↑and↓

1 November 1874, Cambridge, to Anne T. Howells. 4 pp. A.l.s. NAlf.

17 ↑to Church↓   18 successful⟨l⟩   23 There's ⟨*illeg.*⟩
27 turn *w.o.* to   31 as *w.o.* is

17 January 1878, Cambridge, to Anne H. Fréchette. 4 pp. A.l.s. NAlf.

19 ↑eye↓   24 out ⟨without⟩

31 December 1882, Florence, to William C. Howells. 4 pp. A.l.s. NAlf.

13 more *w.o. illeg.*   13 and we] and and we   15 ⟨after⟩ when
16 ⟨talk⟩ takes   18 deal⟨t⟩   19 ⟨p⟩ Americans   27 been *w.o.* by
48 Your⟨s⟩

30 March 1890, Boston, to William C. Howells. 4 pp. Autograph copy
by W. C. Howells. NAlf.

8 said: *w.o.* said,   13 ⟨↑I↓⟩ *love*   19 this ⟨upon⟩   20 mind, ⟨when⟩
22 ⟨a⟩ hotel   28 ⟨*illeg.*⟩ dressed   29 ⟨girl⟩ girlish   30 humorous, ⟨but⟩
31 ⟨*illeg.*⟩ Pilla   32 ⟨the⟩ ↑her↓   32 ↑with↓   35 ↑something↓
35 something which was] something ⟨which⟩ was   35 that] that that
44 But *w.o.* but   46 then] then then   57 ⟨for⟩ against   57 of *w.o.* for

30 June 1899, Kittery Point, to Anne H. Fréchette. 3 pp. A.l.s. NAlf.

10 they *w.o.* though   13 treat *w.o. illeg.*   14 the ⟨the⟩ book
18 ⟨*illeg.*⟩ blunders   21 Journey *w.o.* in   22 which *w.o.* while

16 July 1899, Kittery Point, to Anne H. Fréchette. 3 pp. A.l.s. NAlf.

[*At top and in left margin, first page, in another hand*: To Keep *and*
"A Widow in the Wilderness"]   4 letter *w.o. illeg.*
12 have had] have have had

17 January 1904, New York, to Howells Fréchette. 4 pp. A.l.s. NAlf.

11 friend⟨,⟩"   12 ⟨br⟩ nephew   17 your *w.o.* our   35 ↑in↓

27 May 1908, London, to Anne H. Fréchette. 3 pp. A.l.s. NAlf.

[*In margin, first page, in another hand*: For Howells]

14 what *w.o.* c   14 ⟨I⟩ we   14 ↑but↓   15 place *w.o. illeg.*
21 out ↑of↓   24 Your⟨s⟩

3 April 1910, New York, to Anne H. Fréchette and Aurelia H. Howells.
4 pp. A.l.s. NAlf.

   9 ⟨out⟩ ↑ours↓   11–12 enjoyed *w.o.* enjoys   15 his *w.o.* he
21 was *w.o.* is   24 drives in *w.o.* drives,

29 April 1911, New York, to Achille Fréchette. 3 pp. A.l.s. NAlf.
   17 Kittery *w.o. illeg.*   19–20 ⟨history⟩ ↑experience↓   23 ↑with↓
24 ⟨*illeg.*⟩ never

Word-Division

In the two lists below, entries are keyed to the line numbers of the letter texts; the line-count includes all lines of type of a letter proper, beginning at the internal address or dateline. Entries from "Eighty Years and After" are listed by page and line numbers. List A records compounds and possible compounds hyphenated at the end of the line in the authorial document or extant transcription used as copy-text for the present edition, and indicates how these end-line hyphenated forms have been resolved. If the compounds occur in consistent form elsewhere in the authorial document or in other such materials of the same general period in time, including literary manuscripts, then resolution was made on that basis; if these other occurrences are inconsistent, resolution was based on the form in closest proximity in time to the possible compound in question. If neither of these resources was sufficient, then resolution was based on the evidence of published texts of Howells' works or on the prevalent usage of the period. List B is a guide to transcription of compounds or possible compounds hyphenated at the end of the line in the present text: compounds recorded in this list should be transcribed as given; words divided at the end of the line and not listed should be transcribed as one word.

LIST A

23 October 1912, to F. A. **Duneka**	9	simple-hearted
17 January 1913, to A. H. **Fréchette**	17	overdone
3 May 1913, to A. A. **Fields**	4	ex-New Yorker
22 November 1913, to S. W. **Mitchell**	23	forenoon
10 March 1914, to H. B. **Fuller**	6	out-living
10 March 1914, to H. B. **Fuller**	14	Noise-Poet
6 May 1914, to F. A. **Duneka**	13	background
12 May 1914, to A. H. **Howells**	22	trustworthy
15 June 1914, to A. A. **Fields**	20	daughter-in-
13 September 1914, to A. H. **Fréchette**	6	Sub-Treasury

2 June 1915, to T. S. Perry	3	-and-butter
2 June 1915, to T. S. Perry	7	to-day
16 February 1916, to T. S. Perry	21	English-born
4 July 1916, to A. H. Howells	7	thunder-storming
31 August 1917, to T. S. Perry	16	goldenrod
20 September 1917, to F. A. Duneka	28	go-ment's
13 November 1917, to Mildred Howells	12	heart-kick
21 September 1918, to A. H. Howells	14	fellow-pupils
21 September 1918, to A. H. Howells	40	mid-October
20 August 1919 to Booth Tarkington	9	midwestern
1 June 1864, to W. C. Howells	21	bright-hearted
31 December 1882, to W. C. Howells	4	-and-dried
30 March 1890, to W. C. Howells	30	half-teasing
17 January 1904, to Howells Fréchette	18	well-meaningest

LIST B

16 October 1913, to S. S. McClure	5–6	self-study
18 January 1914, to Bertha Howells	12–13	Merthyr-Tydfil
13 September 1914, to A. H. Fréchette	41–42	grandmother-country
23 May 1915, to A. H. Howells	32–33	home-Germans
12 April 1917, to Paul Kester	9–10	fool-martyr
1 May 1918, to Salvatore Cortesi	11–12	fellow-citizenship
12 October 1919, to W. C. Hayes	7–8	eighty-one
157.11–12	thirty-five	
163.36–37	fellow-voyager	

List of Howells' Correspondents

The following alphabetical list of Howells' correspondents provides page references for (1) letters written by Howells TO others and (2) letters FROM others addressed to Howells. Page numbers in italic type indicate letters appearing in full or as fully as the source permits; page numbers in roman type indicate letters cited in footnotes, with "cited" used broadly to mean quotation from a letter, description of parts of its contents, or mention of it whether printed in this edition or not. The few cited letters about Howells, e.g., from Henry James to Grace Norton, appear not in this list but in the main index.

Index

This index records all names of persons, organizations, monuments, ships, public buildings, and titles of magazines and books (the last recorded under the names of their authors, if known). It excludes the names of relatives of Howells' correspondents when they are mentioned for the primary purpose of sending love or minor information; the titles, journals, or publishers of post-1920 criticism and scholarship; and geographical names and government divisions. Some topics are listed as independent entries, but most can be found under Howells' name, where information is divided into two major lists: **WORKS** and **TOPICS**. The TOPICS section is further subdivided.

Within entries, the general order of information is: brief and/or general references; citation of correspondence other than that with Howells (e.g., Henry James to Thomas S. Perry); works by that person, including reviews and presumably unpublished work; and descriptive modifications, arranged in ascending page order. Finally, the frequent occurrence of some dozen entries has required the use of "passim" (e.g., "*North American Review*, . . . 61–68 passim").

Italic numbers designate pages on which significant biographical information is given. An asterisk preceding an entry indicates that a full record of correspondence between Howells and the person or institution so marked is provided in the separate "List of Howells' Correspondents," pages 227-228, the headnote of which explains its arrangement.